MASS MURDER
America's Growing Menace

MASS MURDER
America's Growing Menace

Jack Levin

and

James Alan Fox

PLENUM PRESS • NEW YORK AND LONDON

Library of Congress Cataloging in Publication Data

Levin, Jack, 1941–
Mass murder.

Includes bibliographical references and index.
1. Mass murder—United States. 2. Mass Murder—United States—Case studies. 3. Criminal psychology—Case studies. 4. Mass murder—United States—Investigation. I. Fox, James Alan. II. Title.
HV6529.L5 1985 364.1′523′0973 84-26585
ISBN 0-306-41943-2

Plenum Press is a division of
Plenum Publishing Corporation
233 Spring Street, New York, N.Y. 10013

Printed in the United States of America

To
Flea and Sue Ann

FOREWORD

I have handled only one case that could truly qualify as a "Mass Murder" case: That of Albert DeSalvo, much better known as "The Boston Strangler." (One other case—that of the "My Lai 4 Massacre," mentioned in this book—would qualify if I had represented one of those involved. I did defend Captain Ernest Medina, the Field Commander of the invasion force on that sorry day, but he had no part in the slaughter that occurred, didn't even know about it until it was all over, and was summarily acquitted of criminal responsibility. Ernie Medina can contribute nothing to the understanding of this genre, for despite the accusations against him, he was and is a decent and healthy human being.)

The handling of the Strangler case yielded a number of disappointments, but two stand out in my mind. The first occurred when Dr. Silvano Arieti, one of the foremost criminal psychiatrists of that era, informed me after a detailed examination of DeSalvo: "Mr. Bailey, I hate to disappoint you, but I must tell you that I do not find your client to be insane in the legal sense, nor psychotic in the medical sense. He is a sociopath, and only that. The law does not recognize a sociopath as having a mental illness which will excuse criminal responsibility. I thoroughly disagree with the law on this point, but as things are my testimony would not help you."

The second disappointment—perhaps disillusionment is a better word—came after DeSalvo had been convicted of some non-homicidal offenses, and was sentenced to life imprisonment (on my recommendation, joined by the prosecution). I literally begged the authorities of the Commonwealth of Massachusetts not to forfeit a valuable opportunity to painstakingly scrutinize a specimen serial killer who was in captivity. I felt that by learning all we could about Albert from his early years (which were horrendous) until his apprehension in his early thirties, there was much data to be recorded that could, together with other similar histories of multiple murderers, be useful in pursuing a most worthwhile objective: defining a profile of a potential homicidal maniac in his or her early or adolescent years, so that preventative steps could be taken consistent with basic constitutional rights.

In November, 1973, DeSalvo was murdered in his cell in Walpole State Prison, the maximum security penal institution for all of Massachusetts. His offense, in all probability, was selling dope at prices that the inmate "bosses" thought to be too competitive and thus too low. We had learned almost nothing about what he was made of, what made him tick, or why he had killed thirteen women, aged eighteen to eighty-eight, whom he didn't know. To add irony to negligence, Albert had often said he would like the worms in his brain to be exposed, even if it meant radical surgery to his head. No one cared enough to make the necessary effort to study what could have been a most interesting phenomenon: A serial killer who defied in almost every way—as this book points out—the profile that an army of police and criminal psychologists had assembled to aid in his apprehension. Authorities, on the strength of this profile, had been looking for a single, withdrawn male culprit who had a domineering mother. Albert, according to the evidence, was married, held a regular job, was robust, spoke "street talk" with the boys, was overtly solicitous of women and the courtesies due them, and was as crafty as the best of cat-burglars.

How could the experts have been so wrong? The public wondered and still does. The answer, if there is one, is this: When you don't do your homework—often minute, detailed drudgery—don't expect to be in a position to give valuable opinions or make accurate projections. America has done very little meaningful homework on the DeSalvos, the Specks, the Whitmans, the Calleys, and those others who have been shown by substantial evidence to have ravaged human life with sudden brutality and no individual animosity toward the victim—only a desire, or an impulse, or an uncontrollable urge to kill. What should be done about such creatures?

The answer to this question has frustrated judges, lawyers, doctors, and sociologists for many years. Truman Capote, a man of some intellectual power, researched this question in considerable depth as he compiled material for his bestselling "non-fiction novel" about the Clutter murders in Kansas called *In Cold Blood.* He told me in an interview that he felt such people, whom we do not begin to understand and therefore cannot pretend to "treat," should be confined in humane circumstances in a very secure place, and observed every day of their lives. I agree with that. As this book makes clear after surveying many such cases, we simply do not know enough about the "actors" to cure their murderous impulses, or to track them quickly and effectively when they are on a rampage. The inclination to execute them in reaction to the ghastly character of their crimes may satisfy our emotional outrage at their unfathomable conduct, but it does little to enhance what modern society would call our "database."

Normally, in a scientific exercise, we go through a process of observation, data collection, data analysis, the construction of an hypothesis, testing of that hypothesis, and then the advancement of a theory or the construction and testing of a new hypothesis. Much of the time we develop sets of scientific rules and principles to guide us when we again encounter problems such as those which were originally observed. Somewhere out there, if we will but work hard enough, are sets of clues and common denominators, which could, ultimately, permit us to recognize and define potential homicidal extroverts before they strike. The ultimate remedy for disease is not to cure it when it appears, but to vaccinate against it before it takes hold. Until we reach that point in dealing with multiple killers, innocent victims must continue to be sacrificed to our lassitude.

This survey is, in my opinion, a responsible compendium of cases that do have common denominators somewhere, even though we do not now know enough to discern them with any clarity. This excellent book, however, accurately profiles many of the bizarre mass murderers of this century; it affords the public valuable insights into understanding these creatures, which sensational trial coverage inevitably omits. Unfortunately, many of the exemplars it considers are not available for observation and inspection, either because we as a troubled society failed to take such measures while the specimen was still alive, or because we have made inadequate efforts to secure the cooperation of those individuals who are still with us. If a consideration of what is published herein prompts some fund or institution—governmental or private—to take seriously the proposition that we need to focus on this problem, to spend money on it and to stay with it until after the scientific process bears fruit, the authors will have served a noble purpose: the substitution of the mantle of ignorance for a quest for knowledge, knowledge which society badly needs.

F. Lee Bailey
Parkersburg, West Virginia
September 26, 1984

PREFACE

When we first began research for this book some four years ago, we sensed that mass murder was a "growing menace." Now we're sure.

Since 1980, the problem seems to have become more enormous than ever. While writing this book, our attention was repeatedly diverted to the shocking news of yet another mass slaughter or another serial killer on the loose. The first half of 1984 has been particularly bloody. In the past two weeks alone, four mass murders have received national attention. In Norwich, Connecticut, a graduate of an Ivy League college was arrested for the rape and murder of several women. Without warning, a Dallas man shot and killed six patrons of a local nightclub. A suspected killer roaming the Midwest was added to the FBI's ten most wanted list just before a fifth victim was discovered in Ohio. And a middle-aged man entered a McDonald's restaurant in suburban San Diego and shot everything that moved; his toll of twenty-one dead, nineteen wounded makes this the largest single-episode mass shooting in our nation's history.

This book is more than just the story of America's mass murders: it is also an in-depth examination of the characteristics of the killers and their victims, as well as the consequences of the crimes. New atrocities will continue to beg for explanation. We expect that their themes will have been seen before, only with different names and places. The ideas discussed in this book apply not only to mass murders of the past, but also to those that will occur in years to come.

Writing this book required us to research cases of mass murder from many parts of the country and many periods of time. What could have been a nearly impossible undertaking was, however, manageable because of the generous assistance of a large number of people. Although to thank them all by name would not be possible, we do want to recognize those whose contributions were particularly important.

In our travels to collect information for three case studies, we depended a great deal on the hospitality and cooperation of certain key individuals in the communities we visited: Police Chief (and now mayor) George McNally of Hamilton, Ohio; Bruce Mowday of the *Daily Local News* of West Chester, Pennsylvania; and Frank Candida of the *Los Angeles Herald Examiner.*

Four major studies formed the basis for this book. First, our statistical profile of 42 mass killers was supported by a grant from the Northeastern University Research and Scholarship Development Fund. Cathy Thomson was a competent and hard-working assistant during the early stages of this project. Second, we were fortunate to have been provided with a large FBI homicide data set by William Bowers and Glenn Pierce of the Center for Applied Social Research at Northeastern University. Third, we thank the dozens of attorneys general who took the time to complete our questionnaire concerning their states' laws. Fourth, graduate students from the 1984 Research Methods course in the College of Criminal Justice at Northeastern conducted hundreds of telephone interviews concerning the death penalty and mass murder.

We wish to thank the hundreds of people around the country whom we interviewed. Many of them are quoted or acknowledged elsewhere in this book. We are also grateful to our colleagues and associates who commented on drafts of the manuscript or who offered valuable ideas which are reflected in our writing: Arnold Arluke, Edith Flynn, Ronald McAllister, Frank Schubert, and Wallace Sherwood of Northeastern University, Jan

Chaiken of Abt Associates, Marcia Chaiken of Brandeis University, Simon Dinitz of Ohio State University, Myron Lench, Edith and Marty Luray, Richard Moran of Mount Holyoke College, Carol Pollack, Helen Rees, Lionel Takiff, Eliot Werner of Plenum Publishing Corporation, and Margaret Zahn of Temple University.

A number of individuals kept a watchful eye on their local newspapers or professional journals, bringing to our attention material that otherwise we might have missed. Others were helpful resources for inquiries we could not resolve elsewhere. We are indebted to: Ernie Anastos of WABC-TV, Cheryl Archer of the *New Britain Herald,* Fred Bayles of the Associated Press, Jeanne Blake of WBZ-TV, Rebecca Catey of the *Cincinatti Enquirer,* Duncan Chappell of Simon Fraser University, Toni Emrich, Donna Fiorilla, Diana Fishbein of the University of Maryland Medical School, Gary Fox of Miami University of Ohio, Neville Frankel and Ann Frazier of the *Columbus Dispatch,* Robert Keppel of the Washington State Attorney General's Office, Frederick Koenig of Tulane University, Kathleen Moran, Dick Perry of the *Cincinatti Post,* Edith Piercy of the *Register Star,* Frank Rawdon, Jack M. Rentfrow, Paul Roppel of the Chicago Police Department, Wendy Russet, Russ Schach of the *Daily News Tribune,* Sally G. Schlaerth of the *Buffalo Evening Courier Express,* Norma Selden of the Westchester-Rockland newspapers, John Snell of *The Oregonian,* Cheri Titlebaum, Paul Tracy of the University of Pennsylvania, Barbara Ann Ward, Chris Wells of the *State Journal,* Mary Wurdock of the *Bay City Times,* and the staff of the FBI's Behavioral Science Unit.

In addition to our students and colleagues at Northeastern University, we are indebted to Dean Richard Astro, College of Arts and Sciences; Deans Norman Rosenblatt and Robert Croatti, College of Criminal Justice; secretaries Marilyn Churchill and Leslie Lemire; the staff of the Computer Center; the Office of Public Information with special thanks to Joan Koffman; and the Center for Applied Social Research.

We were very fortunate to have Linda Greenspan Regan as

our editor. She believed in the project from the outset, nurtured it through several drafts, inspired vast improvements in both style and content, and contributed a number of ideas that we have incorporated into the final version.

Finally, some very special people gave us support and encouragement. Our families—Flea, Michael, Bonnie, and Andrea, and Sue Ann, David, Jennifer, and Alexander—suffered not only through our absence while we worked, but also through a steady diet of gory stories while together.

Jack Levin
James Alan Fox

CONTENTS

PART IV Conclusion

PART I

THE MYSTIQUE AND REALITY OF MASS MURDER

CHAPTER 1

THE POPULAR IMAGE OF THE MASS MURDERER

To many, the words "mass murderer" bring to mind the figure of a glassy-eyed lunatic who kills innocent and helpless people in order to satisfy sadistic and lustful impulses. The popular view of the mass killer closely fits the likes of one Edward Gein, a man whose name is not widely known but whose misdeeds have become ingrained in our minds.[1]

The break of dawn on November 16, 1957 heralded the start of deer hunting season in rural Waushara County, Wisconsin. The men of Plainfield went off with their hunting rifles and knives but without any clue of what Edward Gein would do that day. Gein was known to the 647 residents of Plainfield as a quiet man who kept to himself and his aging, dilapidated farmhouse. But when the men of the village returned from hunting that evening, they learned the awful truth about their 51-year-old neighbor and the atrocities that he had ritualized within the walls of his farmhouse.

The first in a series of discoveries that would disrupt the usually tranquil town occurred when Frank Worden arrived at his hardware store after hunting all day. Frank's mother, Bernice Worden, who had been minding the store, was missing; so was Frank's truck. But there was a pool of blood on the floor and a trail of blood leading toward the place where the truck had been garaged.

The investigation of Bernice's disappearance and possible homicide led police to the farm of Ed Gein. Since the farm had no electricity, the investigators conducted a slow and ominous search with flashlights. Methodically scanning the barn for clues, the sheriff's light suddenly exposed a hanging figure, apparently Mrs. Worden. As Captain Schoephoerster later described[2]:

> . . . Mrs. Worden had been completely dressed out like a deer with her head cut off at the shoulders. Gein had slit the skin on the back of her ankles and inserted a wooden rod, 3½ feet long, and about 4 inches in diameter, and sharpened to a point at both ends, through the cut tendons on the back of her ankles. Both hands were tied to her side with binder twine. The center of the rod was attached to a pulley on a block and tackle. The body was pulled up so that the feet were near the ceiling. We noticed that there was just a few drops of watery blood beneath the body on the dirt floor, and not finding the head or intestines, we thought possibly the body had been butchered at another location.

Apparently, "deer" season had begun in the mind of Edward Gein too.

This heinous crime was not the only gruesome act of the man whom no one really knew. In the months that followed, more of the macabre practices of Ed Gein were unveiled. Not only was he suspected in several other deaths, but Gein admitted to having robbed corpses and body parts from a number of graves. Gein used these limbs and organs to fashion ornaments, such as a belt of nipples and a hanging human head, as well as decorations for his house, including chairs upholstered with human skin and bed posts crowned with skulls. A shoe box containing nine vulvas was but one part of Gein's grim collection of female organs. On moonlit evenings he would prance around his farm wearing a real female mask, a vest of skin complete with female breasts, and woman's panties filled with vaginas in an attempt to recreate the form and presence of his dead mother.

The news of Gein's secret life devastated Plainfield. The townspeople were shocked to learn of the terrible fate of Mrs. Worden and to hear of the discovered remains belonging to 51-

year-old barkeeper Mary Hogan who had disappeared years earlier after being shot by Gein. They were outraged by the sacrilege of their ancestors' graves. They were literally sickened remembering the gifts of "venison" that Gein had presented them.

Any small town is shocked by a murder in its midst. But the horror of Gein's rituals surpassed anything that the people of Plainfield had ever encountered or even imagined.

Curiously, people often resort to humor in situations that are unfamiliar, embarrassing, or uncomfortable; wit and laughter are convenient cover-ups for emotions and reactions that we are unable to show directly. For the people of Plainfield, "Gein humor" provided a common and popular mechanism to deal with acts too disgusting to accept. Jokes such as "What did Gein say to the sheriff who arrested him? 'Have a heart'," became part of the local heritage.[3] One might be tempted to call this humor sick, but perhaps it is instead a reasonable and healthy way to cope with an inexplicable and sickening event.

Outside of Wisconsin, few people had heard of Edward Gein. As bizarre and offensive as his crimes were, Gein never really made headlines in other parts of the country; what happens in Plainfield is not nearly as important, at least to the national media, as what happens in a large city like Chicago or New York. Very few eyebrows are raised at the mention of the name Ed Gein. Hardly a household name or a box office attraction, he might have been immortalized like Charles Manson in *Helter Skelter* had he killed in Los Angeles. Had he lived in a metropolis like Boston, Tony Curtis might have played the role of Ed Gein in a large Hollywood production like *The Boston Strangler*. A killer from Plainfield, Wisconsin—which rings very much like Anywhere, USA—will, however, probably never be seen as important enough to warrant "The Edward Gein Story."*

*Location is hardly the only reason why cases like the Boston Strangler and the Manson killings are so widely publicized: The style of killing, the identity of the victims, and the nature of the manhunt all influence the degree of infamy. However, the location of the crime is probably the most important determinant.

Yet, although the name of Edward Gein is unknown to moviegoers, he was discovered by Hollywood. His legendary place in the history of crime has inspired a number of fictional films, both popular and obscure.

The promoters of *Texas Chainsaw Massacre* claim that it was based on fact, although a crime of this description cannot be found. One thing for sure: the film contains numerous elements reminiscent of Gein. For instance, the farmhouse of the family of killers, like Gein's house, is littered with spare body parts and bones. Also, like Gein, the family has an armchair with real arms.

A less popular film imported from Canada more closely parallels the Gein theme. In *Deranged* a killer, known as the "Butcher of Woodside," slaughters and stuffs his victims. At one point, he parades in the skin of a woman he has just killed, similar to Gein's moonlight charades. Also, a poster ad for the film depicts a woman hanging from her ankles, just as Bernice Worden was found.

The most noteworthy cinematic product inspired by the Gein case, however, was the classic thriller *Psycho*, directed by Alfred Hitchcock. Operating out of a warped sense of reverence, Norman Bates (played by Anthony Perkins) stuffed and preserved his deceased mother—as Gein tried in using female body parts to symbolize and resurrect his mother. Both conversed with their dead mothers, and both struggled with strict moral constraints that had been enforced by their dominating and sickly mothers. Finally, Bates was implicated in the deaths of two adolescent girls, just as the excavation of undersized bones near Gein's farm suggested his role in the disappearance of two teenage girls.

The popular image of the mass killer, fostered by Hollywood depictions such as these—as well as scores of purely fictional portrayals of homicidal maniacs—emphasizes clearly the "psycho" theme. The curious childhoods and strange misadventures of ignominious celebrities like Ted Bundy and David Berkowitz have been explored in several novel-like books, whereas other "less interesting" mass killers have received very little coverage.

It is far from surprising, therefore, that the popular conception of mass murderers as sadistic "weirdos" pervades our culture.

Bizarre activities may not be, however, as typical of mass murderers as Hollywood, television, and newstand paperbacks would have us believe. Is Edward Gein exceptional or typical of mass murderers? Are mass killers really loners who have a psychotic thirst for violence? Are mass killers really glassy-eyed, pale lunatics who are distinguishable from the rest of us? Do mass murderers really kill innocent strangers who happen to be at the wrong place at the wrong time? These are among the many questions that motivate this book.

There has never been a comprehensive exploration of the characteristics of and the circumstances which precipitate mass murder. While a number of psychiatric studies of mass murderers have been undertaken, they are without exception based on very small numbers of cases (and often just one) as well as on the most unique and deviant cases. The scope of this book is different. In the pages which follow we shall discuss and analyze dozens of cases of mass murder, representing a wide range of motivations from sexual lust to love of money, from jealousy to racial hatred, in an attempt to create a more realistic, if less "romanticized," portrayal of the typical mass killer. We hope this study will help us to explain—not condone—what has seemed incomprehensible, and we will suggest ways to deal effectively through the criminal justice system with those who do commit this most heinous form of human aggression.

CHAPTER 2

TOO MANY VICTIMS

Carol DaRonch felt fortunate to have struggled free from the light-blue Volkswagon of her abductor, but she had no idea just how lucky she was. Not until almost five years after her 1974 kidnapping, when she journeyed from her home in Utah to testify in a Florida court at the sentencing hearing of Theodore Robert Bundy, did she acknowledge the full murderous potential of the man who is suspected of killing dozens of women in four states and had tried to kill her.[1]

Carol was young, unusually pretty, shy, and very naive. She was a small-town girl, having just graduated from high school and working as an operator for Mountain Bell. On Friday evening, November 8, 1974, Carol drove her Camaro to the Fashion Place Mall in Murray, Utah to shop for a birthday gift for her cousin. While browsing in Walden's Bookstore, she was approached by a handsome stranger dressed in a sports jacket, green slacks, and patent leather shoes, identifying himself as Officer Roseland of the Police Department. "Officer Roseland" told Carol that there had been an attempted burglary of a car in the parking lot that might have been hers. After revealing her plate number, the "officer" asked Carol to accompany him to check her vehicle.

Carol didn't think immediately of how strange it was that he knew where to find her. Not only was she generally trusting, but her strong family upbringing in the Mormon faith taught her to respect and obey authority. So, Carol went with the "officer" to her car to check for any stolen articles. When it was clear that the car was undisturbed, he asked Carol to continue on with him to the Police Substation at the Mall. She hesitated and asked to see the officer's identification. "Officer Roseland" responded by stealthily flashing his counterfeit gold shield; Carol did not question his identity further. The substation door, which in reality was the rear of a laundromat, was locked, so he then requested her to go with him in his car to the central Police Station. Carol thought how unlikely his beat-up "Bug" seemed as a police vehicle, but then, she recalled TV undercover cops like Starsky and Hutch and the Mod Squad. Coaxed by his commanding manner, she went along for the ride.

Appearances can change quickly. "Officer Roseland" turned out of the parking lot in the direction opposite the police station. Then, when Carol refused his order to fasten her seat belt, his demeanor turned suddenly to rage. This was too unbelievable, even for Carol. When the man attempted to corral her with handcuffs, she lurched from the car, kicking her abductor. He attacked her with a crowbar, but miraculously she was able to muster enough strength to catch his swing before it crushed her skull. Finally, she ran, hobbling on one shoe, to the safety of a passing motorist. Mary Walsh, who was out riding with her husband that rainy evening, would later testify in court about the girl they rescued: "I have never seen a human being that frightened in my life. She was trembling and crying and weak, as if she was going to faint."[2]

Like Carol DaRonch, dozens of other girls trusted and believed the man who would become well known through a nationally televised trial. A bright law student who was respected in Seattle's Republican ranks, Ted Bundy was a likeable and engaging fellow. His many victims were lured into his bloody net by his reassuring tone, which he polished from working the hotline at Seattle's Crisis Clinic. But while the others were bludgeoned, strangled, sexually molested, and buried, Carol

DaRonch was a survivor—most probably the only one to escape the clutches of Bundy until his bungled assault on the Chi Omega Sorority at Florida State University in 1978. However, all of this was meaningless to Carol when she escaped from Bundy's car. She had no idea at the time of the fate of those before her and after her who did not escape. Not only was Carol spared her life, she was spared the greater and perhaps ultimate terror suffered more than eight years earlier by Corazon Amurao, an exchange student nurse from the Philippines, who survived a very different type of episode.

Late on a typically warm and humid July evening in 1966, 23-year-old Corazon Amurao opened her bedroom door of the Chicago townhouse she shared with fellow nursing students from the South Chicago Community Hospital to welcome someone she thought was a roommate. Instead, a somewhat inebriated man, with dark short-cropped hair, a pockmarked face, and dressed all in black, forced his way into the large room. He claimed he only wanted money to travel to New Orleans, threatening with a knife in one hand and a pistol in the other. Corazon watched in fear as the man tore bedsheets with which to tie and gag her and her friends who he had forced together into the back bedroom. Deliberately, the roommates decided to yield to the intruder so as not to anger him into a violent rage.

One at a time, he led away his victims. After a few repetitions it was clear to Corazon and the others remaining that they were to die that night.

Corazon, however, as later described by her dean at the nursing school, was characteristically very calm in times of stress. Under this most extreme test of her nerves, she managed to struggle her way underneath a bunk where the slaughterer could not find her among the helplessly and hopelessly waiting victims. Throughout the night she too waited, but in hiding, mortally afraid that she would be discovered, as she watched the number of her friends dwindle one by one. Each time the stranger was out of the room, she would plead with her friends to join in an ambush to overtake the enemy, but they were all too frightened to act and simply waited for their turn to die. As Corazon huddled beneath the bed, the room soon emptied of all her friends. She prayed that the man had not counted his victims and wouldn't return to search for her.

It was not until her alarm clock stopped ringing the next morning, six hours after the nightmare had begun, that she felt confident enough to leave her sanctuary to scream the screams that she had kept inside. Only then, as she saw the strangled, stabbed, and ravaged bodies of the other eight nurses in the house, could she cry. Crawling out onto the balcony, she awakened the neighborhood, and the world, with her shouts, "They are all dead! They are all dead! My friends are all dead. Oh God, I'm the only one alive."[3]

The scene of the massacre was full of bloody fingerprints, easily identifying the killer as Richard Franklin Speck (he used the alias Benjamin rather than Franklin), a Texas drifter who had worked sporadically as a construction laborer and a seaman, among other things. The police report indicated that he had served time for passing bad checks, burglary, and a knife assault on a woman. Ironically born on the eve of the Pearl Harbor attack, one of his many tattoos read "Born to Raise Hell."

Two days after the wholesale murder, Speck was found in a nearby flophouse, weak and bleeding from an apparent suicide attempt. But he lived to remain a public curiosity for perpetrating what was called, at least for the two weeks until another killer made even bigger headlines, "the crime of the century."

What Carol DaRonch and Corazon Amurao had in common was trust. Like many others who have ended up dead, Carol trusted a man posing as a police officer. Like many others who have ended up dead, Corazon and her roommates trusted a man who claimed that he planned only to rob them. Where the two women differed is in reacting to the peril of their situations. Carol can feel fortunate to have been unharmed; Nurse Amurao's ordeal is a continuing nightmare.

Some mass murderers are so brutally sadistic—torturing bodies or coercing victims into the most demeaning acts—that we mourn not only the deaths but the agonizing last moments of the victim's lives; whereas in other mass slayings the perpetrators extinguish their victims with almost merciful quickness, seeking only to kill but not to cause prolonged suffering. Still other acts of mass destruction that involve the practice of repulsive and bizarre rituals—like removing genitals and rectums from corpses or eating the flesh—are patently offensive, even if the victims die without an ordeal.

Some mass killers are so despicably evil that we can feel no compassion, while others are understood to be expressing impulses that they cannot control. Some mass murderers kill so obtrusively that their crimes are featured in the news across the country; others hardly disturb the night as they massacre their entire sleeping families and so are renowned only in their own communities.

Even with the many features that make each mass murder unique, there is one distinction among mass killings that will persist throughout this book and is central to understanding the motives, the detection, and the punishment of this crime. The fundamental dichotomy is between serial killers—mass murderers who slay their victims on different occasions—and simultaneous killers—those who murder their victims at the same time or in one episode.

Serial murderers, although they may strike over a period of days, weeks, or years, may kill in one place. John Wayne Gacy is a case in point. His home in suburban Chicago was the final resting place for the corpses of many of the thirty-three boys whom he had lured to his den of sadism. Gacy was known as a friendly sort, a sociable and hospitable neighbor who would give extravagant parties for his friends. A large and jovial man, he would dress up as a clown to entertain children. He was also respected as a civic-minded citizen, even nominated "Man of the Year" by the Springfield, Illinois chaper of the Jaycees and photographed posing with First Lady Rosalynn Carter during a Democractic Party rally in Chicago. Unknown to his wife, his children, and his friends, many of whom still deny it, Gacy had a special affection for boys. Some he recruited to work for his construction company and would then seduce them; others he would search for while cruising in his ostentatious black Oldsmobile which sported a large spotlight to help select his victims. All of these boys, however, would share the same fate: an early grave, most of them under Gacy's house. It was not until the smell of the decomposing bodies became unmistakable that the other side of John Wayne Gacy was revealed to the world.

The sudden discovery of the makeshift graves of innocent children lured to their deaths was horrifying. Coincident with Gacy's arrest, the bodies were excavated—announcing for the first time that there had been a mass killing. Although the mothers of thirty-three children were missing their sons, Chicago was not gripped in fear. The killer was in custody as soon as his crimes were publicly revealed. As horrendous as the news of Gacy's activities was, it was also past history.

In contrast, nothing compares to the terror that envelops a community as it slowly begins to face the grim likelihood that a serial killer is on the loose. As one by one the fetid remains of kidnapped coeds were found discarded in fields and roadsides, the residents of Washtenaw County, Michigan became increasingly seized with panic.

In July 1969, public transportation between the University of Michigan in Ann Arbor and nearby Eastern Michigan University in Ypsilanti was not very good. Students would commonly hitchhike the five-mile length of Washtenaw Avenue that connected the two campuses in order to see their friends or to use the schools' libraries. Karen Sue Beineman was a freshman at EMU when she uncharacteristically accepted a ride from a stranger, thus joining a group of seven young women whose disfigured and decaying bodies were found discarded around the county. Karen was last seen by a clerk at a wig shop who remembered the girl well. The salesclerk recalled her as a pretty, petite girl who had joked that she had done two foolish things in her life: buy a wig and accept a ride from the motorcyclist waiting outside. Like everyone else, Karen had heard the recent reports about girls found dead, but she probably doubted that it could happen to her and, besides, the handsome guy waiting outside for her hardly seemed the mass murderer type. Appearances can be deceiving, however. Karen's body was found three days later in a ditch off the side of a road, her form so disfigured and decomposed that fingerprints were needed for positive identification.

The string of unsolved murders lasted from 1967 to 1969, holding the community in terror. Even years after John Normon Collins was caught, convicted, and imprisoned, his impact remains. The secure, peaceful, college-town life-style of Ann Arbor and Ypsilanti will never be the same.

Mass slayings in which victims are slaughtered in one enormous attack do not suspend communities in a state of alarm, yet they often are far bloodier and more immediately shocking. Chinatown in Seattle was not prepared for, and perhaps will never fully comprehend, the slaughter that occurred in its once orderly neighborhood. Early on the morning of February 19, 1983, three Chinese youths crashed the Wah Mee Club (meaning "Beautiful China"), a private gambling spot strictly for people of Chinese ancestry, to rob its patrons. The three then methodically executed all of the thirteen present by shooting each in the head, just to cover up a robbery by eliminating the witnesses.

The most dramatic characteristics of simultaneous multiple killings are their suddenness and their ferocity: the speed with which so many lives are destroyed is as inconceivable as it is chilling. Ironically, the aftermath of these bloodbaths often leaves a scene of carnage that is strangely serene. When the police arrived at the Wah Mee Club in Seattle's Chinatown, the stillness sharply contrasted with the gruesome slaughter of just a few hours earlier. But as unsettling as this was to the city of Seattle and, in particular, the residents of the Chinatown district, few episodes remain so fixed in the minds of Americans, epitomizing the horror of mass murder, as the ninety-one-minute outburst that shook the nation in August of 1966.

The August 12, 1966 issue of *Time* magazine leads with a story of national pride—the wedding of Luci Baines Johnson—daughter of President Lyndon and Mrs. Lady Bird Johnson. Americans certainly love a wedding, but apparently they are more fascinated by murder. The presidential wedding was unceremoniously upstaged by a story of national sorrow. The cover photo of *Time* highlighted another Texan, Charles Whitman. On August 1, 1966, Whitman had climbed atop the 307-foot tower on the campus of the University of Texas in Austin and had opened fire on the campus from a vantage point behind the tower's huge clock. Ninety-one bloody minutes later, fourteen were dead or dying. Thirty more lay injured in a sixteen-block area surrounding the tower which, strewn with casualties, looked more like a war zone than a college campus. Another victim of Whitman's rampage was the fetus of a woman eight months pregnant that was stillborn. In addition to these casualties, Whitman had killed his mother and his wife the night before, and Whitman himself was gunned down by a team of four officers at the top of the tower.

To those who knew Charlie casually, he was the "all-American boy," certainly not the popular image of a deadly killer. A committed and hard-working student, he had earned all A's during his final semester at the University of Texas; over his entire college career as an architectural engineering major, his average was in the B range. He also seemed to be a friendly and caring fellow. After having been an eagle scout in his youth, Whitman as an adult served as a scoutmaster, and impressed the scouts' parents as being good with the children. Being a bright student and a respected member of the community, he seemed to have a promising future. But his parents, his wife, and his friends knew the real Charles Whitman, a troubled man who, according to his psychiatrist, was "oozing with hostility."[4] Whitman had in fact told the doctor that he thought about "going up on the tower with a deer rifle and start shooting people," but the therapist considered this to be merely one of the many idle fantasies that depressed college students entertain about the tower.[5] Whitman also beat his wife on occasion, as reportedly his father—whom he hated passionately—had done to the mother Charles so passionately loved.

Charles Whitman was proud to have served in the Marines. However, his military career was not as honorable as some believed. He had been demoted from corporal to private for a number of transgressions including assault, gambling, and the possession of illegal firearms. But in the Marines, he was decorated for achieving the class of sharpshooter. Whitman was well acquainted with guns from an early age. "He was always a crack shot," said his father, in a dramatic example of understatement.[6] During Whitman's spree at the tower, an onlooker three blocks away remarked to a friend that they were safely out of range; then he was shot.

Whitman had the hostility to commit the crime, and the skillful shot, needing only to amass the large arsenal of weapons that Texas law permitted him to purchase. It was only the delay of a few minutes when Whitman stopped to shoot a receptionist and some tourists, who stood between him and his gunpost, that prevented him from opening fire between class periods on the thousands who would have been under his gun.

Psychiatric theories and explanations for killers like Whitman have filled pages of professional journals. Writers have also popularized theories of the "murdering mind," reaching millions of readers of magazines sold at supermarket checkout counters. Stories of the rocky childhoods and wild fantasies of people like David Berkowitz or Kenneth Bianchi appeal in much the same way as soap operas do. They may be entertaining, but they don't tell you much about mass murder.

Cases of mass murder have been told with a dramatic flair in books and movies like Capote's *In Cold Blood* or Bugliosi's *Helter Skelter.* Other strictly fictional characterizations, like *Prom Night* or *Halloween,* capitalize on our voyeuristic desire to witness first-hand the suspense of a mass slaughter. Few of us, of course, wish in reality to be in such a state of peril, to be hiding under a bed during a mass killing, like Corazon Amurao did to survive. At the same time, however, we want to get just close enough—at least in our minds—in order to make sense of one of the most heinous of human acts.

Mass murder is a notion that few of us can really comprehend, even in our imaginations. Mass murder happens in the movies, but is too incredible to ponder except in our worst nightmares. The ultimate irony, however, is that reality may be incredible even for fiction. Recently, a screenwriter spent time in Los Angeles researching a proposed fictional movie based loosely on the famous Hillside Stranglings. He abandoned the project after reaching the conclusion that as fiction no one would believe it!

Almost every night on the news we are confronted with the topic of murder. Indeed, there are approximately 20,000 homicides each year in the United States. Few of us have in one way or another been unaffected. Whether or not we have known someone who has been slain, feared being murdered, or perhaps even momentarily comtemplated murder ourselves during a fit of anger, we realize that the risk that we will kill or be killed does exist. But mass murder is different; it seems so bizarre, so vast a crime, that it's out of our frame of reference, and thus seems out of the question. By maintaining this viewpoint, we can distance ourselves from the harshness and horror of mass murder, and remain as fascinated yet uncomprehending spectators.

If one morning we were to awake to learn that our neighbor had shot his wife in a rage, we would consider it tragic. But to learn that the entire family next door had been wiped out by their son would be inconceivable. This is just how it seemed to the residents of Amityville, New York when Robert DeFeo, Jr. shot his mother, father, and four siblings in their home. Later the house became the setting for a series of macabre motion pictures about the Amityville horror. The horror was real enough, but the movie plots were pure fiction.

Despite our emotional distance from the crime, we must face the fact that the incidence of mass murder is growing. The 1960s mark the onset of the age of mass murder in the United States. The names of mass killers over the past two decades are numerous and well known; the names of their predecessors are few and obscure. Further, not only are mass killings more frequent and visible in the last twenty years, the number known may even be understated.

For various reasons, we may have grossly underestimated the size and scope of mass murder in the United States. First of all, offenders are not always charged with all of the crimes they are suspected of having committed. Ted Bundy was convicted of brutally murdering two Florida women and a 12-year-old girl, but he was a suspect in many more deaths. Similarly, dozens of young blacks recently died in Atlanta, yet suspect Wayne Williams was charged and convicted of only two counts of murder.

Some claim to have killed large numbers of people, but authorities are not always able to validate their confessions. Convicted murderer Jesse Bishop, who died in the Nevada gas chamber for killing David Ballard during an armed robbery, confessed before his execution that he had been involved in another eighteen homicides. Likewise, convicted murderer Bruce A. Davis, imprisoned in the Menard Correctional Center at Chester, Illinois, recently confessed to the murders of thirty-three men in more than a dozen cities across the country.

Justice Department official Robert Heck estimates conservatively that 35 mass murderers are currently on the loose nationwide. Some missing persons may actually be victims of a few serial killers, as may be known to be murdered victims whose killers have never been found.

A string of unsolved slayings recently occurred in the area of Joliet, Illinois. Located forty miles southwest of Chicago, fifteen brutal murders took place in this city during a two-month period, and very few clues surfaced. The threads that tied together the fifteen deaths were inconclusive at best. Almost all of the killings occurred on weekends and all of the victims were white. Some were stabbed; others were shot with the same caliber gun. Eight victims were murdered in their cars, but three were in their homes and four were in a ceramics shop in town. Six victims were men, nine were women. Their ages ranged from 18 to 75. Robbery appeared to be a motive in half the deaths. Based on the evidence collected so far, authorities in Joliet are unable to determine precisely how many of the slayings were committed by the same person or persons. They raise the unsettling possibility that several mass killers may be at large in the Joliet community.

Since 1980, the number of mass murders that have made headlines in the newspapers has grown noticeably, even as the rate of homicide itself on a national level is beginning to subside. The nation is faced, if by this time not shocked, by an average of three mass murders each month. The state of Texas alone was hit recently with three mass slayings in one month. Yet more dramatic than the increase in the number of mass killers are the changes in the size of their kill.

Just ten years ago, twenty-seven bodies of young boys were excavated in Houston, Texas after Elmer Wayne Henley confessed to his part as an accomplice in the homosexual rituals of Dean Corll. The Corll–Henley murders broke both a Texas record and a national record for most killings, almost doubling the previous high set by Charles Whitman's tower snipings. Since then, the victim counts are staggering: Williams is suspected of killing two dozen boys in Atlanta; Gerald Eugene Stano claims to have taken thirty-two lives in Florida; Gacy buried thirty-three in suburban Chicago; Joseph Fischer may have killed as many as forty in the New York and Connecticut area; and most horribly, Henry

Lee Lucas has claimed responsibility for the death of more than 360 victims.

Serial murderers, like society in general, have become geographically more mobile. Unlike their counterparts in earlier years, some serial murders now travel around the country, leaving a trail of human carnage. For example, Bundy is suspected of having murdered thirty-three females across four states from one corner of the country to the other. More frightening, Lucas is suspected of killing in more than twenty states!*

The increase in mass murder may partly result from technological advances which enable law enforcement investigators to link similar killings in different cities or states. Yet, some killers remain particularly adroit at avoiding apprehension. If and when the police catch up with the serial killers at large, or when still-undetected serial killings become identified, even Lucas's record death count may be short-lived.

In reaction to a very real trend, the news media have headlined the growing incidence of mass murder, particularly serial killings. Not only have newspapers carried daily reports of mass killings, manhunts, trials, and sentencings, but the wire services have run feature stories on the topic of serial murder. In addition, television's ubiquitous impact has enhanced public awareness of the "epidemic": On its *Frontline* series, the Public Broadcasting Service aired an outstanding documentary portraying the mind and motives of mass killer Kenneth Bianchi; ABC-TV News *Nightline* featured a half-hour program on serial murder following the capture and shooting of killer Christopher Wilder in New Hampshire; and even HBO, which customarily televises only

*Lucas's willing confessions have provided an excellent opportunity for police investigators from around the country potentially to clear up unsolved homicides in their jurisdictions, no matter how tenuous the evidence. Moreover, given the dates and locales of some of these murders, it is questionable that Lucas is responsible for as many as he claims. There is, nevertheless, little doubt that he committed numerous killings.

entertainment, produced an hour-long special on the topic of serial murder.

The extensive news coverage given mass killings may have the unintended consequence of encouraging others to commit murder. For example, the so-called "copycat murder syndrome" has produced outbreaks of poisonings linked directly to well-publicized cases of murder. One well-publicized case was that of Dr. Thomas T. Graves who sent a wealthy Providence, Rhode Island widow a New Year's gift of a bottle of whiskey laced with arsenic, after he had gained control of her assets. A midnight toddy made from the poisoned brew left the widow dead and a close friend who shared her gift became ill but survived.

Shortly after the Providence incident received national attention, a jilted mistress in the San Francisco area mailed a collection of delicious, but arsenic-seeded candies to her lover's wife. The mistress had discovered that a reconciliation between her lover and his wife had taken place, and decided to put a stop to it. What she succeeded in doing, however, was to put herself on trial for murder.

She also succeeded in spreading the outbreak of poisonings to another city. A few weeks later, the director of the Knickerbocker Athletic Club in New York City found a one-ounce bottle of Bromo Seltzer in his mailbox. The next morning, his wife drank some of it to cure a headache. Little did she suspect that the painkiller had been spiked with a fatal dose of cyanide. An hour later, she was dead.

The Bromo Seltzer murder and the poisonings which apparently inspired it took place in 1898![7] Long before television was invented, murderers were taking their cues from print media—newspapers and magazines. A 1982 version of the copycat phenomenon was aided by the presence of powerful electronic media which bombarded us with daily reminders of poisoned pain pills.

The first victim of the "Tylenol scare" was 12-year-old Mary Kellerman of Elk Grove Village, Illinois, whose parents gave her an Extra-Strength Tylenol capsule to relieve an irritating runny nose and sore throat. Just a few minutes later, she was found on the bathroom floor, dying of what doctors believed was a stroke.

The next victim was 27-year-old Adam Janus who took Tylenol and then collapsed in his Arlington Heights, Illinois home. A short time later, he died in the emergency room of Northwest Community Hospital, despite his doctors' efforts to counteract what looked like a massive heart attack. The tragedy continued. Hours later, Adam's grief-stricken brother and sister-in-law were admitted to the hospital, sharing not only his symptoms—dilated pupils and low blood pressure—but also the Extra-Strength Tylenol they had found in his home. By the weekend, Adam's brother and sister-in-law were counted among the seven Chicago-area residents who lost their lives after going to the medicine cabinet for Tylenol capsules.

It didn't take investigators long to find the missing link: An unknown person had replaced the dry white powder in Extra-Strength Tylenol capsules with a lethal dose of moist, gray cyanide. Most frightening, his victims apparently were chosen totally at random—either as a smokescreen for getting at one particular person or as an impersonal attempt to get at society in general. The killer went into several different retail stores across the Chicago area, bought bottles of Extra-Strength Tylenol, filled some of the Tylenol capsules with the deadly poison, and then returned the tampered bottles to the store shelves for unsuspecting customers to purchase.

But the impact of the Tylenol tragedy was to spread far beyond Illinois. Following nationwide television and newspaper coverage, copycat killers soon turned up everywhere. Indeed, there were at least a hundred copycat poisonings during the next four weeks alone. In more than a dozen states around the country, poison was discovered in pies, candy, mixed nuts, eyedrops, mouthwash, and a variety of over-the-counter drugs. Excedrin was recalled from Colorado store shelves after William Sinkovic of Aurora took an Extra-Strength Excedrin capsule which had been poisoned with mercuric chloride. While Sinkovic lay in serious condition in Aurora Community Hospital, officials at Stanley Aviation in Aurora reported that a bottle of mercuric chloride was missing from their company plant.

Meanwhile, storekeepers in Cape Cod, Massachusetts began removing bottles of Anacin 3 after several separate cases of tampering were discovered. No sooner had they finished when a Tylenol capsule was reportedly found in a jar of Planter's Unsalted Mixed Nuts.

By October 31, 1982, parents in communities across the nation were panic-stricken that their children might be victimized by a diabolical Tylenol-type Halloween trick. Fearing candy and cookies laced with cyanide, dozens of towns banned trick-or-treating or restricted it to the daylight hours. Some communities held city-sponsored Halloween parties to keep the kids off the streets; and the Department of Health and Human Services warned parents to inspect all of their children's Halloween candy for signs of tampering. Chicago Mayor Jane Byrne sternly advised: "I would not allow my children to take candy this particular Halloween."

News coverage of violence is as traditional in our society as the newspaper itself; but the sudden escalation of mass murder has given new form to an old theme. Just as murder sells newspapers, violence has become an integral part of television programming. More than two-thirds of all prime-time programs contain at least some violence—the average show has almost seven violent episodes per hour.

At least half of all adult Americans believe that violent television fare may be harmful for their children. They voice concern that serious, even fatal, acts of aggression like murder may actually be triggered by what is shown on TV.

A 1983 study by sociologist David Phillips suggests that parents may be right.[8] He examined the homicide rates immediately after televised heavyweight prizefights and found a brief but sharp increase in homicides, an overall rise of almost 13%. This effect peaked the third day following the prizefights and especially after heavily publicized events. The biggest third-day peak occurred after the fight that received the most publicity: Muhammad Ali and Joe Frazier's "Thrilla in Manilla." Some viewers apparently imitate the violence they witness on TV.

Even the form of violence portrayed by the media may be imitated. Women tend to be the victims of "random" murder in movies, soap operas, and prime-time series as well as in real life. Unlike its common portrayal of women as victims, television has not often dared to dramatize serial killings of children. This would probably offend more and titillate fewer. Similarly, the serial rape-murder of homosexuals has been underplayed because many viewers would be repulsed by the homosexual theme itself.

Just as children mimic their favorite violent television heroes, so may adults who are already predisposed toward aggression. Several studies indicated that violent pornography in which women are victimized contributes to male aggressiveness. For example, Dr. Edward Donnerstein showed that men who had watched sexual violence were more willing to punish another person with an electrical shock, especially if that person was a female.[9] Even nonviolent pornography depicts women as submissive and vulnerable. Consequently, a recent study by family sociologists Murray A. Straus and Larry Baron found that rates of forcible rape were higher in states where *Playboy* sold better.[10]

Curiously, a presidential commission formed in the late 1960s concluded after a large-scale investigation that pornography had no deleterious effects on the sexual behavior of adults. A similar study conducted now might very well reach the opposite conclusion, because the nature of pornography, both soft- and hard-core, has become increasingly more violent and sadistic. In the extreme, "snuff" films of the last few years have depicted the sexual murder of women; it is rumored that some of the killings actually occurred. But even mainstream entertainment has begun to dramatize repeated sexual murder of women.

Television has been around for decades and so has violent programming. But things are different now. First, people are watching more TV—the average child, for example, watches five to six hours a day. Second, parents have less control over their children's television habits. In many homes the children have their own sets. Most important, however, television content has changed. The portrayal of violence is now often laced with either explicit sex or sexual innuendo, making aggression seem an intrinsic part of the erotic experience. Violence interpreted as pleasurable is far more likely to be imitated, especially by those who are predisposed—by environment or heredity—to do harm to others.

CHAPTER 3

THE PSYCHIATRIC MISTAKE

The literature on mass murder is full of complex psychological theories based on case studies of uncommonly bizarre or hideous murders. To account for their specimens of destructiveness, researchers have studied everything from family structure to brain structure, from biography to biology. Their analyses make for engrossing reading, but their overall validity as applied to more than a few individual cases needs to be examined.

A set of childhood characteristics held by many to be associated with violent behavior has been named the "Macdonald triad," after psychiatrist John M. Macdonald, who first suggested the possibility that three factors could predict violent behavior.[1] He speculated that those shown to be homicidal commonly have three characteristics in their childhood histories: bedwetting, firesetting, and torturing small animals. Kenneth Bianchi, one of the two men responsible for the Hillside Stranglings, reportedly had had a wetting problem during childhood and once had killed a cat as a prank. David Berkowitz, "Son of Sam," set numerous fires. He even kept a diary of his firesetting activities, calling himself the "Phantom Fireman."

According to psychiatrists Hellman and Blackman—who endorsed this triad—enuresis represents a form of sadism or hostility, since the act of voiding is equated in fantasy with damaging and destroying.[2] Urine can, of course, ruin sheets and the mattress. Similarly, urinating may symbolically express hostility, as in the phrase "pissed off." Drs. Hellman and Blackman conjecture that enuresis is a reaction to parental rejection or abuse in that the child rebels and resists the type of sphincter control demanded by the mother.

The second element of the triad—firesetting—has been found statistically to be associated with enuresis. A further indicator of "violence-proneness," as a number of studies have shown, is the connection between the act of arson or the setting of small, relatively innocuous fires and assaultive behavior. In other words, it is suggested that children who are violent with peers also tend to set fires for fun.

The final element of the triad is perhaps the most obvious of the three. Torturing small animals is a precursor of cruelty to human beings. Psychiatrist Alan Felthous points out, further, that the torture of dogs and cats is more an indicator of future violent behavior than that of flies, toads, and turtles.[3] Not only are dogs and cats more human-like in their level of intelligence and behavior, but the torture and killing of them violates the human bond with pets—a bond of affection that this type of disturbed child is not able to feel.

Macdonald's triad has been implicated in a mass murder that occurred on November 1, 1955 aboard a commercial airliner.[4] Minutes after takeoff from Denver's airport, a four-engine aircraft burst into flames, and all forty-four of its passengers perished in the fiery aftermath. One of the victims was specifically killed by design; the rest were just along for the ride. Two weeks later, tall, well-mannered, 23-year-old Jack Gilbert Graham confessed that he had placed a time bomb in his mother's suitcase in order to collect her inheritance and insurance money. He also happened to hate her guts. The other forty-three deaths were merely a camouflage for the real target of the twenty-five sticks of dynamite.

Jack Graham could have been the prototype for Macdonald's triad. He was a frequent bedwetter until the age of 6, when his grandmother died, at which time he was sent to an institution for fatherless boys. He later set fire to a garage while playing with matches and, as an adult, burned down a car repair garage, resulting in $100,000 damage. In addition, he had a long history of cruelty to animals.

Graham's trial focused on his plea of insanity: whether he knew "right from wrong" and whether he could resist his murderous impulses. Psychological tests indicated that Graham had average intelligence and no gross distortions of reasoning; that he possessed adequate knowledge of social conventions, and felt guilty for his wrongdoing. Psychological evidence further suggested that, despite his impulsiveness, Graham was capable of controlling his violent behavior. He was found legally sane and guilty of murder. After refusing his attorney's advice to appeal, Jack Gilbert Graham was executed in the Colorado gas chamber in 1957.

It is important to note that the Macdonald triad is proposed, not as a cause of violence, but as a set of symptoms. Advocates of the theory, like Drs. Hellman and Blackman, emphasize that the behaviors of bedwetting, firesetting, and cruelty to animals are reactions to parental abandonment, neglect, or brutality. While their position suggests that preventive measures are possible, they do not provide any specific preventive strategies.

While Macdonald's triad gives childhood symptoms of future violent activity, Drs. G. S. Evseeff and E. M. Wisniewski have proposed a theory of childhood experiences which cause "homicidal-proneness."[5] This theory builds on the case of "Bill," an anonymous mass killer who axed his wife and five stepchildren to death in less than ten minutes. Based on this single example, they suggest that the traumatic childhood experiences of being sexually abused, brutally beaten, and abandoned may be important factors in creating a mass murderer.

Bill's early biography is ripe with the elements of Evseeff and Wisniewski's triad. The only child of a turbulent marriage between a man and woman who "indulged themselves in sex, violence, and the excessive use of alcohol," Bill would be beat on the back of his head whenever his mother felt the need to express her anger. When he was 4 years old, his father nearly beat him to death. Six years later, he walked into the house to find his father breaking his mother's toes one by one. Next, Bill was abandoned by his mother in bus depots and a train station. His father's abandonment was more final: He committed suicide by shooting himself in the head, but not before he had made homosexual advances toward his only son. Finally, Bill, from an early age, watched from the couch next to his mother's open bedroom door as she had sexual relations with his father and other men. Bill often slept in the same bed with his mother, where he fondled her genitals when she was drunk or pretended to be asleep. At the age of 10, he was severely beaten by his mother after she caught him masturbating.

There is widespread acceptance outside of professional circles of the notion that a troubled childhood is the root cause of homicidal behavior. A less popular and more fatalistic view rests on the possible existence of a "bad seed." This theory has been dramatized in an early classic film of the same name in which a young innocent-looking girl kills because of her volatile inherited trait.

In the mid-1960s, some researchers purported to demonstrate that inmates in institutions for the criminally insane were significantly more likely to possess the "XYY syndrome," that is, men given to violence were born with an extra "Y" or male sex chromosome. Some medical researchers of the day proposed that the XYY genetic disorder predisposed its estimated 100,000 victims to criminality. Others even inferred that punishment would do little to dissuade those with the genetic affliction from committing criminal acts. It was, after all, a matter of genetic destiny.[6]

The XYY anomaly later became a standard explanation for mass murder, after it was falsely rumored that Richard Speck was an "XYY." The report was eventually proven wrong, but not before the press had publicized this explanation for Speck's outburst. In newspaper articles and even some scientific accounts, Speck's XYY constitution was reportedly apparent in such phenotypical characteristics as facial acne, tallness, long extremities, mild mental retardation, and a history of mental illness. He was falsely labeled "supermale"—the prototypical XYY man.

Genetics is but one of many biological explanations that have been used in an attempt to understand violent behavior. At least 14 million people in America are the victims of some form of brain dysfunction involving epilepsy, mental retardation, minimal brain disorders, strokes, brain tumors, head injuries, or malnutrition. Many individuals with cerebral disturbances are detected by such neurological signs as temporal lobe epilepsy as well as electroencephalogram (EEG) abnormalities. Others exhibit irregular EEGs only under special circumstances (for example, after drinking alcohol).

Clinical studies suggest that brain disease or injury can result in outbursts of anger and less frequently in episodes of violent behavior. In a Polish study, for example, an organic lesion to the central nervous system was discovered in fourteen of twenty-four killers. Psychiatrist Dr. Mortimer Gross similarly concludes: "There is a large body of evidence pointing to an association between organic brain disease . . . and violence, particularly of the sudden-impulsive kind."[7]

Experts from many disciplines were eager to account for Richard Speck's massacre of eight nurses in one evening. Chicago psychiatrist Dr. Marvin Ziporyn, for example, revealed that Speck had had eight major brain concussions before the age of 14 as well as an EEG taken after his capture which showed that Speck was abnormal for a person of his age.[8] But abnormal psychology has not provided a complete explanation for unpredictable outbursts of violence. The 1966 slaughter was uncharacteristic even for Richard Speck, whose criminal record displayed little indication of a propensity for mass murder.

The Texas Tower sniper, Charles Whitman, was another anomaly to be hotly debated by specialists. This case illustrates just how easy it is to create the false impression that brain disorder explains the problem of mass murder. Whitman's postmortem examination revealed a walnut-sized, highly malignant tumor of the brain (a glioblastoma multiforme). Could not the presence of a profound abnormality in Whitman's brain explain his "sudden, episodic attack of violence" in which fourteen died and thirty were wounded?

University of Michigan psychologist Dr. Elliot Valenstein reminds us that Whitman's violent behavior was anything but episodic or sudden.[9] In fact, Whitman had written his detailed plan for mass killing in his diary days before the actual massacre, describing not only how he intended to protect his position on the tower and how he planned to escape, but even what he was going to wear. Moreover, Whitman's killing spree did not occur in quick succession: The night before, he killed deliberately. First, he traveled to his mother's apartment in Austin where he stabbed her in the chest and shot her in the head. Returning home, he wrote "I have just killed my mother. If there's a heaven, she is going there. If there is not a heaven, she is out of her pain and misery. I love my mother with all my heart."[10] Whitman then stabbed his wife three times in the chest, and recorded in his diary "12:30 a.m.—Mother already dead. 3 o'clock—both dead."

Some interest in recent years has centered on the relationship between diet and crime. Advocates of the well-known diet developed by Dr. Ben Feingold, for example, claim that the removal of all artificial colors and flavors, as well as foods with naturally occurring salicylates, such as aspirin, may reduce hyperactivity in children. The syndrome of hyperactivity is marked by impaired ability to concentrate, short attention span, and, most notably, impulsivity and aggression. Vitamin specialists, such as Dr. Carlton Fredericks, have suggested similarly that chlorine or other chemicals in tap water may cause "mental disturbances" and that vitamin deficiencies may even contribute to depression and schizophrenia.[11]

The viewpoint widely accepted in psychiatry is well represented by Dr. Donald Lunde who studied murderers in his role as a court-appointed psychiatric expert.[12] Over a five-year period, he accumulated information about forty murderers—including a few mass killers—based on cases that went to trial, many of which called into question the defendant's state of mind.

Reflecting the majority opinion in psychiatry, Lunde claims that almost all mass murderers are "insane" and that they usually do not know their victims well, if at all. It is not unlike the popular Hollywood image of a glassy-eyed, deranged madman whose thirst for human blood drives him to butcher at random and to stalk his victims wherever he finds them. Based on the cases he has worked on, Lunde asserts that two kinds of mentalities account for most cases of mass killing: (1) paranoid schizophrenia characterized by an aggressive, suspicious demeanor, by hallucinations (usually "hearing voices"), and by delusions of grandeur and/or persecution; and (2) sexual sadism characterized by killing, torturing and/or mutilating victims in order to achieve sexual arousal. The latter type dehumanize victims by viewing them as objects, specifically as life-size dolls or enemies of decent people.

To illustrate the paranoid schizophrenic type, Lunde uses the case of John Linley Frazier who, on October 19, 1970, murdered a well-to-do, well-known eye surgeon and the doctor's wife, two children, and secretary. Each of Frazier's victims was blindfolded, bound, and shot to death. He then threw their bodies into the swimming pool of the doctor's house.

As many psychiatrists contend, the most obvious symptoms of paranoid schizophrenia usually do not appear until adulthood; and, true to form, John Frazier was not "frightening" or "exceptionally strange" until he was 24, only five months before carrying out the mass killing. He began to hear God's voice commanding him to devote himself to the mission of saving the world from the ravages of materialism.

Frazier became convinced that a number of people including his own wife and mother were conspiring to prevent him from carrying out God's mission. Moreover, he would disappear into the woods for days at a time, where he was occasionally spotted scanning the horizon with a rifle, presumably in search of those who were plotting to destroy him.

A slave to his delusions, Frazier carried out what to him was a "divine mission," but to the rest of the world was a senseless slaughter of five innocent people. Four days later he was found by the police, frail and exhausted, in a dilapidated cow shed downhill from the scene of the mass killing. Tried and convicted on five counts of murder, he was judged legally sane, and given a life sentence in San Quentin.

For Lunde's second type of mass killer, the sexual sadist, he draws on the case of six-foot nine-inch, 280-pound Edmund Kemper, who, at the age of 15, shot and killed his grandparents. He was committed for his crime to a maximum security hospital. But that was only the beginning. Upon his release four years later, Kemper shot, stabbed and strangled to death six young coeds as each hitchhiked from the University of California at Santa Cruz. He cut off their limbs and heads, tried to have sex with the corpses, and finished them by devouring their flesh. His ultimate reward, however, was the exceptional orgasm that only the act of killing could provide for him. Kemper also preserved his victims severed heads by wrapping them in cellophane so that later he could masturbate into their mouths. On April 2, 1973, Kemper struck again, slaying his mother and her close friend. After decapitating his mother, he tore out her larynx and threw it down a garbage disposal. His purpose was fulfilled: She would never again "bitch, scream, and yell" at him.

Kemper had displayed signs of psychological disorder at an early age. As a child, he had been fascinated by weapons, especially guns and knives. He once cut off the head and hands of his younger sister's favorite doll. By the age of 13, he had graduated to torturing and killing the family's cat, which he beheaded and cut into small pieces. Feeling totally inadequate with girls, Kemper fantasized about killing them. As he later explained, " . . . if I killed them, you know, they couldn't reject me as a man. It was more or less making a doll out of a human being . . . and carrying out my fantasies with a doll, a living human doll."[13] Kemper's necrophilia was tied to his feelings of inferiority; dead sex partners could not sense his sexual inadequacies or comment on his small penis.

Undoubtedly, psychiatry has provided valuable insights into the minds of particular mass killers such as Graham, Frazier, and Kemper. Unfortunately, psychiatric explanations are often generalized from a few unrepresentative cases—sometimes even a single case—to larger populations of mass killers, murderers, or even those with a propensity toward violence. Drs. Evseeff and Wisniewski, for example, concocted their triad of childhood experiences to explain the general notion of "homicidal-proneness" primarily on the basis of one mass murderer, "Bill." In a similar way, Lunde characterized mass killers generally from his knowledge of a few cases for which he had served as a court-appointed expert.

Not only are many of these psychiatric theories inferred from small numbers of cases, but the cases tend to be special, irregular, or particularly bizarre. These killers have committed acts so heinous, even for mass murderers, that their legal sanity has been seriously challenged in court. To develop and illustrate their theories, psychiatrists have used sexual sadists who mutilate and dismember their victims; paranoid schizophrenics who hear voices or talk to dogs. Missing, however, are the cases of mass killing for the purpose of silencing informants, eliminating witnesses, and collecting inheritances. Absent too are the acts of mass murder carried out by cold-blooded killers who calculate every detail of their crime and know precisely what they are doing. Similarly underrepresented are the multiple murders by killers who know their victims very well, who kill their family, neighbors, or coworkers.

The problem with generalizing the traits observed in specific mass killers to larger groups of offenders is demonstrated in the predictive limitations of elements of the Macdonald triad. It is, for example, not surprising that a sexually sadistic murderer like Edmund Kemper practiced on animals as a youngster, gaining pleasure that may even be sexual from the torture. Nevertheless, the connection between the torturing of animals as a child and the torturing of women as an adult is incomplete at best as an early warning sign of mass murder. Torturing animals is certainly far more common than is mass murder. Many who are so "evil" as youngsters will simply not persist in torturing for pleasure as adults. Others will find more socially acceptable ways to prey on people, such as using shady business practices. Any attempt to utilize childhood behavior to predict adult criminality is doomed to fail, since the so-called false-positives—those predicted to be dangerous who in fact will not become homicidal—exceed in number the rare cases who will.

Another element of Macdonald's triad which has been evident in the biographies of murderers is bedwetting. While the psychological effects of not being able to control one's bodily functions may be severe, there are millions of children with this problem who do not grow up to become murderers, much less mass murderers. Instead, most of them become law-abiding citizens.

Even when an individual has all three symptoms of the Macdonald triad, the ability to predict whether he may or may not become a mass murderer is very limited. Some psychiatrists had endorsed the triad, based on their own isolated clinical observations. But even Macdonald himself was forced to rethink the predictive value of the triad upon further research. Comparing the personal histories of violent and nonviolent psychiatric patients, he failed to find differences between the groups in terms of the triad of symptoms. Contradicting some psychiatric speculations, Macdonald also found no differences between the groups with respect to parental brutality and seduction (that is, excessive stimulation) during their upbringing.

We believe it is quite imprudent to consider seriously policy recommendations such as those proposed by Drs. Hellman and Blackman. They maintain: "It is the detection and early management of children in the throes of the triad that might well forestall a career of violent crime to the adult."[14] The labeling and manipulating of "murder-prone" kids prior to any expression of serious criminality is as dangerous, in a different way, as the behavior itself. Not only is it unethical to treat or incarcerate people—innocent or otherwise—for the crimes they might commit in the future, but the stigma of "dangerousness" might itself cause rebellious behavior.

A common observation of mass killers is that in early childhood they were rejected by others. Indeed, a large proportion of mass killers—like Kenneth Bianchi, the "Hillside Strangler," and David Berkowitz, the "Son of Sam"—were adopted early in life; adoption is sometimes viewed by the child as the ultimate form of rejection by his biological parents. Some psychologists suggest that the frustrations engendered from such early rejections can explode into a violent rage, provided that a sufficient triggering event occurs. We consider this viewpoint to be incomplete. Hundreds of thousands of people have been adopted, yet most will never come close to committing mass murder. Frustration of any kind early in life can predispose certain individuals to commit heinous crimes; but it can more easily motivate someone to strive to overcome his limitations by succeeding in a brilliant career.

The flaw in the theories discussed above is essentially one of overprediction. Even if *all* killers were adopted, rejected bedwetters, they would not approach the number of "normal" adults sharing these childhood experiences. Indeed, these characteristics are more predictive of nonviolence than violence. We should not stigmatize those millions of people who were bedwetters or were adopted for the acts of a few true deviants among them; certainly we don't attribute responsibility to the population of "normal" people for the many among them who violate the law.

Beyond the problem of false-positives, other psychiatric observations are distorted because they are typically formulated on biased (and sometimes small) samples of cases. A psychiatrist is consulted either if a defendant requests it (when an insanity plea is considered) or if the judge orders it (when the defendant's competency to stand trial is questionable). It is the most bizarre murders and the potentially insane killers that are examined by court-appointed psychiatrists, not "ordinary" criminals and noncriminals about whom guilt or innocence is to be determined. Hence, these psychiatrists are exposed to a very extreme population of killers.

The difficulty in generalizing from unrepresentative cases is clear in attempts to establish a link between the XYY condition and violent behavior. The highest prevalence rates for the XYY syndrome have been found in prisons and security mental hospitals. But a limited number of all XYY's ever come to the attention of the criminal justice system. Even fewer XYY's are convicted of a major crime. And even fewer of them are placed behind bars. Finally, a much smaller and more atypical number is placed in maximum security mental hospitals at some point in their processing.

Therefore, inmates and particularly those labeled criminally insane undoubtedly constitute a highly biased sample of all who commit criminal acts. First, they tend to be severely disadvantaged, whether by lack of intellect, education, money, or prestige. It would not be surprising to learn that such institutions also house greater numbers of men physically or socially disadvantaged by the XYY anomaly. As a result, it would be wrong to generalize such a finding to large groups of violent individuals, many of whom escape detection by the criminal justice system or, at least, do not get committed to special institutions.

Finally, though the theories proposed to explain mass murder have been extremely varied, they share one feature in common: a narrow-minded focus on the killer. It has been the mistake of psychiatrists and other scientists who study the mass killer in terms of his psychological or physical constitution to focus exclusively on individual characteristics. Indeed, most who possess "bad seeds" or "sick minds" never kill anyone, and many who appear in body and mind to be perfectly normal have committed the most hideous acts of murder. Mass murder is not just a symptom of disease or pathology.

The role of biology and early experience cannot, of course, be ignored. These factors do apparently dictate a range, albeit wide, of potential behavior for the individual. Situational factors—experiences and learning beyond the fifth year of life, successes and failures in career and family, and social and cultural influences—are at least as critical in encouraging a murderous response from someone who may or may not be predisposed to violence. Some individuals, by their biology and nurturing, may be more prone to homicide and rage than others. Nevertheless, the final behavioral outcome within the spectrum of possibilities, we contend, depends on later experience as well.

CHAPTER 4

DISSECTING THE MASS MURDERER

He talked to dogs; or, more precisely, dogs talked to him. David Berkowitz, the "Son of Sam," the .44 caliber killer, a chubby, pathetic man, remains one of America's most notorious and perplexing murderers.[1]

The story of David Berkowitz is well known, although the truth about his mental state may never be completely understood. He claimed that he attacked his victims when commanded to do so. These orders supposedly came from a man named Sam (Sam Carr, David's neighbor) and were relayed by demonically possessed dogs. Usually it was a bark, a howl, or a certain glance from a dog that would indicate to David when to attack and whom to attack. In one instance it was simply a sign of crossed dog feces on the ground that gave him the go-ahead. Some have disputed the authenticity of David's demonic fantasy, seeing it as an attempt to escape blame. Regardless, the story of Berkowitz's debilitating effect on millions is a fascinating and instructive case.

Berkowitz first struck unnoticeably on Christmas Eve, 1975, twice attacking young females on the street with knives, wounding but not killing them. One of the victims, a Hispanic woman, has never been identified, because she failed to report the assault to the police and didn't seek aid from a medical facility for her knife wounds. Some have speculated that this victim may have wished to keep her status as an illegal alien concealed.

Berkowitz was surprised at how messy and difficult stabbing could be; it always seemed easy on television. He even found the encounters distasteful, repulsed by his victims' screaming and struggling. For David, unlike a number of other mass murderers, physical contact with the victim was not an important form of gratification. Instead, killing was but a means toward an end. If David obeyed dutifully Sam's command to kill, he would get his reward: a strong, satisfying orgasm. So David switched to a gun, a light .44 caliber Bulldog pistol he purchased while in Texas that would be very effective at close range.

Jody Valenti and Donna Lauria were in close range on July 29, 1976. It was very late, past one in the morning, when David Berkowitz approached the car in which the girls were sitting and talking. David was "hearing voices" that ordered him to kill. Donna saw the man approach, saw him pull a gun from a bag, but died before she saw his .44 Bulldog fire for the fifth and last time. Jody, hit only in the thigh, screamed hysterically and leaned her body on the horn. Out of bullets, David could not silence his frantic victim. David fled in terror to his Ford Galaxy and drove away.

Following his July attack on Valenti and Lauria, Berkowitz struck again in November wounding two girls with his .44 Bulldog, struck again in January killing a 26-year-old woman and wounding her boyfriend, and then again in March fatally shooting in the face a 19-year-old Columbia University coed only a hundred yards from the spot where he had killed his previous victim. The police noted, as did newspapers, that the similarities among these attacks were curious coincidences. But on March 10, 1977, two days following the latest killing, New York City Police Commissioner Michael Codd convened a press conference to announce frightening news. Ballistics comparisons confirmed a link between the July 1976 shooting of Donna Lauria and the recent homicide of a Columbia University student: both women were killed by bullets from the same .44 caliber firearm. Newspaper headlines dramatically called the unknown assailant the ".44 caliber killer."

The attacks then began to quicken in frequency. The next assault on April 17, in which a young couple parked in a car was ambushed and shot to death, left clues that significantly intensified both the police investigative effort and the public fear. Aided by ballistics evidence, the police established a definitive link among all six of the attacks since the previous July's shooting of Lauria and Valenti.

The nature and extent of newspaper coverage changed too. The man whom reporters had nicknamed the ".44 caliber killer" now went by a different name: He called himself the "Son of Sam." At the scene of the April shooting Berkowitz left a childishly scribbled note for Captain Borelli of the Queens Homicide Squad, complaining about lies in the newspapers and revealing his "true" identity[2]:

> I am deeply hurt by your calling me a wemon hater. I am not. But I am a monster.
>
> I am the "Son of Sam." I am a little "Brat"

The strange note written by a previously anonymous killer, dubbed by the press the ".44 caliber killer" for lack of any other name, transformed the murderer into a real person. The message which continued from there showed a frightening mix of emotions: sadness and anger, helplessness and despair. Berkowitz even expressed love for the people of Queens and wished them a happy Easter. But, finally, the note closed with this warning:

> POLICE—let me haunt you with these words:
>
> I'll be back!
>
> I'll be back!
>
> To be interpreted as—Bang, bang, bang, bank, bang—Ugh!!

The next few months were unprecedented in New York's history. As the temperature rose during the summer of 1977, so did the level of fear. Newspaper sales spiraled—the amount of space devoted to the "Son of Sam" could have spanned Yankee Stadium. New York City was in panic.

New Yorkers desperately searched for patterns to the attacks, patterns which they hoped would buffer them from danger. A popular belief, for a time, was that the .44 caliber killer chose only young females with long brown hair; this sent thousands scurrying to the hairdresser for haircuts and colorings. Such a response, however, was the understandable but futile fruit of mass hysteria. His final victim had short, blond hair.* According to Berkowitz's explanation later in custody, his attacks were random. He simply obeyed the orders of Sam relayed to him by signs from dogs and by the voices of demons.

The "Son of Sam" did strike again, in June and in July. Open correspondence in the papers between columnist Jimmy Breslin—who pleaded for a surrender—and the "Son of Sam"—who fashioned himself as the "Duke of Death"—further fueled the public's anxiety. Neysa Moskowitz, the outraged and outspoken mother of the latest victim Stacy Moskowitz, loudly demanded action, and the New York Police Department responded by adding hundreds more detectives to the investigation.

Even heads of organized crime reportedly mobilized their underlings to search for the killer. Apparently, business at underworld-owned bars, clubs, and restaurants suffered as New Yorkers stayed home; it was even rumored that the Mafia got involved because some of the victims were of Italian descent.

Finally, on August 10, David Berkowitz was arrested in front of his apartment, ending a rampage which left six dead and nine wounded, including one paralyzed and one blinded, in the boroughs of Queens, Brooklyn, and the Bronx. In an almost anticli-

*One could speculate that Berkowitz purposely chose to shoot a blond in response to publicity which claimed that he only liked brunettes. He might have wanted either to prove a point or to throw off the police.

mactic conclusion to the drama, David Berkowitz pleaded guilty to murder.

The Son of Sam is an extraordinary case; extraordinary not because of the killer's explanation for his crimes, since other killers have claimed to be following divine instruction; not because so many were killed, since other murderers have killed far more people; and not because of the style of killing, which was comparably less gruesome and bizarre than that of others. This case was extraordinary because it gripped in fear what many consider the most important city in the world. Nevertheless, the crucial question here is whether the "Son of Sam" accurately represents most mass murderers. Certainly, few mass killers are as well known as David Berkowitz. Because *The New York Times* is in a sense a national newspaper and because events in New York are often highlighted in network newscasts, David Berkowitz, to many people, became synonymous with mass murder. But is David Berkowitz a typical mass murderer or is he indeed extraordinary; and, more important, what is the typical mass murderer like?

The names of some mass murderers like Berkowitz and Manson are more familiar to many Americans than the names of recent vice presidents of the United States, and thus these two men dominate the popular image of the mass killer. However, an attempt to assemble a representative profile of the typical mass murderer requires the inclusion of both the well known and the obscure. Not all mass murderers, despite the enormity of their crimes, attract widespread and continuing publicity like Berkowitz did. Some killers, after slaughtering a house full of people, have their flash of national notoriety, and then fade back into obscurity as they spend their lives behind bars. Other killers, upstaged by some event of greater national interest, make only the second section of newspapers outside their locality.

Regardless of the extent of notoriety, however, most, if not all, mass murderers are publicized to some degree on a regional or national basis. We have capitalized, therefore, on the availability of newspaper indexes to compile a diverse and representative collection of mass killers to study.

Indexes of the following newspapers were searched for incidences of mass murder: *The New York Times, Los Angeles Times, The Times Picayune* (New Orleans), *Detroit Free Press, Chicago Sun-Times,* and *Chicago Tribune.* Any simultaneous mass slaying or series of killings involving at least four victims killed and falling within the period 1974–1979 were investigated further. We obtained newspaper clippings from these papers as well as local journals, conducted telephone and personal interviews with key individuals, e.g., attorneys, judges, and police investigators, and studied biographies and in-depth interviews with mass murderers to acquire additional information about these cases. The time period for our study was ended in 1979 to ensure that most of the cases had achieved a final resolution. Although a few cases had to be dropped from our sample because the legal proceedings were ongoing or pending, thirty-three cases of mass murder involving forty-two offenders constituted our sample. (Each case of mass murder represents at least four victims and often more than one killer.) Thirty-one of the offenders were convicted of murder, four were found not guilty by reason of insanity, five had committed suicide, one was killed by a relative of one of his victims, and one died in an automobile accident.* While each offender was responsible for at least four deaths, it is impossible to determine exactly how many deaths were caused by these offenders in total. Some of the serial offenders are suspected of killing many more than the number for which they were directly blamed. Others were charged with only a few of the murders for which they were likely responsible, often simply to keep down the cost and effort of prosecution.

*One of the four defendants found insane was also convicted of murder in the first of a two-phase trial. In the second phase, criminal penalties were removed because of his state of mind.

For many of our findings and observations concerning these forty-two killers to have full meaning, a basis of comparison is necessary. We made use of FBI information available on all homicides in the United States for the years 1976–1980, 96,263 cases in total. Fortunately, this source of data enabled us to isolate cases of simultaneous mass murders, in which four or more people are killed in the same incident. We removed those cases in which the motive was clearly arson rather than murder itself. We were thereby left with 156 cases involving 675 victims. In some of these cases, obviously, certain information was not known to the police. Thus, for those concerns focusing specifically on characteristics of the mass killer, we had 107 cases involving 137 offenders for which information on the perpetrator(s) was available.*

Based on our study of the forty-two mass killers and the FBI data on simultaneous homicides, we have developed a composite profile of a mass murderer, which we will examine in the next chapter: He is typically a white male in his late twenties or thirties. In the case of simultaneous mass murder, he kills people he knows with a handgun or rifle; in serial crimes, he murders strangers by beating or strangulation. His specific motivation depends on the circumstances leading up to the crime, but it generally deals directly with either money, expediency, jealousy, or lust. Rarely is the mass murderer a hardened criminal with a long criminal record, although a spotty history of property crime is common. The occurrence of mass murder often follows a spell of

*Our data set of 42 offenders includes both serial and simultaneous incidents, while the FBI data set does not permit us to link together the victims of serial homicides. Because of the extended newspaper coverage of serial murders compared to the intensive short-term interest in simultaneous killings, our data on 33 incidents are perhaps more complete on serial than simultaneous mass murders. Conversely, the FBI data are complete in simultaneous killings, but do not identify serial killings. We were pleased to find, however, that the results of similar analyses of the two sources—our 33 cases and the 156 FBI cases—were very consistent.

frustration when a particular event triggers sudden rage; yet, in other cases, the killer is cooly pursuing some goal he cannot otherwise attain. Finally, though the mass killer often may appear cold and show no remorse, and even deny responsibility for his crime, serious mental illness or psychosis is rarely present. Most unexpectedly, in background, in personality, and even in appearance, the mass murderer is *extraordinarily ordinary.* This may be the key to his extraordinary "talent" for murder: After all, who

would ever suspect him?

CHAPTER 5

PROFILES OF MASS MURDERERS

To most people, the St. Valentine's Day Massacre refers to the famous 1929 gangland slaughter in Chicago in which members of Al Capone's gang double-crossed the gang of George "Bugs" Moran. Having previously arranged a meeting to deal in bootleg liquor, Capone's men masqueraded as police officers, lined up six of Moran's gangsters against the wall, and sprayed them with machine gun fire. To the people of New Rochelle, New York, however, Valentine's Day recalls a day in 1977 when a 33-year-old man who called himself the "Second Hitler" killed six and wounded four while attempting to exterminate his Jewish boss.[1]

Frederick W. Cowan was a huge, 250-pound weightlifter, who adorned his bulging biceps with tattoos of iron crosses, skulls, knives, and a swastika. Yet Cowan was considered gentle and kind by his friends and neighbors. Sometimes he would take neighborhood boys on day trips to auto races and ballgames. However, Cowan, on the inside, was full of hatred. A Nazi cultist, he had inscribed his philosophy on one of his many books on Hitler: "Nothing is lower than blacks or Jews except the police who protect them."[2] The inevitable expression of the frustration and disdain that boiled within him exploded on February 14, 1977 in a form bloodier than even Cowan might have predicted.

Those close to Cowan, including his parents with whom he lived, knew about his fanatic adoration of Hitler and Nazi SS General Reinhard Heydrich, commander of the concentration camps. Some had seen Cowan's attic room which was oddly decorated with Nazi regalia, including a variety of German guns and Lugers, a German army helmet, dummy hand grenades, knives and bayonets, an official Nazi flag bearing the black swastika on a white field bordered with red, and posters of Hitler and Himmler. Everyone thought this collection was nonetheless a peculiar but harmless hobby. When he talked about "shooting up a synagogue," his friends took it as a joke. After all, thousands of Americans belong to right-wing hate organizations and yet maintain a nonviolent coexistence with the many minorities in this country; they don't become mass murderers.

Cowan's ability to coexist eroded as his failures in life left him shoulder to shoulder with the blacks he hated, and worse, subordinate to a Jew. Despite his outstanding academic performance in parochial school, Cowan dropped out of college in his first year, dashing his hopes to become an engineer. He then pursued a career in the United States Army, but this too was aborted by a discharge that followed two courts-martial for going AWOL and fleeing the scene of an accident. Needing work, Cowan took a menial job at the Neptune Worldwide Moving Company. Identifying with the authority and power of the Third Reich, he couldn't stand taking orders from his boss, Norman Bing, a Jew. One day, after refusing his orders to move a refrigerator, Bing suspended Cowan for two weeks.

Those two weeks gave Cowan ample time to think, to fester, and to scheme. On his first day back to work, February 14, 1977, Cowan arrived early, at 7:45 AM, carrying a fifty-pound arsenal of weapons which he then set up in the company warehouse; his target was Norman Bing. Bing, however, was not around. So Cowan instead opened fire on the black employees, yelling to the other whites to move out of his way. Cowan never reached his nemesis Bing, who had hidden beneath the desk in his office when the shooting started. Despite Cowan's failure to shoot his intended victim, he was not a total failure. The dead included three blacks, one dark-skinned man from India, and a white police officer; five more were injured, one of whom died months later from gunshot wounds.

After the initial barrage of bullets, stillness remained for hours, during what became an all-day siege. Cowan still hoped to find Bing; and the police, a SWAT team, and throngs of interested onlookers waited to see what Cowan would do next. At 12:13 PM Cowan telephoned police headquarters to order some potato salad and hot chocolate. He also left a message of apology to Mayor Vincent Rippa for "causing the city so much trouble."[3]

At 2:40 PM a single gunshot was heard, which many in the crowd secretly prayed was Cowan ending the vigil and his life. After two more hours of silence, the police dared to move in on Cowan. There they found him dead, wearing a black beret emblazened with an emblem of a skull and crossbones and torn by the fatal bullet hole. Later the police found his car in the parking lot, bearing a sticker that read "I will give up my gun when they pry my cold, dead fingers from around it."[4]

Murders, instigated by racial hatred, are surprisingly rare in a country that has experienced so much racial conflict and violence. The case of Frederick Cowan is, in this sense, an unusual mass murder. Similarly, less than 10% of single-victim homicides cross racial lines. Those murders and specifically mass murders that do cross racial lines tend to be extremely brutal, fueled by racial antagonisms that may have existed and festered long before the victim and offender met.

Mass murders, however, do differ significantly from other murders in at least one important respect: Whereas blacks commit half the homicides in this country, only one in five mass killers is black; thus, the racial composition of mass murderers more closely approximates that of the population itself. This discrepancy between the presence of blacks in single and multiple killings can be understood by focusing on situations in which blacks do lead in homicide statistics. FBI statistics show that blacks are more likely than whites to kill in response to a fight or argument. For example, a dispute over money or honor may escalate until one person is dead. Criminologists Marvin E. Wolfgang and Franco Ferracuti describe a "subculture of violence," where violence is a learned and rewarded response to a variety of situations.[5] They claim that this pattern of learned violence is prevalent in many black neighborhoods where opportunities for educational and economic advancement are limited.* In the case of mass murder, however, this widely accepted explanation for homicide does not fit. Rarely will one person start a fight with four or more people and end up killing them all. Instead, mass homicides emerge from entirely different settings, those in which blacks and whites are equally likely to be found.

If you picture the image of a mass killer, he may be white, but could be black; he may be large and mean-looking, but could be deceptively harmless in appearance. One thing for sure, few people will imagine the killer to be a woman.

That most mass murderers are male should surprise no one. Only one of our sample of forty-two killers was female. Moreover, less than 7% of the FBI's simultaneous homicides implicate a female offender. What is noteworthy, however, is that the prevalence of men in mass killing far exceeds their 85% representation among all killers. The dominance of men in mass murder requires, therefore, an explanation beyond simple "male aggressiveness." Rather, to understand the overrepresentation of men, we need to focus on the weapon that facilitates the crime and the situation that instigates it.

Whereas knives, clubs, and other weapons can be lethal, the firearm is certainly the most effective means of killing. Furthermore, in terms of the simultaneous killing of a number of people, most weapons other than a handgun or better yet a rifle would be less effective. (An exception here would be a case like that of Jack Graham who blew up a planeload of people with a home-

*The theory of the "subculture of violence" has been used to explain higher rates of homicides among youthful males, in the lower class and the South, as well as among blacks.

made bomb.) Men are more likely to own and have access to a gun. Also, men are better trained in the use of firearms, because of military training, hunting, or law enforcement aspirations or simply different expectations for the male role in our society.

The ownership of and ability to use a gun or rifle are, of course, insufficient to make one a mass killer; many men *and* women are quite competent in shooting firearms and do not commit homicide, much less mass homicide. A gun is but an instrument, a means of executing an internal desire which builds from external circumstances. The circumstances which culminate in mass murder are more likely to occur to men.

It is obvious that certain types of mass killing—for example, serial raping and murdering—are the sole province of men. The fact that sex offenders, including rapists, child molesters, and serial killers, are almost without exception male derives primarily from their greater need to dominate. While society allows a woman to maintain a submissive role, a male who feels weak, passive or inadequate may feel strong pressure to live up to the powerful role that he believes he is expected to fulfill.

By contrast, family slayings theoretically could just as easily be committed by a mother or a daughter as by a father or son. The female member of the family is rarely the one, however. Among our forty-two mass murderers, we found only the case of Margaret Potter, who deliberately burned her family to death in Redondo Beach, California by torching their home.

The prevalence of men among family slayers would seem to contradict statistics which indicate that mothers are more often than fathers guilty of child abuse. The more frequent abusiveness of mothers, however, is probably a result of greater time and frustration with the children. When it comes to murder, however, "it's a man's job." Fathers more often kill than mothers; the maternal bond, for whatever reason, tends to run much deeper, prohibiting filicide. Apparently, Margaret Potter was an exception.

Following a marital separation, males are more apt to suffer a loss of kinship, because they are usually the ones who, voluntarily or involuntarily, leave the home and the family; a few, unable to cope, return to kill them all.

Not unlike separation or divorce, unemployment is one of life's changes which can leave an individual at the mercy of his uncontrolled impulses. Men are especially vulnerable to the effects of joblessness, because they are generally still expected to be the "breadwinners" in the family—those basically responsible for the family's economic well-being. Despite the best efforts of the women's movement, many people continue to feel that women "hold jobs" while men "have careers." Thus, when a man loses his job, he also loses an important source of self-regard and self-control which he can hardly compensate for in other ways. Therefore, it is usually the male as the breadwinner who directly suffers both financially and, more important, psychologically from unemployment.

In May 1977, James A. Girardi, an unemployed construction worker from Briarcliff Manor, New York, was beginning to wonder whether he would ever work again. After all, the unemployment rate for his type of job was somewhere between 30 and 40%; and prospects for the future hardly seemed brighter, at least not in Briarcliff Manor. That's why Girardi began to think of alternatives—like leaving his four children with his ex-wife and moving to Texas where the job market looked better.

Thirty-eight-year-old Girardi was tall and husky with black curly hair; friends described him as "a ladies' man who wore hip clothes and tried to act young."[6] But after Girardi's second wife had left him with four children from his first marriage, he began to develop a reputation around the neighborhood for his harsh and threatening discipline. Some said he had once broken his youngest son's arm and might do it again.

During the first week of May, Girardi's first wife and the mother of his four children tried in vain to contact him by phone. As a last resort, she finally called Girardi's brother Alfred who immediately drove to the red clapboard home, where he discovered his brother's grisly solution to his problems. Girardi had taken his own life with a shotgun—but apparently not before he had made sure that his children weren't abandoned. The Girardi offspring—Cindy, 16; Thomas, 15; Bonnie, 13; and Albert, 10—had been slain while asleep in their beds.

When the frustrations of life become overwhelming, the gun often provides the means toward an end, an effective instrument of mass destruction against those perceived as the source of "the problem." For Girardi, this apparently meant either getting a job—which he couldn't—or getting rid of those who depended on his employment and were therefore a constant pressure.

Some psychologists believe that the very presence of a gun makes people behave more aggressively. Psychologists Berkowitz and LePage observed, for instance, that children were more likely to act in a violent manner when a handgun (fortunately unloaded) was present in the room.[7] They concluded that the weapon, more than just serving as a convenient instrument of aggression, can actually stimulate or trigger violence.

Guns and rifles decorated the Montvale, New Jersey home of the De La Roche family. For Harry De La Roche, Jr. the firearm was the great equalizer, since marksmanship was his way of succeeding.[8]

Harry De La Roche was the eldest of three sons and thereby earned the right to carry his father's name. But with that right came a responsibility, which to Harry Jr. became a burden. Harry Sr. expected a lot from his son; he wanted him to be handsome, bright, and athletic; that is, a success. Unfortunately, Harry Jr. was not handsome, bright, or athletic, and he was also rather unpopular at school. Officer Michael O'Donovan noted, for example, that Harry Jr.'s high school yearbook contained only about eight inscriptions from his graduating classmates, most of which were nasty, such as "You're the stupidest kid I met."[9]

While Harry Jr. had little going for him in the eyes of his peers, he did find one area in which he could compete and earn the pride of his father: Harry Jr., with practice, became an excellent marksman. Harry Sr. taught all of his sons how to use guns, and he was proud of how good a shot his eldest had become.

Because of Harry Jr.'s expertise with firearms, it seemed natural to all—all except Harry Jr.—that military college would be perfect for him. He had never done that well in his studies and his vision was rather poor; thus, he was rejected from the major military schools including West Point, Annapolis, and the Air Force Academy. He did manage, however, better results in his application to two other schools: he was accepted by The Citadel in Charleston, South Carolina and placed on the waiting list at local Ramapo College.

Being rejected from the academies of the armed forces was another major failure in Harry Sr.'s eyes. He was, however, pleased about The Citadel; a military career for his son was his dream.

Harry Jr. felt differently: "As I considered The Citadel I wasn't sure that I wanted to go since it wouldn't be exactly the same as attending the academies I'd chosen."[10] Unlike government-supported academies where there is no tuition and cadets receive a salary to defray costs of uniforms and books, The Citadel is strictly a private institution which attempts to mimic West Point. The most important difference between these schools is that all graduates of West Point receive a regular army commission and enter the army at the rank of second lieutenant, whereas graduates of The Citadel receive only a reserve commission. Graduates of The Citadel who complete the ROTC program may apply for a regular army commission if they graduate with distinguished accomplishments, but this was an unlikely prospect given Harry's mediocre scholastic skills.

Harry Jr. would also have preferred to stay near home in more familiar surroundings than to go to South Carolina. But again complying with his father's onerous demands, Harry Jr. went off to The Citadel. Even up to the day he left for college, he expressed his ambivalence about what lay ahead.

As it turned out, Harry Jr.'s reservations proved to be correct. He was miserable. The Citadel, noted for its "knob system" for freshmen, employed an extremely strict code of discipline. Like West Point, it strongly emphasized military regimen. The freshman year at The Citadel seemed at that time much like a yearlong fraternity hazing.

The obvious purpose of the "knob system" is to teach submission to military authority and to "separate the men from the boys." An additional consequence of this type of initiation may be to enhance the bond of the freshman to the institution. Social psychologists call this process "cognitive dissonance." Some freshman "knobs" may drop out of The Citadel deciding that it just is not for them. But those who survive the first year have learned to justify their harsh treatment by evaluating the school more favorably. Essentially, after going through all that they had to, upperclassmen will find it difficult to see the school as "not worth it." Harry De La Roche, however, soon proved not to be a survivor of his freshman year.

As in high school, Harry was unpopular and was even ostracized. During the first week at school, he had an inauspicious start. Harry's commanding officer was embarrassed when he mistakenly marked Harry present at formation when Harry had actually forgotten to appear. Of course, the CO took his embarrassment out on Harry, and the other cadets followed suit. As the weeks passed, Harry's peers forgot the incident but never forgave him. Still, as Harry continued to suffer from scorn, letters from his father urged him on, telling him "No matter how tough they make it, you know you can take it."[11]

As Thanksgiving of 1976 approached, he could stand no more and left The Citadel for what he hoped was the last time, telling the school that his mother was sick with cancer. But military school was not all that he could no longer take. He was fed up with living the way his father wanted him to. He was tired of being pushed. Yet he couldn't bring himself to tell his father about not wanting to return to school. His father had always told him that "quitters were failures."

On November 28 Harry Jr. returned home late, around three in the morning, after visiting some of his former high school friends. He took a pistol, one of several in the house, and went to his parents' room where they were asleep. He paced the room for some time deciding what to do: should he stand up to his father or simply release himself from the bondage? He held the gun to his father's head for fifteen minutes. He then fired. His mother stirred from the explosion, and he shot her. He then shot his father again. Next he proceeded to his brothers' room. His 15-year-old brother Ronald lay there motionless, his eyes wide open. Harry shot and killed him. The other brother, Eric, age 12, made a rush for Harry. Harry shot him twice in the face and once in the chest, but he was still alive and struggling to get up. Harry bludgeoned him to death with the revolver and stuffed his body in a metal cabinet in the attic.

Harry Jr.'s entire life revolved around guns. It provided his uppermost achievement as well as his greatest tragedy. For Harry the gun represented an instrument, a means not only to kill his persecutor but to measure his own self-worth.

By contrast, psychiatrists have focused on the deeper psychological meaning of the firearm in the act of homicide. Freudian psychiatrist David Abrahamsen suggests that "sexual elements are always involved in the violent act."[12] He illustrates his claim with a case of a serial killer for whom he sees the gunshot as a "symbolic substitute for ejaculation." As intriguing as the gun as a phallic symbol may be, we view the gun as more instrumental than expressive, as a means toward an end rather than an end in itself. Among serial murders that are sexually inspired, the use of a gun is, in fact, remarkably rare. For those killers, physical contact is so crucial to satisying their murderous sexual impulses that a gun robs them of the pleasure they receive from killing with their hands. Interestingly, they have sodomized their victims with bottles but not with the shaft of a gun. A gun distances the killer from his victims. Not only effective as a deadly weapon, it is psychologically effective for those who don't want to get their hands dirty.

Whereas Harry Jr. was just 18 years old, most mass murderers tend to be older than other killers. FBI statistics show that the age distribution for those arrested for homicide peaks during the early twenties. Specifically, 45% of homicide arrestees are under 25. In contrast, only 15% of mass killers are under 25. The reason for this striking distinction seems to be partly situational and partly hormonal. Family mass murders tend to be committed by the male parent who, of course, is one of the older members of the household, if not the oldest; the De La Roche killing was an exception in this regard; the Girardi case was not.

Advanced age is even more typical of serial murderers. Many of these killers grow old ungracefully; they may find it difficult accepting their diminishing sexual desirability and perhaps prowess; they take matters into their own hands—forcefully. This may seem to contradict the notion that the sex drive declines in men after adolescence. To the contrary, this decline means that more stimulation might be needed for arousal and satisfaction. The element of torture and sadism may develop as a new erotic dimension. Thus, while simple intercourse may be satisfying for an adolescent to whom the sexual experience is still a novelty, for some aging men, only whips, chains, and leather will do. The sexual murderer, however, crosses the line between consensual sex, no matter how kinky, and the lust murder of unwilling partners. It is not surprising to find, therefore, that Dean Corll, homosexual killer of twenty-seven boys in Houston, was 33; that John Wayne Gacy, homosexual killer of thirty-three in Chicago, was 37; that Christopher B. Wilder, suspected slayer of eight young women from coast to coast, was 39; and that Angelo Buono, who raped and murdered ten girls and young women in Los Angeles, was 44. Despite the expression that "men become more distinguished with age," many males in our youth-oriented culture feel "over the hill" upon reaching their thirties and forties.

Homosexual killers, like Gacy and Corll, are particularly noteworthy in this regard. Not only does their sexual preference make them outcasts in the eyes of some people, but the greater emphasis on physical appearance and youth in the gay world may exacerbate the emotional trauma of reaching middle age.*

In terms of a personal profile, therefore, the mass killer typically is a white, middle-aged male who can look like anybody. At one extreme, Ted Bundy was noted for his attractiveness and charm; at the other extreme, Nazi cultist Frederick Cowan was balding, fat, and ugly. Edmund Emil Kemper III stood six feet nine inches; mass murderer Charles Starkweather was only five foot five. Just like the rest of us, mass murderers run the gamut in terms of appearance; most are quite ordinary.

Aside from the characteristics of the killers themselves, we found some striking patterns in the geography of mass murder. It may be noticable, for example, that many of the mass murderers discussed thus far lived in the vicinity of New York City: Harry De La Roche, Jr. slew his family in the Montvale, New Jersey home just fifteen miles from New York City; Frederick W. Cowan's spree, in which six were shot to death, occurred in New Rochelle, a suburb of New York City; James A. Girardi murdered his children in Briarcliff Manor, fifteen miles north of the Bronx; and, of course, David Berkowitz murdered his victims in Queens, Brooklyn, and the Bronx boroughs of New York City.

The repeated appearance of mass killers within commuting distance of New York City is, admittedly, a coincidental product of the cases with which we have chosen to illustrate points. However, it does reflect in part the fact that New York City has experienced many mass murders in recent years. While the very size

*The older age of the mass killer, in contrast to the single-victim killer, may help explain why the incidence of mass murder is not now waning as is the overall murder rate. Since 1980, the homicide rate has declined significantly because of a shrinking proportion of the population under 25, whose propensity toward violence is the greatest.

of the population of New York City would lead us to expect a large representation of mass killings in New York, our statistics indicate clearly that New York is overrepresented in greater proportion than its population would predict.

Our data indicate, in any case, that mass murders occur more often in cities, as do, for that matter, homicides in general. Some massacres do apparently occur when the killer breaks under the strain of urban life. Nonetheless, a comparison of urban and rural statistics on mass murder may be misleading, because of the difficulty in an urban center of detecting serial crime.

In cities, loners like David Berkowitz are able to operate in relative anonymity. Moreover, small towns and rural communities are not bogged down with the bureaucracies of the large cities. If a serial murderer is operating in a small town, assuming that the crimes are localized, his existence becomes unmistakable, and he is thus more likely to be caught. As a result of his early detection, the killer might be less likely to accumulate a high victim count.

Yet there are regional patterns to be discerned for mass murder, which are both curious and dramatic. First, a low incidence of mass murder in the South and its near absence in the Deep South sharply contrast with the usually high prevalence of violence in this region. For the years 1976–1980, for example, 42% of the homicides nationwide took place in southern states which hold only one-third of the nation's population. On the other hand, only one in four (specifically, less then 27%) mass murders occured in the South. Most dramatic, only 9 of the 156 mass murders in the U.S. occurred in the eight states constituting the Deep South.

The image of "the duel" pervades the culture of the South, where violence is often viewed as an appropriate means for settling a dispute. The popular sociological theory of a "subculture of violence" discussed earlier—that within certain subgroups of society, violence is a learned and rewarded response to a variety of situations—has also been applied to the higher incidence of violence in the South. However, the South has a relatively low rate of mass homicide. Given the South's propensity for violence, availability of guns, yet low rate of mass murder, the notion that this crime rarely grows out of an argument or dispute is reinforced. Instead, it seems to stem from circumstances, motivations, and strains that are less prevalent in the South.

Many areas of the Deep South—particularly rural sections—were largely immune from the tumultuous social changes that swept America in the 1970s. In part, its mass murder rate remained low as a result. Traditional support systems, such as the church, fraternal organizations, and close neighborhoods, were strong buffers against alienation during the 1970s. Even an unemployed or divorced man in the rural South was far less likely to be alone. His kin, congregation, or lodge were there to help.

While most of the South has experienced few cases of mass murder, one state, Texas, still produces more than its share. Texas is renowned, of course, for the tower snipings by Charles Whitman in 1966 and the first major homosexual serial crime perpetrated by Dean Corll in 1973. More recently, however, Texas has been responsible for approximately one-tenth of the cases of mass slaughter, outnumbered only by New York and California. Our statistics show that these three states, while only 24% of the U.S. population, account for 42% of the mass murders.

During the late 1960s and into the 1970s, a healthy job market in Texas and California inspired many to look upon these states as the new promised lands. In a final desperate move to find a better life, Easterners migrated there in droves, giving up the security of family and old friends to look for work. For some, the journey paid off handsomely in a successful career and an affluent life-style. For many others, however, the promise of streets paved with gold was broken by the cruel reality of failure—no money, no place to stay, no job, and nowhere to turn for help.

In particular, boom cities like Los Angeles, Houston, and Dallas, with their rapid growth in electronics or oil drilling and refining, acquired a reputation for tremendous wealth; they also soon acquired countless disillusioned, down-on-their-luck transients who couldn't pull themselves up by their bootstraps and had no one around to give them a hand out of the gutter. This move for them had been their "last resort" for prosperity or happiness. Dashed hopes and missed opportunities became pills too bitter for some to swallow.

Forced out of a job by the closing of the plant where he worked, James Oliver Huberty decided it was time for a change. At the age of 41, his options were few in his hometown of Massillon, Ohio. So he moved his family in December 1983 to San Diego for a new start and a second chance.

Though fortunate to be hired as a security guard in San Ysidro, a suburb of San Diego just north of the Mexican border, Huberty was fired months later. Seeing his high hopes vanish and feeling he had nowhere else to turn, Huberty became increasingly despondent and angry at the world. By July 18, 1984, his desire to get even had peaked. He chose a rifle, a shotgun, and a pistol along with hundreds of rounds of ammunition from his large arsenal of weaponry, and told his wife he was "going hunting for humans." She didn't realize it, but he meant every word.

James Huberty strode just a few hundred yards to the nearby McDonald's restaurant, a hangout for local kids. He opened fire, shooting everything and everyone that moved. Bicycle riders in the parking lot and children inside eating were stunned by the sudden, furious attack upon them. Eventually, the SWAT team gunned Huberty down, but not until he had gotten revenge: Twenty-one died—mostly children—and another nineteen were wounded in the largest single mass shooting to date.

The West Coast, more than any other region, has experienced the highest rate of mass murder per capita. Further, while the Seattle area was home to Ted Bundy, and the San Francisco area was plagued by the interracial Zebra killings, no other place has been the site of as many bizarre, ritualistic, sadistic, and gory mass killings as Southern California. A heritage was passed on by Charles Manson and Juan Corona to the more recent killers named by the press for their crime-scene and acts: the Skid-Row Slasher, the Freeway Killer, the Sunset Strip Killer, and the Hillside Strangler, to name but a few.

Relatively few Southern Californians were born there. Many came for the sun and fun; others for jobs—leaving behind stabilizing influences in their lives. Even if unsuccessful in the pursuit of their goals, most adapt in some legitimate way or return east; few respond so violently as to commit mass murder.

Therefore, certain personal factors, beyond the issue of transiency, are necessary to distinguish those who kill from those who do not; we consider these factors in the next chapter. The large number of mass killings—and particularly serial killings—in Southern California might also reflect a "sunshine syndrome," which ironically both encourages killers and provides them with victims.

The life style of Southern California—the "do your own thing" ethic—might attract those who want few social and cultural sanctions against behaving in an outrageous manner. The same spirit of adventure and experimentation which has also attracted creative, ambitious people may have inadvertently lured those with depraved and bizarre desires to what they view as the "sex capital" of the United States. Furthermore, those who "never made it" or simply came to California to run away provided a wealth of potential victims for the more depraved. The abundance of prostitutes on the streets, hitchhikers on the freeways, and pretty young women on the beaches has created a veritable "playground for murder" in Southern California.

CHAPTER 6

"OUT OF CONTROL"

For Lawrence Sigmund Bittaker and Roy L. Norris, Southern California was the perfect place. They would cruise together in Bittaker's customized van, looking at bikini-clad teenaged girls at the beaches. The two buddies liked to stop and take pictures of "beachgirls," and if the girls objected they gave them some marijuana to placate them. Bittaker loved teenaged girls, especially blondes. And California provided him with plenty of targets for his passion.[1]

Bittaker, aged 38, and Norris, aged 30, had met in 1978, while imprisoned at San Luis Obispo. Norris, who earlier had served four years at the Atascadero State Hospital as a "mentally disordered sex offender," had after his release raped a housewife in her home and was this time sent to the State Prison at San Luis Obispo. Bittaker also had spent most of his adult life behind bars. In 1978, their friendship grew as they made plans for the future. If prisons are not "schools for crime," then at least they are "study halls."

Bittaker had a wish: to kill a girl corresponding to each teenage year, like trophies. Bittaker's silver 1977 GMC van, which they nicknamed "Murder Mac," was selected especially for its sliding door, which would facilitate his method of abduction. From summer through fall 1979, Bittaker along with Norris kidnapped, tortured, raped, and murdered a 13-, 15-, 16-, 16-, and 18-year-old girl, mistakenly duplicating the 16-year-old category.

More important than the strange pursuit to score one per age was the excruciating pain inflicted on each of the victims.

Cindy Schaefer, visiting the West Coast for the summer from her home in Wisconsin, was abducted while walking along the street. Her screams were muffled with a gag and by the blasting stereo. They took her to a secluded mountain spot they had staked out earlier. There they each raped her several times. Cindy pleaded with the men; "If you are going to kill me let me know ahead of time, so I can pray first."[2] They assured her they weren't going to kill her, then they strangled her to death. They threw her body down the mountainside for animals to devour. Her body was never recovered.

As is typical of many serial crimes, the killings became increasingly more brutal. The next victim to be drawn into "Murder Mac" was 18-year-old Andrea Hall, who had been hitchhiking. First, Bittaker raped her. Then Norris tried to rape her too, but he was disgusted by the blood from her period. They took photographs of Andrea in her subjugated, frightened state, as they did with all their victims. Bittaker asked her to give him some good reasons why she shouldn't be killed. But he didn't like her answers. Andrea Hall was stabbed in the ear with an icepick, then strangled to death with a coathanger and pliers.

The next two victims were the youngest. Thirteen-year-old Jacqueline Lamp, who went by her middle name Leah, and fifteen-year-old Jackie Gilliam never expected their hitchhiking would take them where it did. Bittaker and Norris took their newest prey to their mountain retreat where they held them captive for days, repeatedly raping them. To add to the disgrace of having to act like they were enjoying their rape, Norris made Leah pretend she was his cousin to satisfy his longtime, incestuous desire for his own cousin. Jackie was then tortured—her nipples were crushed with vise grips and her breasts were pierced with an icepick. Finally, both girls were murdered.

Their last killing was the cruelest. Sixteen-year-old Shirley Lynette Ledford was captured, mutilated, and murdered inside

"Murder Mac" while the radio blasted to drown her screams. She was tortured, poked, her nipples torn off with Bittaker's pliers, while the pleas of the girl reduced to an animal-like state were recorded on cassette tape. After death had mercifully come over her, Bittaker and Norris gleefully discarded her torn and bleeding nude body on the front lawn of a suburban home to see what kind of reaction its discovery would get in the newspapers.

Multiple slayings that make front-page headlines are typically those in which the killer expresses profound hostility as well as a need to control through grotesquely perverse and humiliating acts. A murderer who rapes, mutilates, or terrorizes; who whips, cuts, urinates on, or otherwise physically assaults his victims is seeking to achieve a feeling of superiority at the victims' expense, to be triumphant over other people, to conquer by destruction.

Approximately 18% of all mass murders involve sex and sadism. As in the case of Bittaker and Norris, such slayings are with few exceptions serial murders, one stranger at a time over a period of weeks, months, or even years. A killer's first victim may be spared an extreme humiliation or brutality. As the serial killer becomes more and more secure with his crime, however, he may also become increasingly more sadistic and inhumane.

Killing apparently gets easier after the first time. This may be important because millions of people—legitimately as police or militia or illegitimately as criminals—have participated in killing at least one human being. According to psychologist Paul Cameron, the experience of killing increases the willingness to kill again.[3] In fact, killing actually affects an individual's attitude toward the value of human life itself. Those who have killed before—for example, in military service—were, according to Cameron, more likely than those who have never killed at all to say they would murder for money and less likely to say they would continue life-support measures for gravely ill patients. For many people, therefore, the act of killing reduces inhibitions against this fundamental cultural taboo; a few may even come to find excitement in their initiation to killing, and want to do it again.

In large part, the pleasure and exhilaration that the serial killer derives from repeated murder stem from absolute control over other human beings. As Roy Norris admitted about his assaults against women, "the rape wasn't really the important part, it was the dominance."

Psychologist Eric Fromm argues that this acquired need for domination derives from a feeling of powerlessness, worthlessness, or lack of self-fulfillment.[5] An individual with these feelings has an intolerable sense of impotence, which he may attempt to counteract by controlling, manipulating, or eliminating those who are momentarily weaker or more vulnerable than he. Control may be achieved by sadistically inflicting pain or seeking to destroy life—by making others who are incapable of defending themselves suffer.

Many mass killers have experienced severe rejection by other people. In most cases, they have not been able to conquer others with their wit, intelligence, or charm. Or they may have been abandoned early in life. Later, they consistently fail to meet objectives, fulfill goals, and satisfy needs. In short, they are the victims of frustration.

Frustration tends to increase various forms of aggressive behavior. Murderers tend to experience a greater amount of frustration in their early lives than do nonmurderers. Sociologist Stuart Palmer has shown, for example, that the fifty-one convicted (nonmass) killers in his study had severely frustrating childhood illnesses, accidents, child abuse, physical defects, isolation, and poverty.[6]

Frustration is a common and recurrent theme throughout the lives of the mass killers that we studied. Nazi-cultist and mass killer Frederick W. Cowan, for example, failed in school, failed in the military, and failed at work; just prior to his shooting spree at the moving company where he worked, Cowan had been suspended by his supervisor.

Most people are able to cope with frustration without committing mass murder. Many try even harder to succeed or modify their goals. Some do become more aggressive, taking it out on themselves—for example, by committing suicide—or on others—for example, by yelling, hitting, or even killing. It is only a few who, seeing a number of people as responsible for their failure, react in the extreme by committing mass murder.

Frustration usually appears as a precursor of a violent attack—a final straw. Yet the source of the frustration is very often something other than total failure. While it is true that most of the forty-two killers we studied were, like Cowan, either manual laborers or unemployed, ten had completed college and one had a Ph.D. in structural engineering. On the surface those who attended college and maintained respected careers may seem fulfilled. In their eyes, however, they may have felt underemployed or useless.

Serial killer Ted Bundy, who is believed to have killed dozens of young women in four states, appeared to his friends to be a promising young law student. Washington's Governor Dan Evans, for whom Ted had worked, wrote a glowing letter of recommendation in support of his application to law school. In reality, Ted Bundy went from law school to law school, floundering in his attempt to earn his degree. The only case Ted ever was to argue, moreover, was his own; in his Florida trial, he assisted his lawyers in examining witnesses. After sentencing Ted to die, Judge Cowart sadly summed up Bundy's failure: "It's a tragedy to this court to see such a total waste of humanity. You're a bright young man. You'd have made a good lawyer. I'd have loved to have you practice in front of me. But you went the wrong way, partner. . . ."[7]

Ironically, the need to control may get played out in courageous, benevolent behavior, especially if it involves risking one's life to achieve a temporary sense of power. Saving a life is a way of controlling someone's fate, just as is taking a life. In 1969, long before his rampage of death and mutilation had begun, Ted

Bundy received a commendation from the Seattle Police Department for capturing a purse snatcher and recovering the stolen bag for its owner. During the summer of 1970, he plunged into Seattle's Green Lake to save a drowning 3-year-old child. And while an undergraduate psychology major, Bundy worked on Seattle's Crisis Clinic hotline. He seemed to be an exceedingly helpful person.

The psychological need to control is often evident in the idiosyncratic life-styles and aspirations of serial slayers. Some are infatuated with powerful automobiles; others dream of careers in law enforcement; still others collect the symbols of power—such as police and military uniforms, instruments of torture and guns. In all cases, the theme underlying every aspect of their lives, including their killings, is the wish to command the fate of those around them.

"Son of Sam" David Berkowitz loved the sense of authority conveyed by wearing a uniform. He wanted to become a fireman, but never did. Instead, he worked the night shift as a security guard for a trucking jobber located near Kennedy Airport. Berkowitz also "benevolently" set (and documented in a record book) thousands of fires to help the fire department justify requests for increased budgets.

To satisfy aspirations for power, many killers imitate figures of authority as embodied in the role of the police. Both Atlanta's Wayne Williams and Chicago's John Wayne Gacy had their cars equipped with police sirens and flashing red lights. And Hillside Strangler Ken Bianchi, who admired police officers since childhood and majored in criminal justice in his abbreviated college career, tried in vain to join the Los Angeles Police Department. He was hired instead for a time as a security guard and later joined the Sheriff's Reserve in Bellingham, Washington.

Thus, from a psychological viewpoint, both helping and hurting can have the same underlying motive: to control the fate of other human beings. Many people who have a profound lack of self-esteem make themselves feel superior by attacking the weaknesses and errors—and, in the extreme case, the bodies—of others. They are frustrated because they feel they have little power and control over their own lives.

Mass murderers aren't the only ones who have a need to control others. Most people with this need, however, find less extreme, if not socially acceptable, ways to satisfy it. Certain jobs afford the opoportunity to manipulate and manage the lives of subordinates—such as business executives who hire and fire, or teachers whose judgements help determine their students' prospects for a career. Sex also provides a vehicle for satisfying the need to control or dominate others. In a relatively mild form, couples may occasionally play out rape fantasies; in the extreme, they may routinely practice sadomasochistic activities in which one hurts the other.

Sexually motivated murder involves the same element of control, except without the consent of the victim. In fact, overpowering the will of the victim enhances the offender's feeling of dominance. Those who go to this extreme in their quest for control have failed to internalize a moral code for the treatment of others. Serial murderers are able to repeat their acts of brutality and sadism because they lack conscience, guilt, or superego—they are called sociopaths.

The terms "sociopath" and "psychopath"—used interchangeably—apply to those individuals who are not mentally ill, not grossly out of touch with reality, but who are incapable of experiencing normal amounts of love and empathy.* Though psychologists don't know for sure, they speculate that some people become sociopaths because of rejection in family relationships or repeated frustration of needs. Whatever the cause, the sociopath lacks a sense of responsibility, guilt, or morality and is

*The labels "sociopath" and "psychopath" refer to the same personality or character disorder. Though the latter is more often used in popular speech, we favor the newer term because it avoids the common confusion between "psychopath" and "psychotic," the latter of which does refer to a serious mental disease.

unable to have lasting or meaningful relationships. He has trouble postponing impulsive behavior, is immature, and is unaffected by the rewards and punishments which might ordinarily inhibit immoral action. This type of individual is often implicated in behaviors ranging from cheating and lying, on the one hand, to rape and murder, on the other.

Lawrence Bittaker's lack of guilt was symptomatic of his sociopathy. Long after being convicted of torturing and murdering teenaged girls, his feeling about his crime was apparently one of pride rather than remorse: he signed autographs for fellow inmates, not with "Lawrence Bittaker," but with the name of "Pliers Bittaker."

Guilt is not an all-or-nothing feeling; people actually vary on a continuum from those who are debilitated by excessive guilt to those who lack a conscience. At some point, we draw a line and label the least remorseful as sociopaths.

The apparently growing number of people who cross the line into sociopathy may stem in part from society's recent war against guilt. For the past few decades, there have been countless books and articles advising us that excessive guilt is responsible for a long and diverse list of ills, and offering step-by-step suggestions for the reduction of guilty feelings. In 1975, a bestseller on assertiveness training, *When I Say No, I Feel Guilty,* recommended that the feelings of guilt, which we learn as children, are later used by other people "to get us to do what they want, irrespective of what we want for ourselves." The book's author, Dr. Manuel Smith, proposed a "Bill of Assertive Rights" which included "the right to offer no reasons or excuses for justifying your behavior," "the right to say, 'I don't care'," and "the right to judge your own behavior, thoughts, and emotions."

In another popular psychiatric self-help manual, *Breaking Through,* Julian Miller argues that guilt has "gotten out of hand" and is now "a disease of incapacitation." He advises his readers to determine why they are guilty, act to eliminate the guilt, and stop punishing themselves.

During the seventies, "getting hung up on guilt" was widely believed to account for failure to find sexual happiness. Dr. David Reuben's famous book, *Everything You Always Wanted to Know About Sex,* set the stage for years to come by asserting that the "fear of doing wrong" was implicated in the absence of orgasm as well as many other sexual hangups. Also during this period, guilt was associated with such diverse personal problems as obesity, agoraphobia, shyness, suicide, and depression.

For the vast majority of Americans, the emphasis on reducing excessive guilt probably had a beneficial effect by allowing them to achieve greater personal contentment and assertiveness. Many otherwise inhibited people were able to blossom and pursue valuable interests. Moreover, this view was clearly compatible with "the new morality" of the young people of the late sixties and early seventies in which the everyday rules of sexual behavior became greatly liberalized. For a while, "doing your own thing" and "loving the one you're with" were more than just tolerated. In some circles, they were socially prescribed codes of behavior.

The same stress on eliminating guilty feelings, however, may also have been responsible for increasing the numer of sociopaths in our society—and, at the extreme, the number of those few sociopaths who become mass killers. Not coincidentally, the exploitation of others as well as the lack of remorse, which are associated with the sociopathic personality, also characterize most serial killers. For them, sex is nothing more or less than an impersonal act, which has little to do with caring or affection. In fact, their partner is usually regarded as a mere tool to be used, in only the most negative sense of the word, to satisfy ego and sexual needs.

Domination unmitigated by guilt is a crucial element in serial crimes with a sexual theme. Not only does sadistic sex—consensual or forcible—express the power of one person over another, but in serial homicides, murder enhances the killer's sense of control over his victims. This dominant role apparently fulfilled a need for Douglas Clark, the so-called "Sunset Strip Killer," as he decided the fate of his victims based on their ability to please him sexually. Like a teacher, Clark graded their performance pass/fail. Though his victims didn't know it, he killed them if they failed.

The "Sunset Strip Killer," named for the Strip where many of the victims were picked up, turned out upon arrest to be a pair of killers. Douglas Daniel Clark, a handsome, 32-year-old boiler operator, and his accomplice Carol Mary Bundy, an obese 37-year-old divorced mother of two (and no relation to Ted), were partners: they lived together, loved together, and killed together. In a patently pornographic murder spree in 1980, they slew and mutilated at least seven people: some were juveniles and some were adults; some were prostitutes and one was male; some they killed together and some they killed independently. Reportedly, Clark was striving to fulfill his fantasy of cutting the throat of a woman during intercourse to feel the contractions of her vagina during death spasms. Bundy initially just wanted to hold onto and please her man, but she too learned to enjoy killing.

The usual scenario, described by Carol Bundy, would start with Clark cruising the Strip for prostitutes, preferably blondes, whom he would get to orally copulate him, often while Bundy watched. The woman's skill at oral sex would determine her fate. If he liked her performance, she was let go; if he didn't like it, she was executed.

One woman, who was never identified, did not please Clark. While the prostitute was still trying to arouse him, he shot her in the head. With the thrill of killing, he then climaxed and ejaculated into the mouth of the dead victim. Before dumping her body, he put her on the hood of his Datsun, and pressed on her stomach forcing her to urinate. He then had intercourse with the corpse. He also saved the victim's panties as a souvenir, and nicknamed her "Water Tower" for the site where her body was dumped.

Two more victims, 15- and 16-year-old prostitutes, Clark killed at the same time. While one girl was orally copulating him, he shot both of them. Returning to his home with them, he had oral, anal, and genital sex with both, one of whom was dead and the other near death. Clark then positioned their bodies to mimic Lesbian mutual oral sex.

Clark nicknamed all of his victims. One victim who had a dental plate was named "Toothless," and her head was kept by Clark. Clark took the head home and placed it in the freezer; Bundy then painted it with makeup. Clark would take the head into the shower with him and masturbate into its mouth.

On some of the victims, Bundy would help out by handing Clark the murder weapon, a .25 caliber automatic pistol. The one male victim, however, was killed by her alone. While performing oral-anal sex on her former lover, she took out her gun and shot him in the head twice, and then decapitated him.

As disgusting and offensive as we may find the crimes of Clark and Bundy, we must feel some degree of relief that the victim's deaths were mercifully quick, and often instantaneous. Necrophilia may rank among the most sacred taboos along with cannibalism, but at least the victims are unaware of their defilement.

According to Bundy, Clark claimed to have killed 50 women (and hoped to kill 100). We will never know for certain, because the majority of them would have been prostitutes whose disappearance may not have been reported. Some may have ended up among the many "Jane Does" in the Los Angeles County Morgue. But Clark's arrest on August 11, 1980 stopped perhaps the most depraved, but certainly not the only, killer ever to stalk the streets of L.A.'s Sunset Strip.

There is little doubt that Bundy and Clark will not even be near the last to prey on the streetwalkers, runaways, and other losers of Hollywood. For as long as there are those who on live the streets, there will be others who will target them as easy marks.

Serial killers almost without exception choose vulnerable victims—those who are easy to dominate. The frequent victimization of prostitutes by serial killers—such as Doug Clark, Seattle's Green River Killer, Alaska's Robert Hansen who confessed to murdering seventeen prostitutes in the Anchorage area, and even Jack the Ripper—derives in part from their accessibility on the street and their willingness to enter an apartment or automobile, domains controlled by their customers. Furthermore, their recurrent victimization stems from the fact that, for a price, they will assume a submissive role in sex, even with pain, which may further stimulate a volatile person to exercise the ultimate act of control and domination—murder.

Besides prostitutes, several other groups of people are particularly vulnerable, even though they may not willingly participate in their own subjugation. Like prostitutes, hitchhikers will voluntarily get into a stranger's car, where they are at his mercy. Some of the victims of Bittaker and Norris were teenage hitchhikers who were overpowered after accepting a ride in "Murder Mac." Serial killer Edmund Kemper slew six hitchhiking female students from the University of California at Santa Cruz who wanted nothing more from him than a ride. Male hitchhikers are not immune either. Freeway killer William G. Bonin killed, mutilated, and castrated a number of young men who were thumbing on L.A.'s freeways.*

A number of killers have capitalized on the vulnerability and naivete of children. If children are not enticed by a stranger offering a "treat" or bullied by a police impersonator, they can simply be grabbed because of their small size. Atlanta's child-killer Wayne Williams, for example, lured his victims with the promise of a record contract. As documented in the NBC television-movie *Adam,* the eight minutes during which 6-year-old Adam Walsh was left alone in the toy department of a Hollywood, Florida Sears store gave serial killer Ottis Elwood Toole enough time to

*In a similar way, stranded motorists are vulnerable to strangers who stop to "help out." In 1979, for example, Steven T. Judy committed what has been called the "flat tire murders" when he stopped to assist 21-year-old Terry Chasteen on an interstate highway near Indianapolis. Disabling the car further, Judy offered Chasteen and her three children a ride. He raped and killed her and drowned the three children, for which he was executed in 1981.

kidnap him. Two weeks later, Adam Walsh's head was discovered in a canal 100 miles away.

Though children are particularly vulnerable, teenagers and adults can also be lured by trickery or snatched by force. Many of the victims of "charming," serial killer Christopher Wilder, for example, apparently bought his story that he was a fashion photographer. More abductive than seductive, Bittaker and Norris customized their van, "Murder Mac," with a sliding door to enable quick apprehensions; their first victim was simply plucked off the street into the van.

Skid-row derelicts are also easy targets. Not only are they alone, homeless, and on the streets, but they frequently look to strangers for help or companionship. Skid-Row Slasher Vaughn Greenwood killed at least nine bums in a run-down section of Los Angeles, while they lay drunk or asleep in alleys or doorways. In a bizarre ritual, the 31-year-old serial killer first slit his victims' throats to the spine, drank cupfuls of their blood, scattered salt around the bodies, and then removed his victims' shoes and pointed them at their feet. Greenwood was not the only one to murder on L.A's skid row; Bobby Joe Maxwell was convicted in 1984 of two of ten stabbings he allegedly committed in late 1978 and early 1979.

The vulnerability of elderly women has similarly made them the prey of several serial killers including the Boston Strangler and the Stocking Strangler of Columbus, Georgia. They are often chosen because they are believed to be frail and defenseless. In addition, they live alone, and may have no one close to call in case of trouble.

Notwithstanding its early reputation for elegance and its opulent facade, the Park Plaza Hotel by 1973 had become a rundown residence for elderly citizens on the West Side of Manhattan. It also became the temporary home of 25-year-old Calvin Jackson, a drifter from Buffalo who had a spotty history of robbery and drug use.[8] Somehow he convinced the management of the Park Plaza to hire him as a porter to take care of the unattached old ladies who lived there.

During a seventeen-month period in 1973 and 1974, police were repeatedly called to the hotel following the discovery of yet another dead woman's body. For the first few victims, the cause of death was initially recorded by the detectives as natural—coronary or alcoholism. However, after Theresa Jordan was found suffocated and raped, and after Kate Lewishon was found raped and tied to her bed, and after Yetta Vishnefsky was found with a knife in her back, a pattern of serial crimes became unmistakable. In addition, various items including televisions had been taken from the rooms of the nine murdered women.

Police wondered if the theft of televisions could really be the motive for this continuing series of murders. Whatever the real motive, the discovery of one of the stolen televisions led to Jackson's arrest. He was obviously ashamed—during his trial, he planted his head in his hands for hours at a time. He apparently had had little fear of getting caught, however. After raping and killing some of his 80-year-old victims, he had taken the time to sit over their bodies while he snacked on sandwiches from their refrigerators.

Not only have psychologists underplayed the role of victim vulnerability in mass killings, but they have overlooked the types of situations or settings which may even encourage the expression of control through murder. Consequently, they have focused on the issue of control through violence as though the actions of the individual killer were independent of his social environment.

The hospital, the nursing home, and other total institutions represent settings in which some individuals must depend on the control and guidance of others. The total dependence of hospital patients on their caretakers, for example, may create the perfect circumstance for the mass administration of lethal doses of medications and poisons. During the months of July and August 1975, thirty-eight patients at the 460-bed Veterans Administration hospital in Ann Arbor, Michigan inexplicably experienced sudden respiratory arrest. Seven of them died. An anesthetist at the hospital eventually diagnosed the situation as mass poisoning by means of the potentially dangerous anesthetic drug, pancuronium. In June 1976, two nurses were indicted on ten counts of poisoning, five counts of murder, and one count of conspiracy to commit murder.

More recently, a male nurse was charged in the mass killing of eleven patients at Riverside, California's Community Hospital of the Valley and a single killing at San Gorgonio Pass Hospital in Banning. According to the prosecution, the twelve patients, all of whom suffered fatal seizures, were murdered with massive, lethal injections of lidocaine, a drug used in the treatment of irregular heart rhythms. The nurse charged in the killings allegedly had access to the drug, was seen leaving the patients' rooms immediately before their seizures, and had predicted the demise of two patients despite their stable conditions at the time of his prediction.

Like police work, nursing is considered to be among the most benevolent of occupations. Therefore, it becomes possible for hospital caretakers such as nurses, though a small minority, to use as a rationalization to themselves or as an excuse to others that they are merely putting their victims "out of their misery."

Genene Jones of Kerrville, Texas took the notion of helping one step beyond mercy killing, earning her the nickname "Death Nurse." In September 1982, 15-month-old Chelsea McClelland mysteriously died after a routine physical examination in the office of a local pediatrician. Eight months later medical examiners found in her body traces of a powerful muscle relaxant, Anectine, which had caused her respiratory system to stop.

The culprit was Nurse Jones. During the six-week period in which she worked for the town's new pediatrician, six patients had stopped breathing and were rushed to the hospital for resuscitation. Nurse Jones reportedly was "euphoric" that she was able to administer CPR to help save their lives. She presumably had created the life-and-death situations so that she could "play

God." Investigating Jones's previous employment, moreover, Kerrville's local surgeon, Dr. Joe Venus, discovered that she had worked the night shift at a San Antonio hospital during which time more than a dozen inexplicable deaths had occurred.

As horrible as these cases may be, they are on a much smaller scale than that of a nursing home director in Orkdal, Norway, who admitted to poisoning to death 17 patients and is likely responsible for another 138 deaths. Acting as the home's first director when it opened in 1977, 44-year-old Arnfinn Nessett was noted for his charitable work and his talent for knitting sweaters. Between 1977 and 1980, he killed his elderly patients one at a time by injecting them with curare, a drug that paralyzes the nervous system in a matter of minutes.

The congenial and talkative Nessett, who sang in a Salvation Army Band when he wasn't killing, was often seen with syringes, alone with his patients, shortly before they died. To obtain the curare, he would list medicines requested by his staff, have the order form signed by the appropriate doctor, and then secretly add the poison to the list. In this way, he was able to procure from the local druggist more than 11,600 milligrams of the poison—enough to kill 300 people. When later questioned about the purpose of ordering such massive quantities of curare, Nessett claimed he needed the nerve drug to kill roaming stray dogs.

Vulnerability, such as that of bed ridden patients to the deadly acts of a cruel caretaker, may be seen in situations far from the hospital setting. An analogous type of dependency facilitated the horror of the Jonestown, Guyana massacre in 1978. Far removed from outside influences, a cultist dictator had total control over the everyday existence of his followers. On November 19, 1978, 913 members of the People's Temple perished, most as a result of mass poisoning in which men, women, and children all lined up to sip a fatal dose of cyanide-laced Kool-Aid.

The infants went first; volunteers squirted the flavored cyanide into their open mouths with syringes. Armed guards stood ready to gun down anyone who disobeyed orders. The older children were next. They stood in line, one after another, to receive a cup of the lethal mixture of poison and Kool-Aid. The promise repeatedly blared over the camp's overhead loudspeakers: "We're going to meet again in another place."[9] Then came the adults who lined up and waited their turn to die. Some accepted with enthusiasm; others were coerced to comply. Most were dead in five minutes.

How could "insanity" have occurred on a scale large enough to account for the murder/suicide of 913 people? The answer to that question must lie with the Temple's 47-year-old, self-styled dictator, Jim Jones, who dominated his followers just as surely as doctors and nurses may exert complete control over the day-by-day activities of hospital patients. Like a hospital, Jonestown was a total institution in which all of its members' needs were addressed, if not satisfied. It was a social environment located literally in the middle of nowhere, cut off from family and friends, and totally isolated from outside reality. The one and only "reality" for the followers of Jim Jones was the power of Jones himself, whose charismatic sermons and later rantings and ravings were the tools with which he exercised absolute control.

Jones's hold over this "flock" was based on the emotional dependence of "children" on their self-proclaimed father and fanatical leader who demanded that members kill their own families rather than turn on "Dad." Preparing his followers to accept the inevitability of their fate, he advocated mass suicide as an alternative to abandoning his deranged vision: "I'd rather bring it all to a gallant, glorious, screaming end."[10] And that's exactly what he did. During the mass murder/suicide he had so carefully orchestrated, Jim Jones committed suicide. He raised a pistol to his head and fired a single bullet through his brain.

The element of control and its psychological counterpart of dependence are fundamental, therefore, to comprehending how such unthinkable acts of human destruction can occur. The need for control may be rooted solely in the psychological state of the offender who requires power that he cannot attain legitimately; Lacking a conscience, he resorts to murder. But dominance may also stem from an imbalance of power between the victim and the would-be offender. The setting itself—be it natural or institutional—may encourage the manipulation and control of other human beings, and sometimes even murder.

Undoubtedly, the meaning of control in mass murder has not always been understood. The killer in many, if not most, mass homicides is not "out of control," as the saying goes; rather, he is very much in control and lets everyone else know it in the most forceful way possible—by playing God.

CHAPTER 7

MASS MURDER AS A WAY OF LIFE

Abnormal situations can make normal people do crazy things. During times of war, combat soldiers routinely commit acts of "murder" on enemy forces or even civilians—acts that they would never even consider during peacetime. Allegedly operating under directives from his superiors, Lt. William Laws Calley, Jr. commanded his platoon to slaughter hundreds of South Vietnamese civilians—unarmed women, children, and elders—in the infamous My Lai Massacre on March 16, 1968.

Calley is not alone in his willingness to obey authority. Social psychologists have repeatedly demonstrated that under the right circumstances, most "normal" people will act to harm others simply because they are commanded to do so by someone in charge. Most notably, Dr. Stanley Milgram found that a majority of his research subjects—people from all walks of life and backgrounds—obeyed an order to administer a severe electric shock to an innocent victim, for the sake of science.*[1] Outside of

*In his series of experiments, Milgram told his volunteer subjects that the purpose of his research was to understand how people learn. Each of the subjects was instructed to teach a "learner" some word skills by administering increasing doses of electric shock whenever the "learner" responded incorrectly. Unaware that the "learner" was actually Milgrim's associate who acted the part, a majority of the "teachers" gave what they thought was an "Extremely dangerous—XXX" shock to the "learner," despite his feigned screams.

the psychologist's laboratory, the same phenomenon occurs, but it is instead for the sake of victory. My Lai apparently is not an isolated incident either in the Vietnam conflict or in any other war.

While their collective actions were unequivocally reprehensible and unforgivable, Nazi S.S. killers, as individuals, may not have been "madmen." Based on interviews with former Nazi S.S. killers, British psychiatrist Henry Dicks challenges the popular view that even such a heinous example of mass extermination as the Nazi holocaust was actually a product of "collective madness" inspired by insane leaders and carried out by their sadistic followers.[2] He contends instead that, under normal conditions, most of the S.S. killers he studied would hardly have become "common murderers" at all, let alone mass killers.

Echoing political historian Hannah Arendt's surprising assessment of Adolph Eichmann as more of an efficient bureaucrat than a sadistic monster, Dicks focuses on the process whereby Nazis were conditioned to murder. According to Dicks, this process was anything but quick. Rather, it extended gradually over a long period of time, facilitated by strong and continuing group pressure and indoctrination. The constant marches and uniformed processions, the all-day group singing of the Party's anthem, and the required cheering—all of these conspired to enhance the group bond. The Nazis were conditioned to believe that no "right-thinking German patriot" could stand to deviate from their doctrine.

Another factor promoting the outcome of the Nazis' program of conditioning was the fragmented nature of their mass extermination. Everyone had a specialized job to do, but nobody felt personally responsible for the overall outcome. As Dicks indicates, "one 'only' drove the trucks, another 'only' marshalled the trains, a third 'only shoved them in' or 'only' sat at a desk making dispositions—always there is a 'buck-passing'."[3]

The Nazis' conditioning procedures were designed to instill the absolute loyalty and dependence of recruits to the movement.

The family was renounced in favor of the fatherland. Under such a code, killing and indifference to the feelings of victims easily became part of the acceptable *modus operandi* of the Nazi recruit. When the Nazis' conditioning procedure worked, it worked well.

Those who try to explain the mass murderer strictly in terms of individual psychopathology typically see him as a killer who operates alone. Actually, however, a number of mass slayings have been carried out by two or more persons. For example, two cousins were responsible for the string of brutal and grisly Hillside Stranglings in Los Angeles; four men were convicted for their part in San Francisco's racially inspired Zebra slayings; the two Lewingdon brothers were the ".22 caliber killers" who terrorized the residents of central Ohio; Ronald Piskorski and Gary Shrager were found guilty of an armed robbery which ended in the slaughter of six residents of New Britain, Connecticut; the Tate/LaBianca massacres were carried out by Charles Manson's "family"; and so on. If "craziness" were behind such killings, then it had to have afflicted the minds and souls of the brothers, friends, or associates who murdered together.

As in the case of the Nazis' conditioning to commit atrocities, the "craziness" that we recognize in mass killers might more accurately be regarded as part of their situation or their way of life. Mass murder may be sickening, but a mass murderer not sick. A group of people may develop, in fact, a culture of its own—a counterculture at odds with the rest of society—in which mass extermination is regarded as acceptable, if not absolutely essential. Mass murder may not only be encouraged, it may be required.

During 1973 and early 1974, fourteen execution style murders and eight assaults occurred in San Francisco, whose police named the case "Zebra" after the special police radio band they assigned for the investigation.[4] Like the black and white animal of the same name, all twenty-two crimes in the six-month spree involved white victims and black suspects. In a highly controversial police manhunt, some 600 young black men were stopped on the streets of San Francisco, then searched and questioned. But this tactic was later ended after being declared unconstitutional by a federal judge who voiced concern about its implications in curtailing civil liberties.

The Zebra killers belonged to a Black Muslim cult called the Death Angels whose doctrine taught that whites were evil and must be destroyed. Inspired by the message of a charismatic spiritual leader, the members chanted in unison during their intensely emotional meetings. They were reminded repeatedly that for centuries blacks had been exploited and persecuted by whites and that black people were actually morally and culturally superior. Members of the sect were pressured to get even with the "evil blue-eyed devils" for their abusive treatment, and were promised that blacks would one day rule the world after winning the final battle between the races. Thus, the Zebra group had declared war against the whites, which, in their minds, justified killing.

Nightly, the Death Angels combed the streets of the city in search of "white devils" who were out for an evening stroll, waiting at a bus stop, or returning from a day's work. Each member of the cult was required to kill four whites for which he received a button to wear on his coat, a free trip to the holy city of Mecca, and respect in the eyes of his fellow cultists. Sometimes the killings were quick—multiple gunshots in the face at close range; other times, however, they were unbelievably brutal and sadistic, involving long, drawn-out rituals of torture in which pain was inflicted in a step-by-step progression ending in death and dismemberment.

One of the early victims of the Death Angels was a 25-year-old man who had stopped to watch a group of street minstrels at Fisherman's Wharf. Four Angels followed him to a deserted city block where one shoved the barrel of a gun into his stomach and threatened to kill him on the spot if he tried to get away. The four men then drove their prisoner to an apartment building where they forced him to a third-floor loft. There, they stripped him of his clothing, tied him to a straight-back chair, and gagged him with adhesive tape after a dirty cloth was crammed into his mouth.

Throughout the day, men climbed the stairs to look at the naked man, where they would curse at him and leave. One expressed his anger more forcefully by urinating all over "the white devil." But the final sequence of events didn't begin until hours later when nightfall came and a number of men entered the loft, where they lined up single-file in front of their prisoner. Each had a weapon—a knife, a meat cleaver, a metal cutter—and each took his turn.

The first in line ripped off the man's ear with a knife. The second cut off a thumb. The next chopped off three toes. And on and on. When they were through removing his head, hands, and feet, what was left of the man's body was bundled up with rope.

Four Black Muslims—31-year-old Manuel Moore, 29-year-old J. C. Simon, 24-year-old Larry C. Green, and 30-year-old Jessie Lee Cooks—were tried on charges of murder, conspiracy, kidnapping, robbery, assault with a deadly weapon, and illegal use of firearms. In the early phase of the year-long trial, the key prosecution witness and surprise informant, 29-year-old Anthony Harris, testified under a grant of immunity that he first heard about the Death Angels while serving time in San Quentin, when two of the defendants asked him for instruction in the martial arts to kill white people. Upon his release, Harris said, he then joined the defendants in their nightly forays which terrorized the city of San Francisco for six months.

The jury of eight women and four men deliberated eighteen hours before reaching its guilty verdict. The four defendants were sentenced to life in prison.

It is conceivable, if not likely, that none of the Death Angels was either psychiatrically or legally insane; yet their acts of human destruction were almost unimaginably grotesque and despicable. The cult developed rules for killing which eventually became part of their way of life, their shared culture. Those who complied were approved and rewarded; any member who dared disobey or ignore the rules was a traitor.

Charles Manson and his followers represent another example of the countercultural elements of mass murder.[5] Their story began on the morning of August 9, 1969, when a Beverly Hills housekeeper telephoned the police to report a ghastly murder at the secluded hillside residence of her employer, Hollywood starlet Sharon Tate and her husband, movie director Roman Polanski. She had come to clean up the house when she discovered the bodies of five people including Miss Tate, who was eight months pregnant. The word "pig" was scrawled in blood across the front door of the luxurious home.

When the police arrived, they found what one called "a bloody mess." Twenty-six-year-old Sharon Tate's body lay in the living room of the house, a nylon rope tied tightly around her neck as though in preparation for a hanging. She had been stabbed sixteen times. Next to Tate on the floor lay the limp body of her close friend, 35-year-old Hollywood hair stylist Jay Sebring. He had been stabbed seven times and shot. A towel partially obscured the rope which had been tied around his neck and then had been draped over a beam on the ceiling.

Two more bodies were found on the front lawn of the house, some fifty feet apart. Thirty-seven-year-old Wojiciech Frykowski, a friend of Roman Polanski, had been shot five times, stabbed fifty-one times, and bludgeoned thirteen times on the back of the head. His girlfriend, 26-year-old coffee heiress Abigail Folger, had been stabbed twenty-eight times. Both Folger and Frykowski had apparently tried to escape, but were caught while running away from the house. The fifth body, that of 18-year-old Steve Parent, was found slumped over the wheel of an automobile parked on the narrow road leading to the entry gate of the property. He had been stabbed once and shot four times. Roman Polanski was in London at the time of the slayings.

Though they lacked firm evidence linking William Garretson to the slayings, the police quickly arrested and charged the 19-

year-old caretaker who lived in a small garage-like cottage at the rear of the main house. Subsequent events, however, made it clear that the police had the wrong man. Garretson had apparently slept through the entire massacre.

The day after the Tate massacre, the 15-year-old son of wealthy supermarket owners, Rosemary and Leno LaBianca, walked into his Los Angeles home to find his parents' bloody bodies. Rosemary LaBianca's body lay in the master bedroom of the house, her hands tied behind her back with an electrical cord and a pillowcase pulled over her face. She had been stabbed forty-one times. Leno LaBianca's body was sprawled across the living room carpet, his hands fastened behind him with a leather thong and his face covered with a bloody pillowcase. The killers had left a carving fork protruding from his abdomen and had scratched the word "war" in his skin. He had been stabbed twenty-seven times. Scribbled in blood on a living room wall were the words "Death to the pigs" and on the refrigerator door "Helter Skelter."

Taken from the Beatles song, Helter Skelter was the name Charles Manson had given to the war between blacks and whites which he believed would shortly engulf the nation. He preached to his flock, members of the so-called Manson family, that they must prepare to move to an isolated desert area in order to avoid the race war he felt would inevitably result in the victory of blacks over whites. Manson also believed, however, that the victorious blacks would be ineffective in governing the country and would eventually be forced to ask him to rule.

Manson never had a direct hand in the Tate/LaBianca slayings, but he orchestrated them through instructions to his followers. He hoped that blacks would be falsely accused and the race war he envisaged hastened all the more. Instead, Manson and two of the female members of his family—22-year-old Susan Atkins and 23-year-old Patricia Krenwinkel—were convicted on January 25, 1971 of seven counts of first-degree murder. A third

Manson follower, 21-year-old Leslie Van Houten, was convicted of two counts of first-degree murder.

According to psychiatrist Clara Livsey, the Manson cult shares a number of characteristics with other violent terrorist groups. First, Charles Manson was a charismatic leader who convinced his followers of his great power. Members of his family believed him to be Jesus Christ. Second, most of Manson's flock were white and middle-class. Third, the violent behavior of the Manson family was deliberate and purposeful rather than accidental or random. Fourth, family members had a "cause"—assuming the leadership of the nation—which justified their staying together. Indeed, being part of the family and serving its cause were seen by the cultists as the ultimate solution to all problems. Fifth, the Manson followers were as "active" as Manson himself. None was hypnotized into joining his family. Rather, each was attracted to Manson by the promise of becoming a very important, extremely special person who was "destined to make [her] mark on the world." Even if Manson himself were totally deranged, it would be difficult to argue convincingly that all of his many followers—both those who killed and those who didn't—acted out of lunacy. Even those who killed didn't join the family for the purpose of committing violence.

The murders and the motives of the Manson family can, therefore, be likened in some respects to those of any attacking militia. The Japanese airmen in World War II would kill and sometimes go so far as to kill themselves on kamikaze missions for the sake of a cause. The Manson family also was indoctrinated into a cause (also a losing one), and chose the Tate residence as their Pearl harbor to stage their violent declaration of war. Manson, Hitler, and Premier Hideki Tojo (who led Japan into World War II) were all leaders who failed in their ambitious designs for domination and who pulled down their admiring followers with them.

In the purely psychiatric view, mass murder is inevitably brought into play by some immediate and irrational psychological motivation. Very much like mob violence, an act of mass killing is seen as uncontrolled, unplanned, and unburdened by logic or reason, following no particular program or policy and having no realistic goals.

Motives are often complex and difficult to identify. Even in everyday life, what originally looks like inexplicable behavior may turn out to have an ulterior motive. What passes for craziness may in fact be craftiness or deceit.

Most of us infer motives from how people behave. That's the only way we have of getting into someone else's head. To attribute motive or feeling, we must not only listen carefully to what a person has to say, but also to how he or she says it. This requires evaluating not only the content, but the context and style of behavior.

Some people are more skillful than others when it comes to hiding their innermost thoughts, feelings, and motives. Certain mass murderers may be particularly clever in this respect. Thus, what appears to be unprovoked catharsis may actually indicate a premeditated cold-blooded act of instrumental aggression. What passes for craziness may really be a well-planned scheme to accomplish what the killer wants. The vast majority of mass murders fall into this category.

Thus, the terrorist elements in mass murder are by no means confined to the work of Charles Manson and his family. When it becomes a way of life, mass killing may be regarded as an act of terror in which deliberation and calculation often play an important role. Not unlike its counterpart in organized political terrorism, a mass slaying typically involves death and destruction as part of a killer's program of action. There is often a psychiatric component, to be sure; but situational factors often trigger the action. One might be tempted to call Charles Manson "crazy" because of his unrealistic ambition to rule the world. But if Hitler had succeeded in accomplishing the same goal, would he have been called "crazy"?*

More often than not, mass murder is a means to an end—a premeditated act which is designed and executed to accomplish some objective or goal. In this sense, it can be highly rational. It is true that a killer may act out of a strictly personal motive or as the representative of an imagined leader or cause. For example, Herbert William Mullin murdered thirteen people between October 1972 and February 1973 as human sacrifices to ward off earthquakes predicted in Southern California. In his mind, he was successful—the earthquakes never came. But many join other people in killing for some larger cause which becomes the basis for a way of life for the entire organization, group, or cult.

We may not be accustomed to thinking of them as such, but certain acts of political terrorism are also mass murders. On December 4, 1773, George Washington bade farewell to his Revolutionary officers in Fraunces Tavern. Centuries later, on the afternoon of January 24, 1975, the Tavern Annex, located in Manhattan's congested financial district, was the target of another revolutionary group. Their hidden bomb produced a thundering blast which shattered the windows of the building, obliterated its heavy wooden front door, ripped apart a marble and concrete staircase inside, and collapsed an internal wall. Thousands of strands of razor-sharp window glass flew onto passersby on the sidewalk outside, while neighboring skyscrapers shook with such intensity that their windows were shattered.

Inside, the crowded dining room was the scene of incredible human tragedy. Dozens of the Tavern's patrons—mostly Wall

*Similarly, we might say that it will take a crazed leader to initiate a nuclear war, because it is "obviously" futile and senseless. Clearly, then, we judge the rationality of acts by their outcomes—their rewards and consequences. President Harry Truman dropped not one but two atomic bombs, causing instantaneous death or terminal illness for hundreds of thousands of Japanese. It ended the war, a war which we won; therefore, he was a hero. Had the bombings escalated the war instead, Truman might have been considered a lunatic.

Street workers on their lunchbreak—were left with mangled limbs, broken bones, and cuts, many severe enough to be hospitalized. Four men died in the explosion; one was decapitated by flying debris.

An hour later, the Associated Press and United Press International received a call from the Armed Forces of National Liberation (FALN), an organization seeking the independence of Puerto Rico from the United States. Claiming responsibility for the explosion, the callers demanded the release of Puerto Rican prisoners and explained that the bombing was in retaliation for the "murder" by the CIA of supporters of the Puerto Rican independence movement. The same organization also claimed responsibility for the October bombing of several Manhattan buildings as well as the December planting of a booby-trapped bomb that blew up in the face of a rookie policeman.

The Fraunces Tavern explosion was clearly political in its motivation and effect. Because it contained so many of the elements that many associate with terrorism, few would describe it as an act of mass murder even though four human beings were killed.

More subtle in this respect were the events in the aftermath of the brutal murder of the New Orleans' police chief in 1890.[6] On a rain-soaked October evening, Chief David Hennessey had been walking alone in a quiet, dilapidated area of the city, when he was cut down by five men who opened fire with shotguns and pistols. In seconds, the ambush was over. Hennessey had managed to draw his pistol and stagger after his assailants. He then collapsed in a pool of blood.

By the next morning, millions of people throughout the nation read in their daily newspapers that the nationally prominent police chief had been shot down by the "Mafia," based only on the word of Captain Bill O'Connor of the New Orleans Police who claimed his dying friend had whispered that his assailants were "dagos."

The New Orleans police lost little time responding to the crime. Almost immediately, nineteen Italians were arrested en masse and scheduled for trial; but they were never convicted. Instead, the trial of the first nine defendants ended in a mistrial for three men and a verdict of "not guilty" for the other six. Even before the second round of trials could begin, an angry "mob" of some 12,000 New Orleanians stormed Parish Prison where the defendants were being held, and slaughtered eleven Italians, three of whom had been previously acquitted, three whose court appearance had ended in a mistrial, and five more who had never even been tried. Another eight men escaped by hiding themselves in closets or under mattresses in their cells.

Incredibly, half of the major newspapers across the country voiced their strong approval of the mass killing. As justification, they charged that the acquitted Italians had carried out a "reign of terror" throughout New Orleans and had bribed the jury with $100,000 to escape imprisonment for their evil deeds.

According to Richard Gambino, Professor of Italian-American studies at Queens College, everyone first assumed that the motive for the mass slaying was vengeance for the death of David Hennessey, one of New Orleans most illustrious citizens and a crusader against the Mafia. It was later discovered, however, that the murder of Hennessey, whatever its impetus, had provided a "cover" for an organized plot to destroy the Italian-American community of New Orleans.

The Italians were widely resented and despised by native New Orleanians who feared the Italians' growing economic and political power. First, the newly arrived Italians were accused of extracting money from the local economy by sending it back to their starving families in the old country and by paying their boat passage to Louisiana. Second, plantation owners were alarmed that Italians who originally worked the sugar fields for slave wages were suddenly buying up cheap land to become property owners and competitors in agriculture. Moreover, Sicilian fishermen and peddlers who worked hard and benefited from their experiences in the old country were seen by the business leaders of New Orleans as monopolizing the fruit, oyster, and fish industries of the city.

The morning after the jury's verdict of "not guilty" was given to the court, local newspapers carried an advertisement inviting the citizens of New Orleans to attend a mass meeting "to remedy the failure of justice in the Hennessey case." Among the sponsors of the ad and leaders of the meeting were William Parkerson, the Mayor's assistant; John Wickliffe, grandson of a former governor of Kentucky; Walter Denegre, a wealthy land owner and lawyer; and James Houston, a political boss with a long history of violence.

At the meeting the following day, thousands watched as Parkerson and his associates angrily denounced the jury for acquitting the "Mafia society," and urged the crowd to "follow and see the murder of David Hennessey vindicated."[7] Parkerson, Denegre, and Wickliffe then led the furious mob toward Parish Prison, where they were joined by a carefully organized "execution squad" of one hundred men carrying Winchester repeating rifles and shotguns.

Forty members of the execution squad were stationed at the prison gate, their instructions being to block entry to the crowd; the other sixty burst through the gate and into the prison courtyard where six of the Italians were huddled together in hiding some twenty feet away. The squad immediately opened fire, pumping more than one hundred rifle and shotgun rounds into the bodies of the defenseless inmates.

Meanwhile, members of the execution squad busily searched other sections of the prison. In a large gallery, they cornered three men who had been attempting to hide. But their executioners raised their shotguns and fired several blasts through the bars of an open window into the helpless victims crouched just a few feet on the other side. All three Italians were struck in the head. One raised his right hand to protect himself from the onslaught, but it was blown off by a shotgun blast that found its mark. Another fell backward as a bullet ripped away the top of his skull. The third died with a club clutched tightly in his fist.

After waiting twenty minutes or more, the mob outside was in a virtual frenzy. They could hear the shots coming from within the prison and demanded to take part in the kill. Parkerson decided to appease the crowd by allowing it to finish off two of the prisoners who had already been seriously wounded but were apparently not dead. The first victim was semiconscious as he was literally thrown into the bloodthirsty mob and hanged by the neck from the top rung of a nearby streetlight. Already unconscious and limp, the second man was tossed above the heads of the mob and then hanged from the limb of a tree.

For five hours, thousands of men, women, and children maneuvered their way through the prison to catch a glimpse of the bullet-ridden bodies of the Italians. Some even dipped their handkerchiefs in the blood of their victims as souvenirs of the "joyous event."

One might reasonably contend that mass murder committed by groups brings together people of like minds, that is, those who are already predisposed to violence. Could one really insist, however, that the thousands of citizens of New Orleans who participated in the mob action were actually insane or demented? These New Orleanians—like the Death Angels of San Francisco, like the Fraunces Tavern terrorists of New York City, like the family of Charles Manson, or even Lt. William Calley of the United States Army—were indoctrinated into a movement or "a way of life" that demanded killing.

FRITZ GOES MARCHING IN

'Frisco latest Pages 4-9

TODAY
Mostly sunny, low 80s

TONIGHT
Clear, 60s

TOMORROW
Sunny, mid 80s

Details, Page 2

NEW YORK POST

METRO
SPORTS FINAL

TV listings: P. 87

THURSDAY JULY 19 1984 30 CENTS R

© 1984 News Group Publications Inc. Vol. 183, No. 212

AMERICA'S FASTEST-GROWING NEWSPAPER

ABC AVERAGE SALES EXCEED 960,000

BIG MAC MASSACRE

21 DEAD

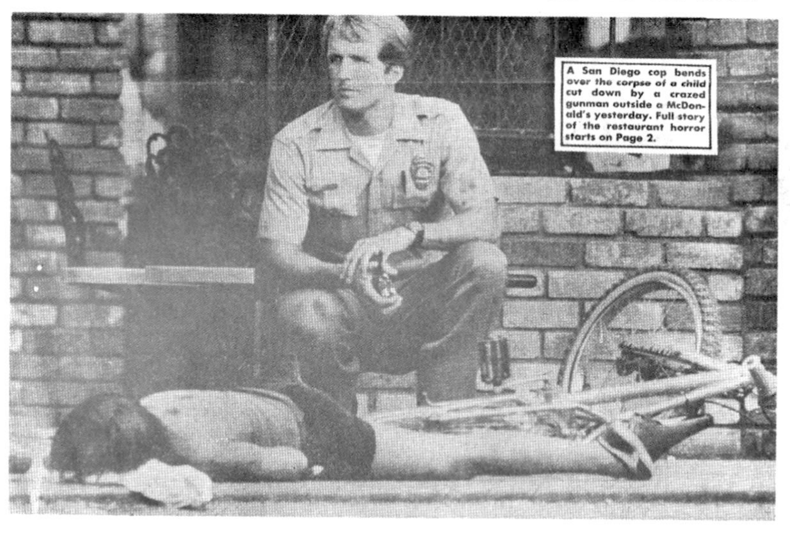

A San Diego cop bends over the corpse of a child cut down by a crazed gunman outside a McDonald's yesterday. Full story of the restaurant horror starts on Page 2.

1. The biggest headlines are made by the most unusual mass killings: James Huberty's random shooting at an American institution will be remembered for years as the "McDonald's Murder." Reprinted by permission of *New York Post*, copyright 1984, News Group Publications, Inc.

2. First Lady Rosalynn Carter posing with John Wayne Gacy at a local Democratic reception. She signed an autograph: "To John Gacy, Best Wishes—Rosalynn Carter." Copyright News Group Chicago Inc., 1979. Reprinted with permission of *Chicago Sun-Times.*

3. The caskets of his victims reveal the other side of John Wayne Gacy. By permission of Wide World Photos.

4. Mass murderers don't stand out in a crowd. This file photo of a campus scene was reprinted on the cover of the Eastern Michigan University directory. After its publication, someone looked closely and recognized former student and convicted murderer, John Norman Collins. Courtesy of Eastern Michigan University, Office of Information Services.

5. Ted Bundy (top) and Fred Cowan (bottom) represent the extreme diversity in the appearance of mass killers. By permission of Wide World Photos.

6. For years Edward Gein, necrophile and murderer, tried to prove that he had regained his sanity. His 1974 court hearing attracted some local publicity but failed to win his release. Gein died in the state hospital in 1984. By permission of Wide World Photos.

7. The Manson women, photographed during their vigil outside the courthouse in Los Angeles, shaved their heads to symbolize their unified and abiding loyalty to their leader who was on trial for the Tate/LaBianca murders. By permission of Wide World Photos.

8. In Jonestown, Guyana, the total dependence of hundreds of American citizens on their autocratic and charismatic leader, James Jones, made them extremely vulnerable to all his demands. His last commandment—to drink from a bucket of cyanide-laced Kool-Aid—resulted in their deaths. By permission of UPI/The Bettmann Archive.

PART II

CASE STUDIES IN MASS MURDER

CHAPTER 8

THREE TYPES OF MASS MURDER

There are three major types of mass murder: family slayings, mass murder for profit or expediency, and killing for the sake of sex or sadism.* These categories differ in terms of why the killer commits the crime, what he tries to accomplish by the deed, and how he justifies his actions.

Not unlike assailants who commit less serious crimes, mass murderers are often aware of the wrongfulness of their offense and may even express a sense of guilt or shame about having committed it. Indeed, many mass killers are otherwise law-abiding citizens who belong to the local church, pay their taxes, attend ballgames, play with their children, and complain about corruption in high places. They may generally obey the rules of society but adopt a set of justifications which allows them temporarily or periodically to commit a heinous crime without withdrawing from normal everyday activities. There may be, at one extreme, a few individuals who feel totally guiltless whatever the circum-

*Certain cases cannot fit neatly into any of these categories, for example mass murder inspired by racial hatred. Also, there are a few cases that appear to contain elements of more than one type, such as murders primarily for money in which victims are sadistically tortured. These three types, nevertheless, encompass most incidents of mass murder, and help us to understand this diverse phenomenon.

stances. There are, at the other extreme, mass killers whose guilt is so severe that they take their own lives as an act of self-punishment. For most mass murderers, however, justifying their offense is not only possible, it is essential.

Exactly how are such heinous crimes rationalized? One might argue: If you can justify mass murder, you can justify anything. And history informs us that this is precisely the case. Human beings have proven time and time again that they are capable of justifying even the most atrocious acts imaginable.

Family slayings are by far the most common; they comprise nearly half of all mass murders. These murders seem doubly tragic: not only do they offend our fundamental notion concerning the family as a crucible of love and life, but they also appear to the rest of us as so senseless or pointless—after all, no one wins. According to psychiatrist Dr. Shervert Frazier, however, there may be a payoff psychologically.[1]

In cases of family homicide, jealousy or frustration typically culminates in the sudden annihilation of an entire family. For example, the family breadwinner on whom all depend loses his job and is unable to find another; out of uncontrollable despair, he spares his wife and children the humiliation and hardship of permanent unemployment and the pain of living by "mercifully" executing them in their sleep. At the same time, he assures himself that his family will be reunited in the hereafter. Dr. Frazier calls this "suicide by proxy": a parent may identify so strongly with his children that he sees them as an extension of himself. Therefore, to kill his children is, in his mind, to commit suicide.

Another theme in family killings stems more from anger than love. Following relentless conflicts with his wife, a man may be forced to leave the security and emotional support of his family. Feeling lost, angry, and alone, he returns to get even with his wife by killing all of "her" children as if he were attacking his offensive partner. The husband or wife who slays all of the children as an act of revenge against the spouse is, in Frazier's terms, committing "murder by proxy."

In many parts of the country, one out of every two marriages ends in divorce. At the same time, families tend not to "stick together" as they once did. Frequently, a middle-aged man, who has had a profound emotional attachment to this family, is forced out of the home by an estranged wife or a mother on whom he has depended for years. Whether or not he deserves to have been thrown out is immaterial. He has come to rely emotionally so much on family members in the past that he now finds himself distraught. He is without social connections or controls. In effect, his entire world has been torn apart. He, in a very real sense, becomes an individual who lacks rules for living in the absence of family structure. Without a reason to live or to let live, he may find that revenge becomes an all-consuming passion.

As we will describe in Chapter 9, the horrible prospect of being alone faced 41-year-old James Ruppert of Hamilton, Ohio, whose mother was on the verge of forcing him out of the house. On Easter Sunday, 1975, James slaughtered eleven relatives, including his mother, believing, as defense psychiatrists later argued, that she and his brother had conspired with the FBI to sabotage his career.

Like many other family killers, Ruppert led a life filled with frustration and disappointment. He had trouble relating to other people, especially women, and had recently lost his job. His facility with firearms permitted him to carry out an act of mass destruction precipitated by his worsening economic situation, strained relationships with important family members, and his imminent forced departure from his mother's home.

The first reaction of Ruppert's neighbors and other townspeople was predictably one of disbelief or denial. Very few, if any, truly understood the inner tensions of the Ruppert household or James Ruppert's long-standing antagonism toward his older brother. Once public denial was no longer possible, the citizens of Hamilton—like citizens of other locales in which family massacres have occurred—became intensely angry about the crime that to them seemed utterly senseless.

The profound emotion—love, passion, jealousy, revenge—that pervades a family murder is by contrast entirely missing from murder for profit or expediency. That is, those who kill for practical reasons are cold, calculating, and dispassionate. For them, murder is purely instrumental—a means toward an end.

Brooklyn's Devernon LeGrand, self-styled bishop of St. John's Pentecostal Church of Our Lord, for example, killed two of his female followers to stop them from testifying against him for having raped them. These same women had previously given testimony at a trial in which Bishop LeGrand was convicted of bribery. Similarly motivated, Ronald Piskorski, a former bouncer and circus-bear wrestler, snuffed out the lives of six people who witnessed his armed robbery of Donna Lee's Bakery in New Britain, Connecticut. The 280-pound Piskorski and an accomplice shot to death the owner of the popular bakery, an employee, and four customers so that they wouldn't be identified to the police.

The elimination of witnesses to an armed robbery or accomplices who inform about illegal activities occurs more frequently than one might expect. Even though these criminals are primarily out for profit, they may feel compelled to murder in order to avoid detection. For crimes of profit and expediency, the end may seem to justify the means. In other words, the killer doesn't necessarily hate his victims or enjoy the act of murder, but sees his victims as obstacles to fulfilling important goals—goals more important than a few lives.

For the Johnston Brothers of Chester County, Pennsylvania, mass murder was an unfortunate expediency. To illustrate mass killing for profit, we will examine in Chapter 10 how brothers Bruce, David, and Norman Johnston proceeded to kill their accomplices in order to protect themselves from a grand jury investigation of their crime ring.

The dispassionate murders committed by the Johnstons were met with general indifference by the public, since it was "crooks killing crooks." This kind of community response contrasts sharply with that of the third type of mass murder—those motivated by sex or sadism. Murders committed for reasons of sex or sadism are usually serial crimes carried out repeatedly over a period of time. Such killings are often viewed as senseless or irrational, because they are purely expressive—an end in themselves. Unlike other types of mass killers, the sexual sadist chooses his victims more or less randomly—they are not specifically viewed as obstacles to his goals. Rather than killing in order to remove certain individuals—such as family members or informants—from this world, he kills for the thrill or excitement of the act itself. For example, 21-year-old David Bullock of Manhattan murdered six people, ranging from a prostitute to his roommate, just for fun. Following his capture, he explained to the judge that he did it because it "makes me happy. . . . It was in the Christmas Spirit . . . something to amuse myself."[2]

Bullock fits the mold of the sociopathic killer, who feels no need to justify his act since he feels no remorse. Even when he accepts responsibility for his behavior, he may not accept any blame. The sociopath reasons, "Sure I did it, but so what?"

Some sexual sadists never admit to their evil deeds, even when caught "red-handed." Ted Bundy, for instance, against whom the evidence, both physical and testimonial, was overwhelming, continues to insist that he's innocent. Similarly, convicted child-killer Wayne Williams proclaimed his total innocence after a guilty verdict was reached following nine weeks of testimony. He stated: "I maintained all along through this trial my innocence and I still say so today. I hold no malice against the jury, the prosecutors, or the court. I hope the person or persons who committed these crimes can be brought to justice. I did not do this."[3]

In addition to serial killers who deny blame—whether or not they also deny the crime itself—there remain a few who justify their crime by appealing to some cause or force, larger than themselves. Herbert William Mullin of California, for example, justified his murders as human sacrifices to prevent an earthquake near the San Andreas fault, which would have killed many more than his thirteen victims. "Son of Sam" David Berkowitz insisted that he had been ordered to kill by demons who spoke to him through barking dogs. Others have held to loftier causes to justify their sadistic crimes. The Manson family, for example, tortured and killed under the direction of their leader whom they believed was Jesus Christ and should rule the world. San Francisco's Zebra killers belonged to a Black Muslim sect whose members were religiously inspired to rid the world of the "blue-eyed devils."

Some sexual killers, such as Alaska's Robert Hansen who chose his seventeen victims from the streets of Anchorage's red-light district, hunt out prostitutes or other "evil beings" who need to be eliminated from the face of the earth, reasoning that the world would be better off without them. Thus, these killers justify their crimes by denying the basic humanity of their victims. Prostitutes, in particular, are viewed as "pure" sex machines whose sole function in life—and in death—is to serve and satisfy men. As subhuman objects, they can be raped, ravished, and even killed for the sake of pleasure. They may also be the target of displaced aggression for those men who profoundly resent their own mother's promiscuity and sexual perversity, real or imagined.

We will analyze in Chapter 11 the case of the Hillside Strangler which, in so many respects, is a classic example of sexual and sadistic murder. Beginning quite inconspicuously with the killing of "lowly" prostitutes, the murders soon spread to young schoolgirls. As the killings grew in their grotesqueness, public reaction reached a feverish pitch.

During this climate of panic, citizens were quick to point their finger at any stranger or acquaintance who looked the least bit peculiar or acted the least bit oddly. Because of the "perfection" of the crimes, police and reporters speculated that the killer, rather than a crazed lunatic, might be the "neighbor next door," "the worker at the next desk," or even the "cop on the streetcorner." As in the late 17th century Massachusetts witch scare when anyone could have been "Satan's sidekick," or as in the

McCarthy era when anyone could have been a communist, no one was beyond suspicion in Los Angeles in early 1978.

The strangler was, in reality, two men: Kenneth Bianchi and Angelo Buono. As is common in serial killings, they teamed up to prey on "innocent" victims, not out of a psychotic impulse, but more out of a spirit of adventure and fun that developed within their friendship. It is easier to kill when someone else is there to help justify it.

Angelo Buono was in some respects an evil man, who liked his sex with pain; but he was hardly deranged. Many of his friends still hold to his innocence. Ken Bianchi also seemed quite normal to his friends. Like many other serial killers, he aspired toward a career in law enforcement where his confused needs to be helpful and to be in control of others could be expressed. Bianchi and Buono—as well as Ruppert and the Johnstons—may have been murderers, but in most other respects they were extraordinarily ordinary.

CHAPTER 9

JAMES RUPPERT

The case of James Ruppert demonstrates in dramatic fashion that things aren't always what they seem to be.[1] The 41-year-old resident of Hamilton, Ohio hardly seemed likely to commit mass murder: He had no police record and, except for thick glasses and small stature, was undistinguished in appearance. Even after he had brutally murdered eleven relatives, neighbors still recalled the five-foot six-inch, 135-pound Ruppert as being a quiet and responsible member of this industrial community of some 63,000 people. Defense attorney Hugh Holbrock later said of James Ruppert, "He's one of the kindest human beings I have ever met. He would do anything to help people."[2]

The scene of the mass slaying was the house which Ruppert and his mother shared: a small two-story, two-tone wood-frame structure situated on a quiet, tree-lined residential street in Hamilton. The occasion was Easter Sunday, 1975—the day after James's 41st birthday. Ruppert's ailing 65-year-old mother, Charity, had invited the entire clan to the house: her two sons, James and Leonard, and Leonard's family including his wife Alma and their eight children ranging in age from 4 to 17.

The day began happily enough. Shortly after arriving, the members of Leonard Ruppert's family gathered together on the front lawn, where they had an Easter egg hunt. Then, they all went into the house for the yearly family reunion and dinner. Everyone mingled in the living room and kitchen—everyone, that is, except Uncle James, who was on the second floor of the house making his final preparations.

Charity Ruppert was fixing sandwiches at the kitchen range, while Leonard and his wife Alma sat together at the kitchen table. Their youngest child was in the bathroom; one of their daughters stood waiting her turn by the bathroom door, as the other six children played in the living room.

Moments later, James Ruppert, gun enthusiast and crack marksman, walked calmly down the stairs carrying three revolvers—a .357 magnum and twin .22 caliber handguns—and an 18-shot rifle which he immediately propped against the refrigerator door. With his back to the kitchen sink, Ruppert fired first at his brother Leonard, who fell backward onto the floor; he then shot his sister-in-law Alma and his mother, who lunged toward him in a last futile effort to save her family and her life. Before anyone had a chance to think—let alone, escape—Ruppert had fired 31 shots, stopping only to reload. The first round was disabling; the second and third rounds finished off his victims. Ten of them were shot in the head at close range; one was shot in the chest. Nobody screamed; nobody ran. All of them were dead when Ruppert called the police some three hours later. "There's been a shooting here," he told the police over the phone.[3]

Minutes later, the police found James Ruppert standing inside the front door of the house. They also found five blood-splattered bodies in the living room and six in the kitchen. None of the victims had been tied or restrained in any way, yet the only sign of a struggle was an overturned wastepaper basket.

The police had a suspect but no motive. James Ruppert was taken into custody and charged with eleven counts of aggravated murder. He refused to talk to the police about the killings and pleaded not guilty by reason of insanity.

Even the least sadistic witnesses to a gory traffic accident will slow their cars, shine their brights, and turn their heads to catch a glimpse of a blood-stained car seat, a crushed fender, or an injured victim. The same sort of curiosity is often sparked by the gruesome circumstances of mass murder. The crime is so large, so extraordinary, so out of proportion to everyday reality that it virtually begs for definition.

The Ruppert murders and trial provoked what one local observer called "a three-ring circus." For weeks following the tragic event, James Ruppert was the topic of conversation in town. Street sales of Hamilton's only daily newspaper doubled; hundreds of neighbors congregated outside the Ruppert home, sometimes long past midnight. For six hours after the funeral, 400 cars carrying enthusiastic curiosity-seekers—some in taxicabs—cruised past Arlington Memorial Gardens, where Ruppert's eleven victims were buried.

During the trial, curious spectators began arriving early in the morning—some by six AM—to wait outside the stone-faced, three-story courthouse for one of the sixty seats in its warm, stuffy third-floor courtroom. They ran for the stairs or elevator, hoping to beat the crowds to the courtroom door. Those who couldn't get seats stood around the walls of the courtroom or waited outside on benches in the corridors. For the duration of the proceedings, spectators in the hallway peered through the glass in the door, straining to get a glimpse of the defendant who sat impassively throughout most of the trial. As reporter Dick Perry later recalled, "It was a free show!"[4]

One year following Easter Sunday, 1975, the Ruppert home was unlocked to auction off its household possessions—the furniture, appliances, clothing, and odds and ends. Dozens of people came searching for bargains and bloodstains. They wound their way through the tiny backyard into the living room and kitchen and up the stairs into Ruppert's second-floor bedroom. As eyewitness Nancy Baker reported in the local paper, "Babies asleep in strollers . . . housewives in curlers . . . men smoking big cigars—all added to the carnival atmosphere."[5]

It wasn't all fun and games, of course. Indeed, the Ruppert slayings provoked widespread anxiety throughout the Hamilton area. Townspeople had plenty of questions, but very few answers. Until the trial, the local newspapers did little more than report surface information—mostly about the who, what, and where, but little about the why. As though to fill the need for news, rumors were spread everywhere—rumors which attempted to explain why the killings occurred and what effect they might have on the community:

"Alma had wanted to commit suicide and take one of her children with her. She started the whole thing by harrassing Jimmie."

"Ruppert went beserk when he learned his mother had made Hamburger Helper for Easter dinner." (Though said in jest, the police actually found a skillet on the stove in which Charity Ruppert had been preparing Sloppy Joe's for her grandchildren.)

"If Prosecutor John Holcomb loses the Ruppert case, he'll quit."

"The Ruppert house is haunted."

"Kids snuck into the Ruppert house on Minor Avenue and said everything was covered with blood."

"The new occupants of what was formerly the Ruppert house were newcomers to Hamilton who weren't told that the mass murder had taken place there."

"Though confined in a mental hospital since the trial, James Ruppert has an extensive wardrobe, loves to eat ice cream, and continues to receive the *Wall Street Journal* on a daily basis."

Psychiatrists report that grieving over the loss of a close relative or friend frequently begins with denial: survivors reject the reality of a death until such time that they are psychologically ready to deal with it. Denial seems to be especially common in cases of murder where a large number of victims are involved. The enormity of the crime provokes widespread disbelief: "How could only one person have killed all those people?" "Why didn't at least some of them escape?" "How could they have gone to the slaughter like lambs?" The answer, of course, is that even the victims themselves couldn't believe what was about to happen.

Christians went to the lions like lambs; Jews went to the "showers" like lambs; and the Ruppert family members were just as incredulous. The body of one of the Ruppert children was found lying only a foot or so from the back door which she apparently had managed to open slightly before being gunned down by her uncle. None of the other victims even came close.

We like to think of the family as a crucible of love and affection. Hence, murder by the hands of a family member (especially a son killing his mother) can be too much for the mind to fathom. What is more, the family is typically a closed unit in which conflicts and disagreements are kept from the prying eyes and ears of outsiders. Consequently, people who considered themselves to be familiar with the perpetrator and his victims responded in utter shock.

Ruppert's friends and relatives couldn't believe it: James's uncle, Rufus Skinner, insisted that "Jimmie and his brother Leonard were two close soldiers" who "did everything for their mother . . . ever since their father died in 1947."[6] Arthur Bauer said of his close friend, James: "He's not violent at all. I can't believe he did it . . . how could anything like that happen?"

A retired court stenographer, Mrs. Lucille Tabler is an intelligent, active woman who lived in the Hamilton area for seventy years and knew the Rupperts as their family friend and neighbor. The gray-haired Mrs. Tabler denied what she couldn't understand. Upon hearing about the mass killings, she told reporters that she was thoroughly stunned: "I just don't believe it. Why would he want to do something like that? . . . I wish I could talk to Jimmy."[7] Even after being informed of Ruppert's undisputed confession, his presence at the scene of the crime, his fingerprints on the weapons, the victims' blood on his clothing, and his internally consistent recollections of the circumstances of the crime, Mrs. Tabler steadfastly refused to acknowledge that James Ruppert was a killer. Seven years later, she faithfully reconfirmed her confidence in the man she knew from childhood, visiting him in jail and defending his name among the locals. To this day, she asks: "Why was the whole world against the Ruppert family?"[8]

A community can deny only so long after the occurrence of an extraordinary murder. As more and more information about the killings comes to public light, denial quickly turns into anger and community members begin to look for someone or something to blame.

For several months following the slayings, people in Hamilton were profoundly outraged. After all, there were eleven bloody bodies, eight dead children, an entire family whose members had been completely wiped out in one fell swoop. A close friend may not have exaggerated when she told us, "Everybody wanted to go out and shoot Jimmie—I was always arguing for him."[9]

Angry feelings toward James Ruppert sometimes became generalized in a free-floating sort of hostility which could have taken a dangerous turn. Members of the Donald Ruppert family were lucky to have escaped with their lives. The only Ruppert remaining in the Hamilton telephone directory, Donald isn't so much as a distant cousin of James Ruppert. Though not related to the killer, Donald Ruppert's family was constantly harassed by townspeople for at least six months following the mass slayings. He finally decided to change his name for a period of time in order to avoid the dirty looks and obscene phone calls. According to Donald Ruppert, even those people who had known him well weren't really sure that he wasn't implicated in the crime: "At work they thought I did it. . . . Some wanted to know when I was going to get the money. . . . I hate it every time I see something about the trial in the newspaper."[10]

At his June 1975 trial, James Ruppert entered a plea of insanity. Defense Attorney H. J. Bressler argued that the very act Ruppert had committed was itself "insane"—that Ruppert had been insane for ten years and that he was incapable of controlling his actions. Several expert witnesses agreed. Dr. Howard Sokolov described Ruppert as suffering from "a paranoid psychotic state," one symptom of which was "departure from reality in terms of thinking and behavior." Ruppert, he suggested, was inclined to be excessively suspicious, jealous, and angry.

Defense psychiatrists also testified that Ruppert was absolutely obsessed with the belief that family members, the police, and the FBI were involved in a long-standing conspiracy to persecute him. Dr. Philip Meehanick saw an even wider deficiency in Ruppert's personality: "His ability to evaluate is impaired, his view of others is warped, he sees virtually no one in a kindly light."

Harvard psychiatrist Dr. Lester Grinspoon testified that Ruppert's deadly reaction may have been uncontrollable: "His ego was just completely overwhelmed by this rage, this suppressed rage which had been accumulating over some ten years or more, actually since childhood, that there was no way in which he could avoid doing that act. In fact, if there had been more people in the house, they might have been killed also."[11]

Thus, the defense attempted to show that James Ruppert had gone totally beserk—that he was a victim of self-delusion who had acted from sheer impulse; the perpetrator of a brutal yet purposeless crime.

But appearances can be deceiving; and the prosecution called twenty-nine witnesses and presented two hundred exhibits to develop an entirely different line of reasoning, namely, that James Ruppert was as much a victim of self-delusion as Attila the Hun. Rather, he had carefully plotted and schemed to kill his entire family in order to collect more than $300,000—money tied up in life insurance, real estate, savings accounts, and other investments owned by his mother and his brother, Leonard. Prosecuting attorney John Holcomb convincingly argued that Ruppert's arrest and indictment were actually part of his master plan "to enter a plea of not guilty by reason of temporary insanity . . . to be sent to Lima, a state mental hospital where he would eventually be declared sane and then walk out with $300,000 in his pocket."[12]

It was indeed reasonable to posit an economic motive. Under Ohio law, Ruppert could not have inherited his victims' estate if he had been found guilty of murder. If, however, he had been declared innocent by reason of insanity, he could have gotten everything.

The family estate was a sizable amount by almost any standard. A prosecution witness and member of the real estate and probate committees of the American Bar Association testified that James Ruppert, as sole heir, stood to inherit the entire proceeds of his brother's life insurance, his mother's estate, and half of the property of his brother's children. Leonard's home was valued at $40,000; property belonging to Leonard's family was assessed at $19,500; and his mother's home was worth $14,000. Leonard's life insurance coverage at General Electric was $62,000. His personal coverage was another $100,000. And Leonard invested in savings bonds, stocks, and mutual funds. His family also held savings accounts amounting to almost $30,000.

James Ruppert could have used the money, having been out of work for some time, having little money of his own, and being seriously in debt to his mother and brother. What is more, he had invested and lost thousands of dollars in the stock market and was about to be evicted from his rent-free room in his mother's house.

The defense sought to show that Ruppert had acted spontaneously out of impulse rather than deliberately by plan or scheme. But psychiatric testimony for the prosecution consistently emphasized the plausibility of the profit motive. Two psychiatrists and a psychologist testified that Ruppert was aware of what he was doing, knew right from wrong at the time of the slayings, and had the ability to resist his aggressive impulses. Dr. Charles Feuss, Jr. told the court he did not believe the slayings were carried out in a robot-like manner; yet there simply was no explanation for the killing of the sister-in-law and the children, since they had never been implicated by Ruppert in the alleged conspiracy against him. Butler County Coroner Dr. Garret Boone called the Ruppert slayings "pretty much of a deliberate execution."*[13]

What are the factors which led James Ruppert to kill his entire family? One of the most important may have been frustration, that condition which results from failure to meet an objective, fulfill a goal, or satisfy a need. The person is said to be frustrated who works with all his might to obtain a raise or promotion only to be blocked by an unappreciative boss; an aspiring tennis star is regarded as frustrated who spends a childhood in rigorous training but suffers a debilitating illness or accident that ends her career.

James Ruppert looked normal, but a close look at his biography reveals that he actually led a life of frustration. When James was a young boy, the Rupperts lived in a long barn-like structure which lacked indoor plumbing and running water. His father raised chickens and squabs in the rear of the house. At the same time in his life, James began to suffer from a case of asthma—an allergy to dust and feathers—which left him sickly and limited many of his physical activities for the rest of his childhood. He simply couldn't perform like other children his age. He walked hunched over from illness, so sickly that he was not permitted to take gym at school or to play sports with the neighborhood kids. Even without asthma, his frail appearance and short stature could have severely limited his success in competitive sports.

James Ruppert was regarded a "sissy" by the other kids in the neighborhood. He remembered being a shy, introverted child who, from his earliest years in school, was routinely teased by other children and had few, if any, friends. Until his junior year in high school, James remained pretty much a loner, avoiding

*In his retrial in 1982, a three-judge panel found Ruppert guilty in the deaths of his first two victims—his mother and his brother—but not guilty by reason of insanity in the other nine slayings. This decision suggests that Ruppert intentionally killed his two immediate family members for some reason like revenge or money, and the others he killed almost as though he were an automaton, just because they were there.

extracurricular activities, rarely attending ballgames or going to dances, and never dating girls. The events of childhood had a lasting effect: Try as he did, James Ruppert was impotent; he was never able to have sexual relations with a woman, except as they occurred in his rich fantasy life.

Ruppert's memory of his father was that of a frustrated, unsuccessful man who displayed a violent temper and little affection for his younger son. Ruppert also thought that his father had had no confidence in him, recalling his father's warnings that he would not be capable of holding a job or supporting himself as an adult.

It didn't help that Ruppert's five-foot eleven-inch 36-year-old father died of complications from tuberculosis when James was only 12 years old, forcing him to assume adult responsibilities from an early age. Ruppert told psychiatrists that, after his father's death, his mother would beat and taunt him and would encourage his brother Leonard to do the same. From James's viewpoint, his mother had made very clear to him that his presence was a mistake; that she had wanted a girl, not another boy in the family. At the age of 16, things at home got so bad that Ruppert ran away and later attempted suicide by hanging himself with a sheet. Though he failed in this attempt, the thought of suicide was something that stayed with Ruppert for decades to come.

Ruppert's mother showered love on her older son, who became a constant reminder to James of his own inadequacies. Leonard was the male head of the household after their father's death, whereas James always felt like an outcast in his own family; Leonard played sports while James sat on the sidelines; James was very conscious of being five inches shorter than his brother; James's math and science teachers always compared him with his older brother whose grades in the same classes had been superior; Leonard graduated from night school with a degree in electrical engineering, whereas James flunked out of college after two years; Leonard became a successful engineer with General Electric, whereas brother James went from job to job; Leonard was happily married with eight children, whereas James never married, was jilted by his only fiancée, and continued to live with his mother. Moreover, James had dated the woman whom his brother would later marry and had even introduced them to one another.

By his own standards, James was as much a failure as his brother Leonard was a success. To make matters worse, Leonard was, at least in his younger brother's mind, a vicious sadist and torturer—in a word, he was the enemy. Going back to early childhood, James still remembered his brother locking him in closets, tying him with rope, beating him with a hose, and sitting on his head until he screamed out loud. The image only worsened over time; and, by James's 30th birthday, he was just beginning to see Leonard as the executioner—as a major figure in what he believed to be an emerging conspiracy against him.

The paranoia really escalated in 1965, when the Hamilton Police Department determined that James had made an obscene phone call to an employee of the local public library where James spent much free time. Although admitting making the call, James was convinced that his mother and brother were attempting to discredit him by informing everyone of his transgression and reporting to the FBI that he was a communist and homosexual. He also believed that the FBI was tapping his telephone not only at home, but also in the restaurants and bars he happened to visit. Over the years, he felt, the intrusion of the FBI into his personal life continued to grow. Other groups were also implicated by Ruppert in the plot to sabotage his career, his social contacts, and his car. By 1975, he told psychiatrists of being followed by the State Highway Patrol, the local Sheriff's Department, private detectives, and the Hamilton Police.

Ruppert did have a frustrating life, but so do lots of people, and they don't commit mass murder. By itself, frustration simply isn't enough to explain Ruppert's criminal behavior: He must also have had access to an effective weapon of mass destruction—a means of eliminating eleven people at once. That's why Ruppert's long-standing love affair with handguns is important to consider.

Obviously, Ruppert was not unique in his use of handguns—many other brutal murders have been committed in the same way. Handguns are effective weapons, though the dull-silver barrel, brown grips, and tiny bullets give the appearance of a child's cap pistol. Yet handguns effectively distance the killer from his victim; they are easy to obtain, easy to conceal, and easy to shoot. Their high-velocity bullets penetrate quickly, assuring instantaneous results. And, as we have seen, the very presence of a handgun may act psychologically to arouse aggression.

Guns played an important role in Ruppert's life. They represented a "manly" activity that had been denied him as a sickly child with asthma, while other boys expressed their masculinity through competitive sports. Police Chief McNally described James Ruppert as a "gun freak." He collected guns and passed his leisure time alone on the banks of the Great Miami River, "walking" tin cans along the ground with his pistols.

As recently as two days before the Easter Sunday massacre, witnesses recalled seeing Ruppert by the river, where he repeatedly fired his .357 magnum revolver at tin cans. Moreover, a gun store employee claimed that a month or two before the Easter killings, Ruppert had asked him where he could obtain a gun silencer. The implication was clear enough: Ruppert may have been planning for some time to eliminate the members of his family. The exact time of death was yet to be decided, depending on the right events to raise his level of emotion and provide the opportunity.

Though Ruppert had endured a frustrating childhood and had access to guns, his crime depended on the operation of certain triggering events. In general, the triggering events may occur over a period of weeks or even months before a murder, or they may occur immediately prior to it. In a number of family mass murders, the killer had given up trying to find a job and was deeply depressed about it. In other cases, a husband killed all the members of his family upon learning that his wife intended to obtain a divorce or shortly after the separation actually occurred.

Psychiatrist Shervert Frazier argues that family killers are frequently seen as "gentle" and "passive" individuals. They carefully sublimate their hostility toward family members so long as they receive some kind of reward in return, be it psychological or economic. But when such rewards are withdrawn—for example, when they are kicked out of the house or deprived of money—an explosion of anger is likely to occur. Family killers are frequently "loners" who depend almost exclusively on the family to satisfy their emotional needs. The threat of separation by family members is a particularly painful and threatening event.

In Ruppert's case, the triggering mechanism consisted of certain precipitating events which, just prior to Easter Sunday, served to magnify the intensity of his negative feelings and to separate him further psychologically from others in his family. The testimony of Wanda Bishop, a 28-year-old mother of five who was separated from her husband and frequently met James Ruppert at her place of employment, the 19th Hole Cocktail Lounge, shed some light on these feelings. Mrs. Bishop told the court about their meeting at the 19th Hole bar on the evening before the shootings. Ruppert talked about his financial troubles, his unemployment, and his family. He had a "problem" which had to be taken care of immediately: his mother had told him that "if he could drink seven days a week, he could help pay the rent. Otherwise, he would have to leave home."[14]

Mrs. Bishop testified that Ruppert left the bar at eleven PM, only to return later. When she asked whether he had taken care of his problem, he answered, "No, not yet." He stayed at the bar until two-thirty, when it closed.

Notwithstanding his hostile feelings, Ruppert nevertheless depended heavily on his family for both emotional and economic support, and their yearly reunion was special to him. But Easter Sunday, 1975 was to be different: Ruppert was on the verge of eviction, and his mother had been ill, so his brother's family came late in the day.

Ruppert had a severe case of the "holiday blues." He spent the afternoon asleep in the upstairs bedroom of his mother's house. At four PM he awoke and went downstairs where he chatted with his brother about politics and the stock market, and watched his nieces and nephews as they gathered Easter eggs. The opportunity was at hand.

After spending a few minutes with the family, Ruppert said he was going target shooting. He went back upstairs, collected three pistols and a rifle, and came back down to the first floor where his family was gathered together. As he walked through the kitchen—still in a state of apparent calm—his brother asked him "with a mocking smile,"—"How's your Volkswagen, Jimmie?"

According to psychiatrists at the trial, Ruppert believed his brother had been trying for several months to sabotage his Volkswagen. He was convinced that Leonard had gotten into the crankcase, had purposely destroyed the carburetor and the distributor, had sabotaged the windshield wipers, had loosened the bumper, and had blown holes in the muffler. Thus, Leonard's apparently innocuous question precipitated an entire surge of "thoughts, memories, fantasies" about what his brother had done to him since childhood. From Ruppert's point of view, Leonard was mocking him about the car; and Ruppert "reflexively" drew his gun. James would see to it that Leonard never again hurt him; he would finally get the better of the brother against whom he had never quite measured up; he would deprive Leonard of life and of the lives of those whom he loved; and he would make sure that he had enough money to live the life he felt was rightfully his.

A three-judge panel decided in favor of the prosecution. James Ruppert was found guilty of murder and sentenced to the Ohio State Penitentiary. On a legal technicality, however, he was later transferred to a mental hospital and granted a new trial.

Finally, on July 23, 1982, the now-bearded 47-year-old Ruppert was sentenced to two consecutive life terms in prison after being found guilty of murder in the death of his mother and brother, but not guilty by reason of insanity in the death of his nine other victims. The inheritance was forfeited.

CHAPTER 10

THE JOHNSTON BROTHERS

The family business is essentially a thing of the past. Our nation has become one of big business and giant corporations. Most young people today can look forward to working for a large company in a job that bears little, if any, resemblance to that of their parents. Few college graduates, or even high school graduates, end up working in a family-run, family-owned enterprise.

The Johnstons were different, however. Brothers Bruce, Norman, and David operated a family-run million dollar burglary ring in southeastern Pennsylvania.[1] In 1972, two policemen in Kennett Township were ambushed and killed by local tough-guy Ancell Hamm. The police theorized, but were never able to prove, that Hamm was closely connected with the Johnston brothers gang—perhaps as its ringleader—and that his killings were in retaliation for police harassment of gang activities.

From 1972 to 1978, there were many prosecutions, but few convictions for the crimes perpetrated by the Johnston brothers. They specialized in stealing hundreds of John Deere tractors costing several thousand dollars each, as well as trucks, front-end loaders, tailgates, jewelry, drugs, and store safes. During a five-year period, more tractors were stolen in Pennsylvania, Maryland, and Delaware—the tristate region in which the Johnstons operated—than in all other states combined. The Johnstons were proficient in their trade.

Headquarters for the Johnston's criminal activities were situated in picturesque, 960-square-mile Chester County, Pennsylvania. Stretching all the way to the border of Delaware and Maryland, Chester County is a repository of life's ironies. Located only a half-hour's drive from Philadelphia, its 335,000 inhabitants reside in sixty-seven separate political units, representing the extremes of both affluence and poverty, sophistication and simplicity.

The Unionville area of the County is horse country: 11,000 prime acres are home to cowboys, steeplechases, chow wagons, branding irons, and livestock fattened for the eastern beef market. In contrast, Rt. 52 toward Centerville, Delaware is the scene of beauty that only money can buy as epitomized by opulent Longwood Gardens, the former mansion of Pierre du Pont. Heading north, the town of Coatesville, composed of working-class people, has very little wealth of its own apart from the profits of Lukens Steel Corporation. Finally, Chester County's mushroom country, in sleepy little Kennett Square near the Delaware line, is known for its redneck, hillbilly life-style. The Johnston brothers hung out in Kennett Square.

In 1978, "the law" began to close in on 39-year-old Bruce, 30-year-old David, and 27-year-old Norman Johnston: as part of a national initiative to "crack down" on habitual criminals, the local office of the FBI targeted the Johnston gang for investigation. Eventually, several members who were in their late teens and early twenties—the so-called Johnston's kiddie gang—were called to testify before the grand jury. Some of them may have decided to cooperate with the police; at least, that's what was leaked to the senior members of the gang.

At this point, the Johnston brothers apparently concluded that the investigation of their activities was bad for business and could only be ended by silencing the State's key informants. That's when several of the Johnstons' disloyal accomplices—delinquent boys who had been arrested many times for nickel-and-dime theft—became targeted for execution.

According to courtroom testimony, it took the Johnston gang all of six hours to dig the common grave in Brandywine Game Preserve located two and a half miles north of the Delaware border and a few miles south of the Brandywine River Museum; and it took only a few minutes to cover their victims' bodies with the aid of a stolen bulldozer.

The date was August 16, 1978. The first victim was 18-year-old Jimmy Johnston, a stepson of ringleader Bruce Johnston, Sr. Throughout the day, "Big Bruce" had held Jimmy in a room at the Oh Shaw Motel on Rt. 30 in Lancaster County, with the help of enough Quaaludes to keep his prisoner "like a zombie tripping over logs and everything on the way to his death."[2] That night, Jimmy was lured to the gravesite accompanied by the Johnston brothers and gray-haired gang member, 38-year-old Richard (Ricky) Mitchell, on the pretext that they were all recovering a stolen tractor that was stuck in the sand. Everyone piled out of the 1978 Thunderbird, where they climbed a fence and walked the half-mile distance up a tractor path to some dense woods at the top of a hill.

As soon as Jimmy came within a few feet of the grave, polite and farmer-like Bruce Johnston, the boy's stepfather, shone a flashlight into his victim's eyes, then leaned forward and fired two .22 caliber slugs point-blank into his head. The boy's limp body fell immediately to the ground. His killers then rummaged through his pockets and threw the body into the open grave.

It was now almost eleven-thirty. The Johnstons drove back to their mother's house in Kennett Square, where they picked up two more suspected informers who were told the same story about a stolen tractor being stuck in the sand. All of them went to the gravesite and the same procedure was followed; one victim at a time being taken to the grave at the top of the hill, while the other waited in the car with Norman driving around and blasting his radio to cover the sounds of gunfire.

First, 17-year-old Duane Lincoln was escorted to the grave. As before, Bruce shone the light into his victim's face; but this time it was brother David who shot him repeatedly in the back of the head. The long-haired teenager grabbed his head, turned on an angle, and fell forward to the ground. They searched his body for money and then tossed it into the hole.

Then, 20-year-old Wayne Sampson was taken from the car to the gravesite. It was Ricky Mitchell's turn to play executioner. In his words, "Bruce shined the light in the boy's and my eyes. My first shot missed. The boy turned around and asked if that was a real gun. Bruce moved the light from my eyes and I fired two more times. The boy fell down."[3]

The Johnstons went through Sampson's pockets and dumped his body into the grave, where it rested on top of their other two victims. After a night of killing, only two more informants remained to be silenced.

The next victim was, according to Ricky Mitchell, exterminated five days later, on August 21. Twenty-four-year-old James Sampson, Wayne's older brother, naively, went along with the Johnston brothers and Mitchell to an isolated landfill near Honey Brook and just over the county line into Lancaster County, ostensibly for the purpose of committing a robbery. Instead, the youngest of the Johnston brothers, six-foot, 165-pound Norman, shot Sampson in the head and buried his body in a hole covered with garbage. Investigators were never able to locate his grave, though they did find his car at the Philadelphia airport. By the time they knew the location of Sampson's corpse, it was already under seventy-five feet of compacted trash.

Thirty-nine-year-old Bruce Johnston, Sr. was said to be the kingpin of the family-operated burglary ring. He was a physically strong and powerful man at almost six feet tall and nearly 200 pounds; yet he couldn't control his own 21-year-old son, "Little Bruce," who had worked in the family crime ring since age 16 and was part of the so-called kiddie gang.

Little Bruce had lived most of his life in Chester County with his grandmother, Harriet Steffy, and his mother, Jennie Johnston. He had long curly blonde hair, a lanky build, and a cleft chin which he inherited from his father. Like the other younger members of the Johnston gang, Bruce Jr. had dropped out of school to join his father's burglary operation and was known to drive fast cars and to use excessive amounts of marijuana, LSD, Quaaludes, and angel dust. He was arrested a number of times for theft, receipt of stolen property, and criminal conspiracy.

While doing time for stealing truck tailgates and gasoline during the summer of 1978, Little Bruce was visited by pretty, 15-year-old Robin Miller, whom he had been dating for six months and wanted to marry when she would turn 16.

Robin was the daughter of 38-year-old Linda Morris Miller of East Nottingham Township. Weighing 100 pounds, Robin was a slender, attractive girl—little more than five feet two inches—with short wavy brown hair and bright hazel eyes. Her cousin once described her as "one of the happiest little kids—up all the the time."[4]

Despite her "little kid" image, Robin Miller had gotten into a fast crowd and knew her way around. To keep her daughter from running away with Bruce Jr., Linda Miller permitted them both to stay in Robin's second-floor bedroom, but the arrangement created more problems than it solved.

Robin had reason to be scared. She recognized that her love affair with Bruce Jr. had placed her own life in jeopardy. In a letter written to her boyfriend, Robin revealed a premonition concerning her own death: she wrote that Bruce Sr. would soon put an end to her life.

Robin later wrote another letter to Little Bruce which may have played a role in making her worst nightmare into a reality. In this letter, she told Little Bruce that she had been drugged and raped by Bruce Sr. on one of her trips back from visiting him in prison. Furious, Little Bruce decided to get even with his father by telling the police what they wanted to know—the activities of the Johnston clan. In early August, in appearances before law enforcement officials and a federal grand jury in Philadelphia, Little Bruce talked about a number of tractors that he and other members of the kiddie gang had stolen with the help of his father. He also told about thefts carried out by the Johnston gang in which he was not personally involved.

Bruce Sr. was Little Bruce's biological father, but there was little love lost between them. Bruce Sr. had separated from his wife when Little Bruce was only an infant. Afterwards, he had rarely expressed fatherly feelings toward the boy. In fact, they saw one another only a few times while Little Bruce was growing up—until, that is, Little Bruce joined the gang.

Bruce Sr. was extremely concerned about his son's defection to police authorities and its possible effect on other members of the kiddie gang. He considered Robin Miller a "big mouth" who turned Little Bruce against him. In a last-ditch effort, Bruce Sr. tried to get his son to recant his grand jury testimony by offering him large sums of money.

When all else failed, the Johnston brothers apparently decided to repay their debt to Little Bruce. It happened in East Nottingham near Oxford, Pennsylvania on August 30, 1978. Little Bruce sat with Robin in the driveway of her family's rented two-story farmhouse surrounded by corn and barley fields, after an evening at an amusement park in nearby Hershey.

Robin's mother, a nurse at the Oxford Manor Nursing Home, was vacationing in Virginia. Her older sister, 17-year-old Roxanne, had been home an hour before, but had become frightened when she saw an unexplained light coming from the cellar of the house and left before Robin returned.

Neither Little Bruce nor Robin suspected that Bruce Sr. had paid $15,000 to have them eliminated. Meanwhile, Bruce Sr. was waiting with Ricky Mitchell and two women in Mister T's bar in order to establish an alibi. As Bruce Jr. and Robin were sitting in his car in the driveway, Norman and David lay hidden behind bushes only a few yards away. They had staked out the area for four nights and were ready to strike.

Robin fell asleep in the car. Bruce woke her and turned on the light to help her find the pocketbook he had just bought her. They sat for a few moments with the light on.

Little Bruce then stepped from the car. He heard a sound "like somebody threw firecrackers." The car shook as it was peppered by a hail of bullets from the nearby bushes. Stunned, dazed, and covered with blood, Little Bruce staggered around for a moment or so and then fell back into the car with his head between the seats. He looked up at Robin who was still sitting in the front seat, screaming and bloody from a wound to her chin.

A neighbor in the house on the corner, opposite the Miller's duplex, was watching television. She heard two screams which she thought came from the Miller's cat and a series of high-pitched gunshots. Her digital watch read 12:34 AM.

Bruce and Robin somehow made their way to the farmhouse where Little Bruce immediately called the police, yelling "Robin's been shot! They're still shooting!"[5] Robin collapsed in her upstairs bedroom and was beyond help when the police arrived a few minutes later. She was dead from a gunshot wound to the head—a gunshot meant for her boyfriend. The bullet had penetrated the left side of her face near her mouth.

When the police came, Little Bruce was holding his arm, blood running all over his white shirt and down his face. Nine slugs from two .38 caliber handguns had smashed their way into his body: the first shot entering behind his right ear; the second penetrating the back of his head; the third nicking the back of his neck; the fourth exploding through his right shoulder; the fifth burying itself in his chest; the sixth piercing his stomach; the seventh entering his right arm; the eighth piercing his right elbow; and the ninth entering his back near the shoulder blade.

Despite the seriousness of his wounds, Little Bruce survived the ordeal to testify at his father's trial for murder. He testified though his fingers were half numb, his elbow and left shoulder popped and cracked, and a bullet remained lodged in his body.

But he was and still is alive! Little Bruce would later say of the incident, "If it weren't for me, she wouldn't have gotten killed."[6] (He was later arrested on a charge of breaking and entering along with his new 18-year-old fiancée; he was positively identified from his many bullet wounds.)

Nobody likes a "stool pigeon." Parents routinely reprimand their kids for tattling on friends or siblings. Nothing ends a relationship faster than learning that a close friend has been gossiping about you behind your back. From the criminal's viewpoint, any person who informs to police investigators—even if he happens to be a close relative or friend—commits an act of unforgivable treason which is often punishable by death. Prison informers who are discovered to have "snitched" on their fellow inmates are routinely confined in segregated quarters for fear they will be executed by other inmates.

From the beginning, police informants figured prominently in the case against the Johnstons. In October 1978, the State put pressure on one Richard Donnell to testify about a homicide he had committed years earlier with the help of the hitman for the Johnston gang, 39-year-old Leslie Eugene Dale. In 1970, Donnell and Dale beat and drowned their 23-year-old "buddy," dishwasher John "Jackie" Baen, after Baen had decided to cooperate with police investigators and inform on his two companions in crime.

The prosecutor's plan was first to build a strong murder case against Dale with the aid of Donnell's testimony and then to bargain with Dale who would be asked to inform on the Johnston gang in exchange for a reduced sentence. On a foggy Saturday morning in November, some eight years after the murder, Chester County investigators met to exhume Baen's body from the Glenwood Memorial Garden Center in Delaware County. They were determined anew to find a cause of death other than drowning.

According to plan, Donnell got scared, admitted his own part in the killing of Baen, and agreed to testify against Dale. In return, Donnell was permitted to plead to a charge of voluntary manslaughter and receive a prison sentence of no more than one-to-three years. Since he was already doing that much time in federal prison for transporting stolen goods, Donnell did not have to serve extra time for killing Baen.

Having himself been convicted on the word of Donnell—a partner turned informant—Dale then decided to cooperate with the prosecution in another case. He was linked to the mysterious disappearance of 30-year-old police informer Gary Wayne Crouch of Elkton, Maryland, who had been missing for more than a year. Dale, during the early morning hours of December 1, 1978, led police investigators to a secluded clearing in the woods of western Chester County, where they dug up a five-foot grave containing Crouch's decomposed body.

Information uncovered days later was unnerving to those whom Dale directed to the gravesite. First, though shot in the head, gravel found in Crouch's throat suggested that he had been buried alive and thus would not have died for another several hours. Second, the Johnston brothers had intended to get to Crouch's body before it was discovered. It was rumored that they had been hiding in the woods, only a few yards away, for the entire period of time it took searchers to unearth Crouch's remains.

Gary Crouch had been executed because he was a problem for members of the Johnston gang. Only three years earlier, he had testified against them concerning the theft of a trailer carrying food from a supermarket.

On the evening of July 16, 1977, Gary Crouch left his girlfriend's home across the Delaware border to meet Bruce Sr. and Leslie Dale at the Wooden Shoe Inn in Kennett Square. After their meeting, the three men stole a car and drove toward Stottsville, for the supposed purpose of committing a burglary. Instead, they veered off the main highway onto an isolated dirt road. Crouch immediately became "jittery," suspecting that his companions were up to no good.

In the original version of his testimony to the court, Dale claimed that he only drove the car while Bruce did the shooting from the backseat. Subsequently, however, he told Assistant D.A. Dolores Troiani that he had gotten out of the backseat of the car. This slip of the tongue was enough to convince Dale that a full confession was in order. It was actually he who had pulled the trigger to end Crouch's life. It was he who fired a single shot into Crouch's brain, while Bruce Johnston drove the car. According to Dale, however, Bruce's part in the killing was more sinister than it first appeared. Bruce had paid him $3000 plus a "bonus" of $89 from the dead man's pockets to eliminate the informant.

An informant also led investigators to the remains of kiddie gang members Jimmy Johnston, Dwayne Lincoln, and Wayne Sampson. Looking much older than his 38 years, Ricky Mitchell cooperated with prosecutors after becoming convinced that there was a contract out on his life. Mitchell already had more than his share of problems—his face was disfigured from several automobile accidents; he could hardly hear or see; he had trouble walking and was epileptic. He also claims to have suffered gunshot wounds in seven places, the first of which was at the tender age of 9.

Dolores Troiani offered Mitchell a deal that he couldn't refuse: "either life in prison and testify against the others, or walk out and get killed by the Johnston brothers."[7] In addition, the prosecution agreed not to oppose a future bid for Mitchell's parole, should he ever become so ill that prison would threaten his life.

On December 29, Mitchell led local detectives, the state police, and the FBI through corn and barley fields and over a fence to the top of a hill in Brandywine Game Preserve. It was five o'clock and just getting dark when searchers began digging in the spot Mitchell pointed to. Three hours and two and a half feet of dirt later, they hit paydirt: the first of the three corpses they would find. Using spoons to remove loose dirt, the bodies were removed from their grave and carefully lifted into body bags for delivery to Phoenixville Hospital.

Despite the Johnston's reputation as thieves, neighbors and friends described them as clean-cut, polite, and very patriotic, as "moral people" in their own way who believed with all their might in the traditional American virtues of independence and self-reliance, but who valued the family above everything else. The family had always assumed a position of supreme importance in the lives of the Johnston clan. Sixty-six-year-old Louise Johnston, a diminutive woman weighing no more than 100 pounds, raised her children—Bruce, David, and Norman—to believe that members of their family should stick together and care for one another. She demonstrated her own devotion to the tight-knit family unit, for example, by removing her elderly father from a West Virginia nursing home and caring for him until he died at the age of 101.

The Johnstons trace their roots back to the Price family farm in the hillbilly culture of northwest North Carolina and Mountain City, Tennessee. This is the area in which Louise grew up, before she left the South at the age of 20 and met her husband-to-be, Passmore Johnston.

When they met, Passmore was driving a taxi in Philadelphia. But shortly thereafter, he, Louise, and her two children from a broken first marriage settled into the tiny village of Marlboro, Pennsylvania, where they became tenant farmers who ran cattle and worked at local greenhouses to earn extra money. In 1939, Bruce was born. Twenty-two years later, Passmore died and the family moved to Kennett Square.

Prosecutor William H. Lamb called the Johnstons a "family of crime" whose code demanded that "snitches" die. Lamb maintained that Louise Johnston "did not show one shred of remorse in court, despite the fact that some of the victims were her grandsons." As Allen Davis, the managing editor of a local Chester County newspaper, recalled about the Johnston women: "They always said [the Johnston brothers] didn't kill those boys. Bruce loved them. But they never said it's a shame they died."[8]

Over the years, many things about the Johnstons changed. But the family allegiance which they had inherited from the hillbilly culture of backwoods North Carolina remained intact. It was an unspoken, unwritten moral code which no generation of kin dared ignore, let alone defy.

According to Lamb, hillbilly culture also accounted for the patronage that the Johnstons always paid to the head of their family. Louise's house was the focal point for all activities involving "her boys." She was an absolute matriarch. In a similar way, Bruce Sr., the eldest of her sons, expected unswerving loyalty from members of his kiddie gang. It was acceptable by their moral code for Bruce Sr. to have a "little fun" with his son's girlfriend; and any complaints from Little Bruce should have gone directly to his father.

Lamb emphasized the absolute value of family loyalty to the Johnstons: "Junior and Jimmy were snitching and you don't snitch on the family. . . . Their motive was not only to keep people quiet, but to send a message: What ever you do, you don't rat on family. No matter what happens, you don't go to the cops. That was the cardinal sin."[9]

The prosecution of the Johnston brothers was divided into two trials—one for Norman and David, another for Bruce—both presided over by Judge Leonard Sugarman. In maintaining control over an extremely complex and difficult case, Sugarman was praised by both the prosecution and the defense as well as by the media covering the trials.

By a change of venue, the 1980 trial of Norman and David Johnston was moved to Ebensburg, Pennsylvania, some two hundred miles from Chester County. Nestled in the Allegheny Mountains of Cambria County, the 4000 residents of Ebensburg showed only passing interest in the trial. From the beginning, local newspapers focused more on an FBI investigation of a congressman from nearby Johnstown and on the local trial of an accused ax-murderer.

Norman and David's trial brought lots of people and money. The hotels were filled to capacity. But the Johnston brothers were still regarded as outsiders who had no relation to the town—as two Chester County brothers whose crimes were far removed from the steel mills and mushroom houses of the Ebensburg community. The trial was held in Ebensburg for only one reason: pretrial publicity made it impossible to hold it in Chester County. Why should the local Ebensburg citizens care?

The Johnston's Ebensburg trial was situated in a 135-year-old courthouse patterned after the nation's Capitol. During the early stages of the proceedings, reporters and security guards made up most of the spectators in Courtroom One on the third floor. Relatively few local residents took the opportunity to attend. Even when community interest later increased, it never assumed the intensity of feeling that would follow a local event of tragic proportions.

The reaction in Chester County was altogether a different story. Its citizens were absolutely shocked and outraged that such a heinous crime could have happened in the heart of their "pleasant valley." Robin Miller's killing was especially infuriating, because she was a pretty, cherubic 15-year-old girl whose life was tragically ended when caught in the cross fire between the Johnston brothers and their kiddie gang informant.

Certainly, brutal murders happen all the time, but in such big cities as Philadelphia, New York, or Chicago. Chester County always thought of itself as essentially immune from the decadence of urban Armerica. Its residents prided themselves on being different from "city folk." They were moral, upstanding patriots—the very backbone of America.

After their initial amazement, however, local residents reacted predictably enough given the notorious reputation of the Johnston brothers in Chester County ("Hey, that doesn't surprise me coming from that family") and their victims ("Bruce, David, and Norman did the taxpayers a favor" and "They killed scum.").

Unlike mass killers who randomly victimize citizens from every walk of life, the Johnston brothers were widely regarded as "hillbillies killing hillbillies" and "criminals murdering criminals." As a result, Chester County residents were able to distance themselves from the crimes and feel immune from injury. Even the trial lacked an element of apprehension, except for those who were personally involved or who had to testify. The typical reaction to the trial was: "If you didn't get subpoenaed, there was no problem!"[10]

Impaneling an impartial jury, unaffected by pretrial publicity, was just as much an issue in Bruce's trial as it had been in the trial of his brothers. To avoid the incredible inconvenience and cost of again commuting hundreds of miles to and from a place like Cambria County, however, a jury was chosen in distant Erie County and sequestered in Chester County, where the second trial was held.

During his trial, Bruce denounced witnesses against him, calling them "nuts" and "liars," referred to a police investigator as a "dummy," told the court that he hated Chief County Detective Charles Zagorskie whose efforts were instrumental in bringing the gang to justice, and denied he had ever killed anyone. When asked whether he was angry with Bruce Jr. for snitching to the police, he said "Kids are kids. How do you get mad at your son?" Questioned about his part in the rape of Robin Miller, he testified "It is disgusting to me that you even ask me about it. It never entered my mind." And when he was asked about his relationship with victim and gang member James Sampson, he said "I think of James Sampson as my brother. James Sampson and I remained the best of friends until the last time I saw him."

But Bruce was also quoted by witnesses as saying after Sampson's disappearance, "Where Jimmy is he has friends and he doesn't need anything to eat." According to another witness, David Johnston told him, "The worms have taken care of James

Sampson. If he wants to talk to his brother Wayne, maybe they can send messages by groundhog."

Why would law enforcement officials falsely charge Bruce Johnston with masterminding the murder of six persons? He told reporter Bruce Mowday of the *Daily Local News* that he was being persecuted, that the police had harassed him because they were convinced he had participated in the murder of the two Kennett Square policemen in 1972.

Witnesses saw it differently. At the Ebensburg trial,[11] Florida James "Disco" Griffin, himself a professional burglar, testified that Norman Johnston had just managed to get home ahead of the police during the early morning hours after the ambush of Robin and Bruce Jr. According to Disco, Norman's wife Sue held the police at bay until her husband could get out of his street clothes and answer the door as though dressed for bed. Disco also testified that he was with the Johnston brothers in Pottstown 10 days after the ambush, where they paid for repairs to Ricky Mitchell's car. Mitchell had earlier told the court that the repairs were made by the Johnstons in return for his help in carrying out the slayings.

The testimony of Bruce Johnston's brother-in-law was damaging to the defendant's case. He testified that Norman had searched around for a sawed-off shotgun because "we might have to take somebody out with it." A few days later, Robin Miller was dead.

On March 18, 1980, after hearing from 162 witnesses over a five-week period and deliberating for some twenty-eight hours over three days, a Cambria County jury of eleven men and one woman found 32-year-old David Johnston and 29-year-old Norman Johnston guilty of four counts of first-degree murder. Eight months later, a jury of seven women and five men in West Chester deliberated six hours before concluding that Bruce Johnston Sr. was guilty of six counts of first-degree murder.

The case of the Johnston brothers' gang is more typical of mass murder than we might care to believe. What looks like a purposeless, senseless crime may actually be a means to an end—a cleverly conceived and executed plan to eliminate the informants whose testimony would lead to arrest and imprisonment.

The practical grounds for political terrorism are well known and understood. The bombing of an embassy or the shelling of a village is typically designed not only to silence particular individuals but, more important, to send a message concerning future acts of terror, to harass the enemy into ultimate submission.

The Johnston clan sent a message too: No matter what, you don't rat and especially not on the family. The testimony of several members of the kiddie gang could have resulted in lengthy prison terms for Bruce, Norman, and David, and the probable elimination of their crime ring. In the view of the Johnstons, this was totally unacceptable and could simply not be tolerated.

The Johnston gang also reminds us again that mass killing cannot always be explained solely in terms of individual psychopathology. These murders took place in the presence of several gang members, none of them obviously psychotic or insane, who took turns pulling the trigger and covering their victims with dirt. Thus, the Johnston killings were truly a collective effort, rather than the lunatic rantings of a single person. Moreover, even the "moral" decision to commit mass murder was itself a group phenomenon: the norm of family loyalty had been severely violated. In the hillbilly culture of the Johnston clan, the informants had committed a "capital" offense. Death was the rightful punishment.

CHAPTER 11

THE HILLSIDE STRANGLER

It had been six years since the "Hillside Strangler" was on the loose. The people of Los Angeles were trying to forget the string of brutal murders that occurred in their city between October 1977 and February 1978; but the slow wheels of justice in the trial of Angelo Buono kept the memories alive. During a two-year period, nearly four hundred witnesses had taken the stand to describe or to defend Buono's alleged deeds of viciousness, before his guilt was finally determined.[1]

Only one real question now remained to be decided surrounding the famous Hillside Strangler case. Would Angelo Buono, who with his adoptive cousin Kenneth Bianchi had raped, tortured, sodomized, and strangled ten young women discarding their bodies on hillsides and roadsides, be condemned to die in the gas chamber? All that was left now, mercifully, was the final stage—the penalty phase—of the longest trial in the history of this country.

Judge Ronald M. George stared from his bench down at Angelo Buono, who had just been convicted of nine counts of murder. Judge George tried hard to hide his impatience as he waited for what seemed an eternity for Buono to repond to a very simple inquiry.

"Do you wish to testify?" asked Judge George, looking directly at the defendent. Buono sat calmly and coldly, in a navy blue jump suit inscribed "Los Angeles County Jail" on the back, rather than in a suit and tie as he had worn prior to the guilty verdicts. Destined for either the gas chamber or at least life imprisonment without the possibility of parole, Buono chose not to play the role of the humble defendant. The judge waited for Buono to speak, but nearly half a minute of total silence passed.

The judge then repeated, "Do you wish to testify?" The gallery of spectators leaned forward, straining to catch any words that Buono might mutter. The press took notes to back up their tape recorders, which, contrary to courtroom regulations, were turned on, capturing the long spaces of silence.

The courtroom was filled with an air of anticipation. After all, Angelo Buono had sat motionless and without emotion or expression for over two years. His only gesture reported by some court observers had been that of disdain toward Kenneth Bianchi, Buono's accomplice and cousin whose confession had implicated him.

Finally, Buono answered the judge; he wanted to speak to the court. Some observers predicted that Buono would now plead his innocence or maybe plead for mercy; others speculated that he would ask for the death sentence as an ultimate act of martyrdom. Whatever his intention, a few words from Buono would surely be a fitting conclusion to a drama that had lasted for over six years since the death of a Hollywood prostitute in late 1977.

The first of the Hillside Stranglings, which would come to paralyze Los Angeles, was discovered on October 18, 1977. The nude body of a woman was found perversely sprawled alongside of Forest Lawn Drive, near the famous Forest Lawn Cemetery, resting place of "the stars." Homicide detectives conducted their routine search of the area for evidence and questioned nearby residents about any peculiar sights or sounds they might recall. With close to nothing to go on except an obvious cause of death—strangulation, probably manual—the body was sent for an autopsy.

The body was easily identified: Yolanda Washington, a 19-year-old part-time waitress and part-time prostitute, was well known to the vice squad working the Hollywood streets. For

Yolanda, prostitution was simply a profitable business. A "good night" could bring in over three hundred dollars which would go farther than any legitimate job in helping to support her 2½-year-old daughter Tameika. Unfortunately for her, she was not a high-class call girl. She worked the fast and cheap streets of Hollywood, where drugs and commercial sex overshadowed the starlet images. Yolanda knew the risks involved. There was always the chance of injury from some crazy john who liked violence. But the kinkier and the more violent the man's fantasies and desires, the greater was the payoff. While such were the occupational hazards, Yolanda never bargained for murder.

The streets were hardly shaken by the news of the murder. While Washington's death was a top item of conversation at the Howard Johnson's at the corner of Hollywood and Vine, where the pimps and hookers usually hung out, ate, and relaxed, the death of a streetwalker did not come as a surprise, but simply was a reminder to be careful.

The newspapers downplayed the strangling too. Unlike a simultaneous mass slaughter as bloody as that perpetrated by the Manson family or a murder of someone of high position, Washington's death was hardly newsworthy. A brief, well-hidden, back-page report of a body found on a hillside would be the first page of the Hillside Strangler saga.

Nearly two weeks later, on October 31, another body was discovered along a roadside in Glendale, just a few miles from Hollywood. It too was nude and bore ligature or rope marks around the wrists, ankles, and neck. Subsequent examination revealed evidence of rape and sodomy. The victim was identified as 15-year-old Judith Lynn Miller, and her story is sad indeed.

Unlike streetwise Yolanda Washington, Judy Miller was an unhappy runaway living in a rundown Hollywood motel who sought from the streets and her makeshift family of other runaways the love and support she apparently felt she lacked at home. We may never know if her parents even grieved her death; her mother was wanted by the police for welfare fraud and her father jumped probation on unemployment fraud. As in life, she was alone in death. Her body remained in the morgue unclaimed for ten days following her murder.

The details of Judy Miller's killing and the torturous last few hours of her life are similar to the horror suffered by eight more women to follow, though Kenneth Bianchi admits remembering most vividly the terror in Miller's eyes. Indeed, she was the first "child" subjected to Buono's house of unspeakable tortures.

With the exception of Washington who was killed in an automobile, each of the other nine victims of the Hillside Strangler was kidnapped and brought to Buono's home. In order to avoid their involuntarily urinating right after death—like Washington's body had done—Buono and Bianchi first forced each of the victims to go to the bathroom. Each was then tied by the arms, legs, and neck to a special chair in Buono's spare bedroom. Each was brutally raped, sodomized with various instruments, and strangled to death. The nude and bruised bodies were tossed, like refuse, along roadsides and hillsides in Los Angeles and Glendale, hence the name "Hillside" Stranglings. (Cindy Hudspeth, the last victim, was an exception; her body was put in the trunk of her car and pushed down a ravine.)

The murders began shortly after Kenneth Bianchi moved at the age of 26 to Los Angeles from Rochester, New York where he was raised. "I came [to California] hoping to find a better job," Bianchi later explained to psychiatrists; "I always wanted to go to California—the sun, the girls, the beaches, you know, the dreams."[2] Bianchi had also looked up his cousin Angelo Buono, who took him in.

The question of why Buono and Bianchi embarked on their spree of murder is complex. But once they tried it, they found killing exciting and fun.

Up to the point of Washington's murder, neither Buono nor Bianchi had a history of violent crime. Their initiation into murder emanated not out of a psychotic need to taste the blood of another, not out of the frustration of divorce or unemployment, but out of a spirit of adventure rooted in their friendship. By one account, Bianchi and Buono reportedly were sitting around Buono's house one day, when they began talking about what it must feel like to kill someone. Almost as a lark, they went out and tried it.

While some of us might find the act of killing abhorrent, Buono and Bianchi apparently found it to their liking. Characteristic of sociopaths generally, they felt neither guilty nor remorseful about the deed, seeing the prostitute as merely a tool for their personal gratification. In any case, they could always rely on each other to help justify their crimes to themselves, no matter how dastardly.

After the first time, killing gets easier. Just as the addict requires increasing doses of a drug to satisfy his craving, the serial killer who kills for sexual pleasure typically requires more and more perversity to satisfy his sadistic libido.

Though all the Hillside Stranglings were heinous, they grew more brutal, true to form, as the victim count rose. Victim seven, Kristina Weckler, was "for the fun of it" injected with cleaning solution causing her body to convulse and then was gassed with a bag connected by a hose to the oven. Victim eight, Lauren Wagner, was tortured and burned with an electric cord on her hands and body.

Another pattern of change that emerged in the killings played an important role in the development of the Hillside Strangler story. While the early victims were women of the night or of the street, Buono and Bianchi began branching out to suburban neighborhoods for more "innocent" prey.

The deaths of Washington and Miller were considered, by those who even considered them at all, as part of the subculture of the streets. Among the streetwalkers of Hollywood there sprung a new and understandable fear following these murders, yet this was only enough to prescribe greater caution. Coping with the dangers and the role of the automobile in the culture of Los Angeles, hookers worked in pairs; one would write down the license plate number of another's trick as the other hopped into his car. All were quick to be alarmed by johns who were into pain—inflicting it, that is.

It was easy at first for most citizens to distance themselves from the murders, since they were happening just to "common prostitutes." But then came November 20, 1977, the day when the bodies of victims five and six—Dolores Cepeda, age 12 and Sonja Johnson, 14—were discovered together near Dodger Stadium, a week following their disappearance.

Unlike Washington and Miller, these two young friends were schoolgirls who did not understand or anticipate danger as they got off the bus on their way home from shopping. That day Sonja's father, Tony Johnson, had refused to pick them up by car. (His guilt about the refusal later drove Tony to an aborted suicide attempt, excessive drinking, and a fatal liver disease.) Bianchi and Buono, on the other hand, did offer to drive them home, but it was to Buono's home instead.

The news of the brutal deaths of the two girls sparked fear and anger all around the Los Angeles area. For the first time, the citizens of Los Angeles were warned that an unknown serial killer might be responsible for a number of recent unsolved murders, linked by the similar manner in which the victims' bodies were discarded. The extensive media coverage of the case both fueled and reflected public anxiety. Not only were citizens demanding that the police do something about the Hillside Stranglings, but most changed their own life-styles in significant ways. Women frantically enrolled in self-defense courses which sprang up in response to the pervasive and intense levels of fear. One physical education professor announced a special six-hour course in self-defense designed for up to sixty-seven students, and as many as a thousand people called for information on the offering. Residents were not only taking active steps to protect themselves, they also began avoiding any dark street or even going out whenever unnecessary. They were, above all, suspicious of strangers.

The situation worsened with the discovery of one important clue. Witnesses who had seen some of the victims on the nights of their deaths reported that two men posing as police had "arrested" the victims. The police ruse was consistent with the autopsies' strange absence of evidence of struggle. Ordinarily, one would find traces of skin or hair underneath the fingernails of victims who had clawed at their attackers. The police charade explained why the girls—especially the two youngsters—had apparently gone willingly with the killers.

After reading in the papers that the stranglers posed as officers, the public trusted no one. How could one be certain of the authenticity of a man wearing a blue uniform with a shield? Could the strangler be, in fact, a cop gone astray? All rules of order consequently broke down. One high school girl from the San Gabriel Valley, for example, refused to stop for a police officer who had spotted her for a traffic violation; instead she sped home to safety with the police in hot pursuit. Others showed the same caution of the police. Eventually, police officials, understanding the cause for panic, were forced to allow motorists not to stop immediately for the police but to continue driving to a police station where it would be safe. As might be expected, speeding motorists "were getting away with murder" under the new set of rules.

Aside from fear of being the next victim, there was always the chance of being the one to discover another nude and mangled body discarded around the city. Marcia Chaiken of the Brentwood section of L.A., for instance, had planned for a long time to take girl scout troop 1139 on a hiking trip to scenic Griffith Park. After the discovery in that vicinity of three bodies believed to be victims of the strangler, Marcia canceled the excursion.

The citizens were not alone in their state of frenzy. The press wrote strong editorials criticizing the police force for its inability to catch the killer. A Hillside Strangler Task Force was formed, and a reward of over $140,000 was offered for information leading to the arrest of the strangler. The Task Force, a combined effort of the Glendale Police, the Los Angeles Police, and the Los Angeles Sheriff's Department, grew to eighty-four officers, and would frantically follow any lead available. And the apprehensive community gave them plenty of leads to investigate, over 10,000 of them. Chief of Police Daryl F. Gates later admitted that this effort was probably too broad and decentralized, a case of too many cooks spoiling the broth. Lt. Edwin Henderson who headed the Task Force agreed, "When you expand a task force to the size it was, you lose a lot of control."[3]

Astonishingly, at one point, for example, an investigator had questioned Kenneth Bianchi about one of the victims, Kimberly Martin, a call girl whose last assignment sent her to Bianchi's apartment building. But this lead got lost in the shuffle and was never relayed to the proper individuals.

As suddenly as the murders had begun on October 17, 1977 with Washington's murder, they ended after Cindy Hudspeth's body was found in her trunk; ten homicides in five months, and then nothing. As the spring and summer months passed without recurrence of the stranglings, the people of Los Angeles slowly recovered and began to relax. Still the investigation and the work of the Task Force forged ahead toward more and more dead ends.

It was not until almost a year after the killings had stopped that the case broke. It broke, not in Los Angeles, but in a small, industrial, seaport town of 50,000 in Washington, just 20 miles from the Canadian border, as far northwest as one can get in the continental United States.

In January 1979, Bellingham, Washington experienced a double homicide—the only killings they would have that entire year. The bodies of Karen Mandic and Diane Wilder, college roommates, were found strangled, raped, yet clothed in the trunk of Mandic's car, following a report of their disappearance. An investigation of their recent whereabouts uncovered that Mandic had been hired by a man from a security firm to housesit for $100 per hour while the home security system was out for repair. Karen asked her friend along as company during the job; neither was seen alive again. Bellingham police immediately suspected Kenneth A. Bianchi, the man who had hired Mandic; and maneuvered for his arrest. Bianchi's California driver's license prompted a call to authorities there.

Lt. Phillip Bullington of Los Angeles, who received the call from the Bellingham police, will always remember the date: January 13, 1979, the day after his wedding anniversary when his wife had tried to boost his spirits by suggesting that maybe "the call" would come tomorrow. It had been almost a year since the last body was found, a year full of frustration and fruitless clues. The strangler was no longer on everybody's lips, and some suggested that the expensive Task Force should be declared a failure and be disbanded, leaving the case of the Hillside Strangler in the "permanently" unsolved category.

But when this new lead surfaced, Bullington jumped at the bait. The similarities were so strong. The two victims in Bellingham were described as two young coeds from Western Washington University who were lured by "a real smooth talker" and then raped and strangled. The check on Bianchi's driver's license uncovered that he lived in the same apartment building in Glendale where Kristina Weckler had once lived, where Kim Martin was last known to have been, and across the street from where Cindy Hudspeth had lived and been abducted. Investigators from L.A. left immediately for Bellingham.

Though the similarities in the crimes were many, the effects on the communities were hardly comparable. Bellingham, a usually peaceful and quiet community, was stunned by the murder of two young coeds, but the police were led quickly to an arrest, so panic did not result.

The arrest of Kenneth Bianchi on suspicion of murder was a surprise to everyone in Bellingham who had known him. Kelli Boyd, Ken's girlfriend and the mother of his baby, always thought of him as a gentle man who was kind to her and to his friends. "The Ken I knew couldn't ever have hurt anybody or killed anybody—he wasn't the kind of person who could have killed somebody," she explained.[4] Friends who knew him during the nearly eight months he lived in Bellingham described Ken as an "all-around nice guy." His boss at the security firm knew him as a hard worker, an excellent security guard with a bright future. Even Bellingham's Chief of Police Terry Mangan considered Ken a fine prospect for his own police force. Indeed, character references just didn't seem to jive with circumstantial evidence that implicated Ken.

While Ken calmly insisted on his innocence, and his friends confidently awaited his clearance of the charges, detectives were arduously combing the scene of the crime for clues. A microscopic search of the carpet on the stairs in the Bellingham house where the murdered girls had been housesitting unearthed long blond head hairs probably belonging to Karen Mandic and pubic hairs matching those of Ken Bianchi. Ken's position suddenly worsened. His attorney, Dean Brett, decided to resolve the inconsistency between Ken's claims and the extant evidence by seeking the opinion of psychiatric specialists.

Brett consulted with psychiatrist Donald Lunde of the Stanford University Medical School. Lunde saw striking inconsistencies between Bianchi's recollections during interviews and information contained in various medical and psychiatric records from his childhood. Ken had been raised in Rochester, New York by his adoptive parents, Nicholas and Frances Bianchi, who had received custody of him when he was three months old. Generally, Kenneth Bianchi presented a description of his childhood as one filled with love, joy, and tranquility. Psychiatric records, however, described Ken as an extremely troubled boy who had been completely and pathologically dependent on his adoptive mother. Mrs. Bianchi, who herself was portrayed as psychologically imbalanced and paranoid, had dealt with Ken by unconsciously giving a "double-message," a combination of overprotectiveness and excessive punitiveness. On the one hand she would drag Ken to the doctor for the mildest of ailments, but, on the other hand, would discipline him by holding his hand over a stove burner. Dr. Lunde was forced to conclude that Ken was repressing much of his past, and possibly might not remember the stranglings.

As the physical and circumstantial evidence mounted against Bianchi, his attorney became increasingly skeptical not only of Ken's stories and alibis, but of his very sanity. Still, Ken resisted Brett's wish to enter an insanity plea, so Brett decided to probe further into the possibility of amnesia for the crimes. He called in an expert in hypnosis who might be able to restore Ken's repressed memory.

Dr. John Watkins of the Department of Psychology at the University of Montana undertook a series of lengthy sessions with Bianchi, many of which were facilitated by hypnosis. Watkins uncovered a startling revelation which would dramatically change the entire character of the case. During one session of hypnosis, Ken became suddenly agitated, as if his entire being was instantly transformed.

"Are you Ken?" questioned Watkins.[5]

"Do I look like Ken?" his patient replied sarcastically. Hypnosis had produced the emergence of a second personality—"Steve Walker." Steve Walker was crude, sadistic, impatient, and proudly boasted of his crimes in both L.A. and Bellingham.

"Killing a broad doesn't make any difference to me," bragged Steve. "Killing any-fuckin'-body doesn't make any difference to me."

Steve continued to describe in detail the murders in California and in Bellingham. He also named his cousin Angelo Buono as his accomplice in the L.A. killings, explaining "Angelo is my kind of man—there should be more people in the world like Angelo." Yet Steve admitted that Ken knew nothing about the crimes, adding "I hate Ken."

The "multiple personality" theory—that Ken possessed two different personalities, one who did the killing, and another who knew nothing of it—was a way out of the dilemma. The puzzle seemed so clear now, at least to some people. If he had multiple personalities, the loving father, kind friend, and reliable worker could make up one of his characters, and the vicious murderer another.

When Ken was a boy, Dr. Watkins surmised, he had invented Steve as a repository for all his hateful feelings toward his mother. In this way, Ken could remain a loving and devoted son. The Ken personality would stay the affectionate man whom everyone knew, while Steve—unbeknownst to Ken—would periodically emerge with vengeance. Hence, it seemed that Kenneth Bianchi was clearly not legally sane at the time of the murders. Ken himself viewed videotapes of Steve's hypnotic appearances, and reluctantly and despondently accepted his illness and his role in the murders. With his permission, Dean Brett changed the plea to "not guilty by reason of insanity" for the Bellingham murders of coeds Mandic and Wilder.

Judge Jack Kurtz, disturbed by the sudden change in plea, called in an independent advisor to the court, Dr. Ralph Allison, renowned expert on multiple personalities and altered ego states. Dr. Allison also hypnotized Bianchi and confronted the vicious personality of Steve who angrily described the murders.

"I fuckin' killed those broads," Steve boasted, " . . . Those two fuckin' cunts, that blond-haired cunt and the brunette cunt."[6]

"Here in Bellingham?" checked Allison.

"That's right."

"Why?"

"'Cause I hate fuckin' cunts."

Steve also detailed proudly the killings in L.A., beginning with the murder of Yolanda Washington.

"She was a hooker. Angelo went and picked her up. I was waiting on the street. He drove her around to where I was. I got in the car. We got on the freeway. I fucked her and killed her. We dumped her body off and that was it. Nothin' to it."

Allison also explored Bianchi's childhood, taking him back through hypnosis to the age of 9. There he found the climate of fear and hurt from which the alter ego had been invented.

While entranced, 9-year-old Ken explained, "I ran away once, hid under my bed. Mommy was hitting me so bad. I met Stevie."

Allison probed a bit further. "How did you first meet him?"

In a child-like squeal, Ken replied, "I closed my eyes. I was crying so hard and all of a sudden, he was there. He said hi to me, told me I was his friend. I felt really good that I had a friend that I could talk to."

Allison was convinced, and reported his conclusion to the court: Ken Bianchi was a dual personality, was not aware of his crimes, and therefore incompetent to stand trial.

To others, besides Watkins and Allison, the multiple personality theory was just a bit too neat. Many were not convinced, particularly in view of the benefits of such a conclusion. The County Prosecutor, David McEachran, conjectured, for example, that if Bianchi could "con" the psychiatrists into thinking he was insane, then following a not guilty due to insanity disposition, he could possibly "con" them into believing he regained his sanity, and go free. At the strident request of the prosecutor, one further expert was called in, Dr. Martin Orne of the Department of Psychiatry of the University of Pennsylvania Medical School.

Orne, understanding the benefits to Bianchi in possibly faking a multiple personality, set out to analyze not so much Ken's personality, but the assumption of "multiple personality" itself. Orne carefully and expertly devised "tests" of the authenticity of Ken's hypnotic trance; if he could fake hypnosis, he could fake the multiple personalities.

Orne mentioned in passing, just prior to hypnotizing Bianchi, that it was rare in the case of a multiple personality for there to be just two personalities.[7] A few minutes later once Bianchi was hypnotized, out came "Billy," personality number three. On another occasion, Orne asked Ken, under hypnosis, to sit and talk with his attorney who actually was not present in the room. Ken overplayed his part, going so far as to shake the hand of the absent Brett. Then Orne had Brett come into the room. Bianchi immediately shifted his attention to the real Brett, remarking "How can I see him in two places?" This was significant because a hypnotized subject ordinarily doesn't question the existence of two of the same people.

Other tests also suggested strongly that the hypnosis was feigned. Prosecution psychiatrist Saul Faerstein summarily argued "Bianchi was almost a caricature of a hypnotized person, with eyes closed and head bobbing—a pseudo trance."[8] Furthermore, books on psychology were found in Bianchi's home—including one on hypnotic techniques, further endorsing the theory that this was all a well-planned method to escape guilt. However, there was no real proof one way or the other concerning the dispute over the validity of both the hypnosis and the existence of a multiple personality. How one interpreted the evidence and even Orne's tests, which themselves were subjective, depended on one's predisposition in the case.

The police and in particular the detectives in the Hillside Strangler Task Force were dead set against the insanity claim. Los Angeles Police had no real evidence against Angelo Buono except for the testimony of Bianchi. If Bianchi were found to be legally insane, or even if his testimony were determined to have been stimulated by hypnosis, then under California law none of what Bianchi had to say about the crimes could be used in court. Thus, not only might Bianchi escape the death penalty, but Buono might even go free.

What was the truth of Bianchi's mental state? This was either a classic case of a multiple personality, which someday might become the basis for an engrossing piece of nonfiction like *The Three Faces of Eve* or *Sybil*, or just a top-notch job of acting.

The key discovery that convincingly refuted the "multiple personality" theory came from investigators in L.A. as they followed up on Ken's life there. They found a suspicious looking copy of a transcript from Los Angeles Valley College, showing Bianchi's academic record. Not only was the date of Ken's birth wrong, but the transcript listed courses that were taken even before Bianchi had ever moved to Los Angeles. Upon the request of the investigators, the registrar at Valley College produced the authentic transcript. Prior to alteration of the name, it had belonged to a Thomas Steven Walker.

Bianchi was a very good con man. He, in fact, had once convinced a North Hollywood psychologist to give him space in his counseling office until he got his own practice on its feet. Ken had displayed his phony diploma from Columbia University, a master's degree in psychology, and he conversed convincingly about psychology.

As part of his plan to assemble the needed credentials, Ken had placed a job advertisement in the *Los Angeles Times* to hire a counselor, requesting that applicants send a resume as well as a college transcript. When the real Steve Walker responded to the ad, Ken substituted his own name on Walker's credentials and used them to further his own career. An altered ego could presumably mimic a real identity, such as that of Steve Walker. But Bianchi first saw Walker's name as an adult, whereas "Stevie Walker" had appeared under hypnosis when Bianchi was regressed back to the age of 9. It is, of course, possible that by coincidence two Steve Walkers appeared in Bianchi's life—one a childhood fantasy and the other a person who answered an ad years later. More likely, Bianchi was faking hypnosis.

Now that it was clearly a hoax—the multiple personalities, the hypnotic trance, the diplomas, and the "nice guy" facade—Bianchi retracted his insanity plea, and entered a plea of guilty. Part of the deal with the prosecutor—in order to avoid a death sentence—required him to testify against his cousin Angelo. Before the judge in Washington, Bianchi tearfully vowed[9]:

> I can't find the words to express the sorrow I feel for what I've done. In no way can I take away the pain that I've given to others. In no way can I expect forgiveness from anybody. To even begin to try to live with myself I have to take responsibility for what I have done. And I have to do everything I can to get Angelo Buono and to devote my entire life

> to do everything I possibly can to give my life so that nobody else will hopefully follow in my footsteps.

Regardless of the claim of some court observers that Bianchi was faking the tears and the remorse, as he had faked hypnosis, the stage was set for the next chapter in the Hillside Strangler saga, the ordeal of *State of California vs. Angelo Buono, Jr.* After a hearing in California affirmed Bianchi's sanity and clarity of memory, Bianchi's testimony could be used in Los Angeles against his cousin.

Shortly after Bianchi entered his guilty plea in Washington, Buono was arrested in Los Angeles for his part in the murders. Forty-five-year-old Angelo Buono was hardly the convincing type like his cousin Ken. His rough voice and uneducated speech were in sharp contrast to Bianchi's smooth manner and above-average, 116 I.Q. Buono had been married three times, and had at least seven children who not so affectionately called him "The Buzzard." Despite his ninth grade education, Buono learned the upholstery trade, and operated an auto upholstery shop adjoining his home in Glendale. Although his criminal record was far from long—a couple of petty crimes such as stealing hubcaps and disturbing the peace—he was far from a nice fellow.

Buono pimped for young prostitutes whom he himself would often abuse sexually. For example, according to the girls who worked for him, Buono forced them to use unlubricated dildos in their anuses. One of his wives also reported that he liked to tie her up during sexual relations. Angelo apparently liked his sex with pain.

But, all of this, the pimping and the petty crimes, was hardly equivalent to murder. The only "real" evidence against Buono was the story of Bianchi, and everyone knew what kind of liar and storyteller Ken was.

In July 1981, prior to the trial, District Attorney John Van de Kamp, with the advice of his deputy, Roger Kelly, who headed the prosecution team, filed a motion for dismissal of the charges against Buono. The case hinged on the testimony of Buono's cousin and partner in crime. Bianchi's credibility was quite questionable, however, since he kept changing his story. At times he would acknowledge his part in the murders and name his cousin as his accomplice; other times he would disavow any knowledge of the killings, except for what he read in the papers. Kelly and Van de Kamp felt there was just too little to go on to justify the expense of a lengthy proceeding, even though their motion to dismiss the charges would have freed Buono.

Ordinarily, a motion by the state to dismiss a case for insufficient evidence is granted by the judge. But the Hillside Strangler case once again proved to be no ordinary case. In a response that surprised the defense, embarrassed the prosecution, and delighted the media and the public, Judge George read a thirty-six-page prepared decision denying the motion. The seriousness of the case required that Angelo Buono be tried, regardless of outcome, regardless of cost.

The prosecution file was transferred to the Office of the State of California Attorney General, a move which led to some speculation that the entire motion to dismiss was an engineered maneuver to transfer the cost of prosecution from the County of Los Angeles to the state. Highly publicized cases like this are always good material for rumor and gossip; but like many rumors this one was without foundation.

The trial, called a "judicial extravaganza" by the *Los Angeles Times,* began in November 1981. It took all of five months to choose seventeen jurors—twelve regulars and five alternates, who had not formed an opinion about the highly publicized case and who did not reveal overwhelming resistance to taking a projected year from their lives to decide the fate of Angelo Buono. Like most jurors for extended trials, these citizens were mostly either retired or employed civilly and were guaranteed their ordinary wages while performing their civic duty.

But the two years and two days that the ensuing trial took to reach a conclusion, making it the longest in the history of the United States, was more than the jurors had bargained for. With

400 witnesses—including Bianchi who testified for 80 days—1800 exhibits, and 55,000 pages of transcript, the legal proceedings seemed relentless.

The trial was an ordeal for everyone. Prosecutor Roger Boren gained weight from consuming junk food during working breakfasts, lunches, and dinners; Defense Attorney Gerald Chaleff, on the other hand, lost considerable weight from the grueling nature of the trial. All personal relationships, friendships, and marriages were strained, and many other professional obligations had to be ignored. As Judge George remarked, "I see more of the lawyers than my wife."[10] Finally, there were the jurors, twelve women and five men, who stoically performed their civic duty in the two years away from their normal lives.

While the physical and emotional strain of the trial was demanding on all, it was perhaps hardest on the judge. His actions were scrutinized and analyzed by the lawyers and the press. Many saw him as the ultimate hero in the case, the one who insisted the Hillside Strangler be brought to justice. But at any time during the trial, a wrong move on the part of the judge could constitute a reversible error—a violation of Buono's constitutional rights causing an appellate court to overturn the verdict. Compounded by the fact that he was the only one who had insisted on the continued prosecution, a mistrial would make him ultimately "the goat" for wasting two years of everyone's lives and for wasting the two million dollars that the trial would cost California. Crediting jogging as his mainstay throughout the trial, Judge George shined, however.

As incredible as it may seem, the trial was most often boring, despite the goriness of the testimony. As the months dragged on, the gallery was often nearly empty, except for a few regular court watchers or a vagrant looking for a place to rest. The highlight of the trial was the appearance of the prosecution's key witness, Kenneth Bianchi. During his arduous eighty days of testimony, Bianchi described—over and over in several different and often contradictory versions—how the victims were captured, how they were sexually tortured and killed, and how their bodies were discarded. Even this became so tedious for him that he would sometimes stop to yawn in the midst of repeating vivid descriptions of sadism. When the jury brought in the guilty verdicts, most were as relieved that the proceeding was finally nearing a close as they were that Buono was to be punished.

The verdict was guilty of nine out of ten counts of murder. The not-guilty finding was for the murder of Yolanda Washington, the first victim. She had been killed in an automobile, unlike the rest who were killed in Buono's house; and her body did not bear the same "five-point ligature marks" (neck, wrists, and ankles) or microscopic fibers from a chair in Buono's house, found on other victims. Evidence linking Buono to her death, aside from Bianchi's testimony, was just not strong enough. Nevertheless, the nine counts of murder were accompanied by the important finding of "special circumstance of multiple murder."

In California, first-degree murder carries a life sentence with parole eligibility after seven years; furthermore, multiple sentences are served concurrently. However, a range of so-called special circumstances exist covering certain aggravating situations in which the sanctions are elevated. A finding of special circumstances—like a multiple homicide count—dictates only two possible sentences: Life imprisonment without parole eligibility, or death.The jury chooses between the two options during a separate stage of the trial called the penalty phase.

By the time the verdicts had been rendered, communication between Buono and his court-appointed defense team, Attorney Gerald Chaleff and his assistant Katherine Mader, had completely broken down. Against the vociferous protest of his attorney, Buono wanted to defend himself during the penalty phase. Ruling whether or not to permit Buono to act on his own behalf was the task of Judge George. Many observers viewed Buono's request to take over his own defense as an attempt to commit suicide with the aid of the court. For Judge George, it was but one more crucial turning point in a trial that demanded all the prudence, wisdom and care that he could muster.

Ironically, the one who seemed so unaffected by the ordeal was the defendant, the little man who not only had extinguished the lives of so many girls and women, but who continued to demand the time and energy of all those participating in whatever way in his prosecution. Up until this point, Buono had remained silent and emotionless. Throughout the 345 days of trial, 392 witnesses, and 1807 exhibits, Buono just stared into space. What was he thinking about? Was he even listening? No one could tell.

But Judge George was demanding some answers to help decide whether Buono should be allowed to represent himself at the critical penalty phase. The judge warned Buono that should he be allowed to represent himself and it proved a fatal error, "he would have to . . . go with it." Judge George, ordinarily articulate, showed signs of embarrassment while trying to substitute for the axiom "Live with it." George then questioned Buono concerning his understanding of the law and of terms like "aggravating" and "mitigating" circumstances. Buono's inability to answer correctly was pitiful, so pitiful that the judge denied his request.

Demonstrably upset by the judge's refusal to allow him to take over his own defense, Buono sat coldly as Judge George kept trying to get him to respond. Judge George repeated his question once again, "Do you want to testify?" Finally, Buono muttered "Yes, Sir."

Buono swaggered slowly to the witness stand, and the jury was led back into the courtroom to hear him speak. The gallery had suddenly filled with surprised and anxious spectators and reporters. After two years of silence during the trial, Buono summarized his feelings to the jury that had convicted him and would soon be recommending his sentence: "My moral and constitutional rights have been broken. I ain't taking any procedure in this trial. I stand mute."[11]

The penalty phase of the trial was fast and predictable. A series of ten witnesses took the stand to praise the character of Buono as a loving friend and neighbor.[12] Jayne Lowinger testified, "Anyone who loves his mother like him could never hurt anyone." Another witness remarked, "We all loved him." Robyn Miller, who had worked for Buono in 1978, said she was "very fond of Angie." Mary Lou Bustamonte told the court that Buono was "a super guy, one of the best friends I've ever had." But apparently Buono had two sides. None of his wives, whom he had liked to tie up during intercourse, and none of the prostitutes who worked for him and were forced into sadistic sexual acts by him had such nice things to say.

The jury recommended the lesser penalty of life imprisonment without parole eligibility. They may have been moved by the glowing statements of character witnesses on Buono's behalf. On the other hand, they may have been influenced more by the punishment given to Bianchi in exchange for his confession of guilt. Bianchi would escape the gas chamber and be eligible for parole, although in all likelihood it would never be granted. The defense team had painted Bianchi as the main perpetrator; after all, Bianchi killed again, without Buono, after moving from L.A. to Bellingham. Under the notion of "proportionality"—that punishments should be in proportion to those given other similar offenders—the jury spared Buono's life.

The prosecution, which had argued that if any crime deserved the death sentence this one did, was displeased with the sentence. Yet others, like juror Bertha Hollier found subtle justice in it: "Death is too good. He should suffer like the women he killed. I think being in prison is like a slow death."[13]

The case of the Hillside Strangler ended, at least officially, on January 9, 1984 when Bianchi and Buono came before Judge George for formal sentencing. The two killing cousins sat side by side once again, waiting for their fate to be sealed. Buono looked pale and tired; he had grayed a bit during the two-year ordeal after being so close to having the charges dropped. Bianchi also showed his age, now wearing glasses and having put on some weight; he was no longer the bright, charming, handsome ladies' man.

For two years Judge George had remained a dispassionate and impartial overseer of the proceedings. This was his opportunity to express in court his personal feelings about the defendants before putting them away: "I'm sure, Mr. Buono and Mr. Bianchi, that you will only get your thrills by reliving over and over the tortures and murders of your victims, being incapable, as I believe you to be, of ever feeling any remorse."[14]

Buono was, as expected, sentenced to a life term without the possibility of parole. Bianchi, having not fulfilled his end of the plea bargain by wavering on his testimony, was sent back to Washington where he would wait twenty-six years and eight months for his first parole hearing.

The drama that had begun over six years earlier on the bawdy streets of Hollywood had finally concluded. There were two villains who met justice, and certainly Judge George was the hero for insisting that the trial go on. But of course there were many more heroes, the attorneys as well as the investigators and the jurors.

But the heroes and villians were outnumbered by the victims. Besides the ten California girls and the two coeds from Bellingham, many more suffered in their own way. The victims' families had varied successes in coping with their tragedies, from the Wagners who moved to Oregon and founded a group called Crime Victims United, to Tony Johnson, whose guilt and mental anguish over not having agreed to drive home his daughter and her friend from the Mall, drove him to an early grave. Tony Johnson's wife, Mary, who found support in her religion, demonstrated amazing compassion for her daughter's killers: "The Lord spoke to my heart saying 'I, too, lost a child. I forgave. Can't you?' How could I do less? I have forgiven the two men. May God have mercy on them."[15] On the other hand, Judy Wagner reacted more

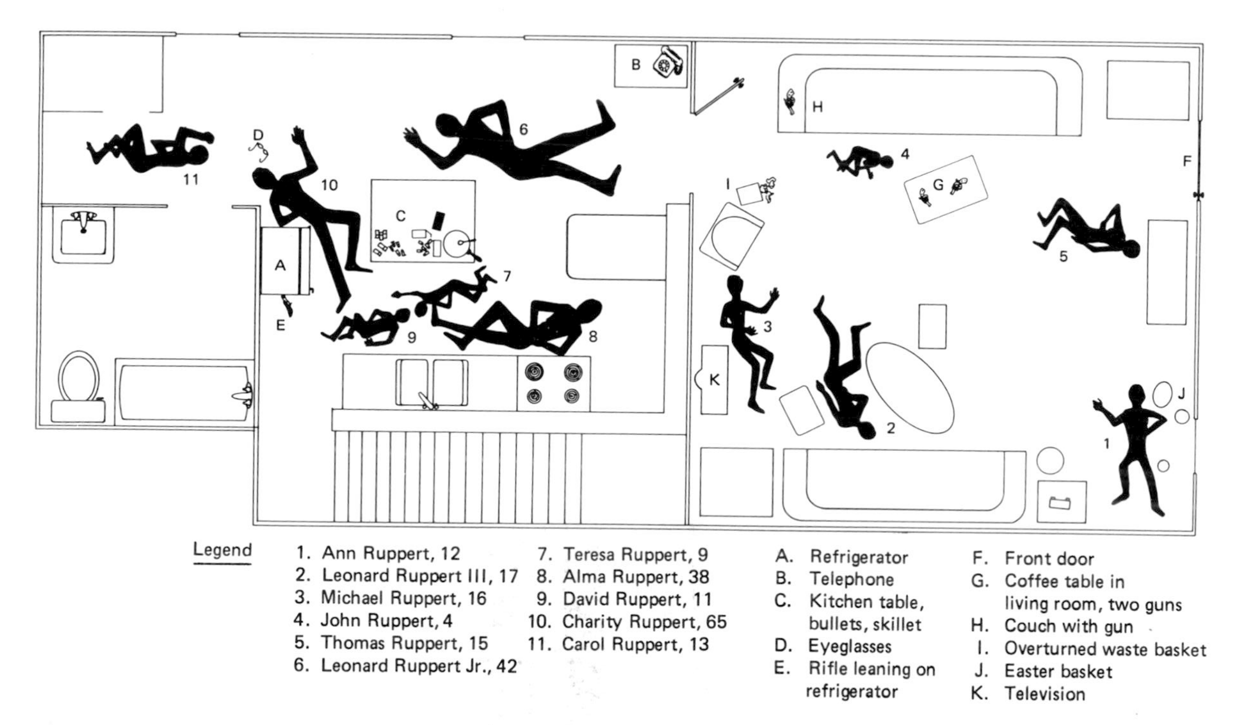

9. Scene of James Ruppert's Easter Sunday massacre. Courtesy of *Journal-News.*

10. The tiny, two-story house in Hamilton, Ohio, where the masssacre of eleven Rupperts occurred (top). Authors' collection. Leonard Ruppert's family during happier times (bottom). By permission of Wide World Photos.

11. The eerie facade of Hamilton's courthouse (top) contrasted sharply with the carnival-like atmosphere among spectators to James Ruppert's trial that took place inside. Authors' collection. James Ruppert (bottom) is escorted by police from the courthouse as curious and bewildered citizens of Hamilton look on. By permission of UPI/The Bettmann Archive.

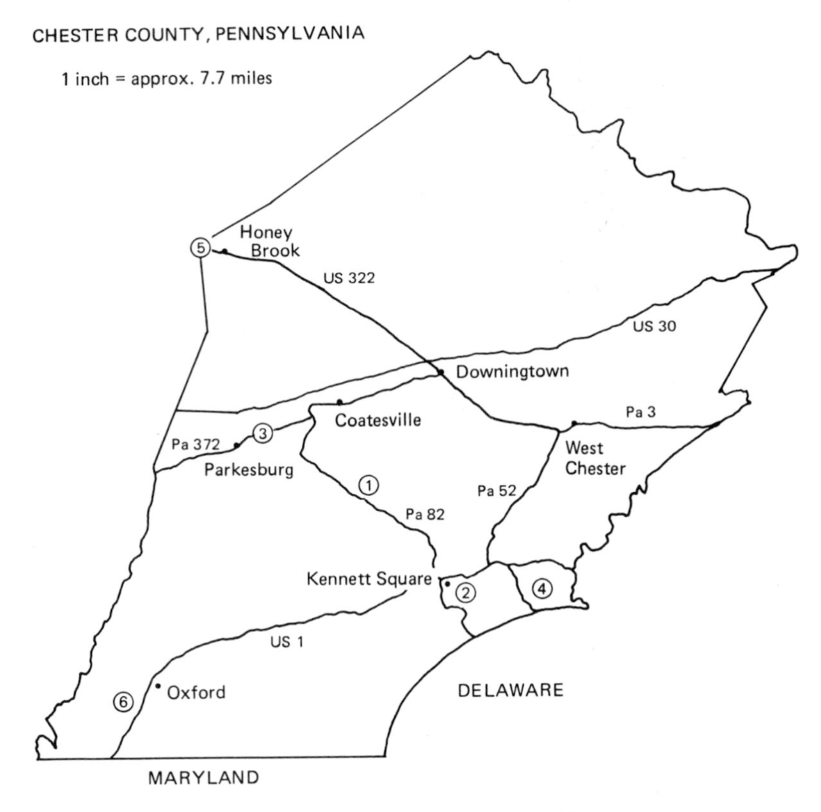

12. Murders in which the Johnston gang was implicated:
    1. John "Jackie" Baen drowned in Brandywine Creek, August 18, 1970
    2. Two police officers shot in Kennett Square, November 15, 1972
    3. Gary W. Crouch shot in automobile near Parkesburg, July 16, 1977
    4. James Johnston, Duane Lincoln, and Wayne Sampson shot in the Brandywine Game Preserve, August 16, 1978
    5. James Sampson shot in a Lancaster County landfill near Honey Brook, August 21, 1978
    6. Robin Miller shot (and Bruce Johnston, Jr. survived) at her home near Oxford, August 30, 1978. Authors' collection.

13. The exhumation of the corpse of Jackie Baen from a Delaware County cemetery was what the prosecution hoped would set off a string of confessions leading them to the Johnston brothers. *Courtesy of Daily Local News.*

14. Bruce Johnston Sr., David Johnston, and later murder victim Gary Crouch relax at a coffee shop in "down home," rural Chester County. By permission of *Philadelphia Inquirer*. Photo by Michael Viola.

15. The body of one of the strangling victims is discovered along a roadside, a frequent occurrence in the Los Angeles area from October 1977 to February 1978. By permission of Michael Haering, *Los Angeles Herald Examiner.*

16. The Hillside Strangler victims and their ages (from left to right): Yolanda Washington, 19; Judith Miller, 15; Elissa Teresa Kastin, 21; Jane Evelyn King, 28; Dolores Cepeda, 12; Sonja Johnson, 14; Kristina Weckler, 20; Lauren Ray Wagner, 18; Kimberly Diane Martin, 18; Cindy Lee Hudspeth, 20. Authors' collection.

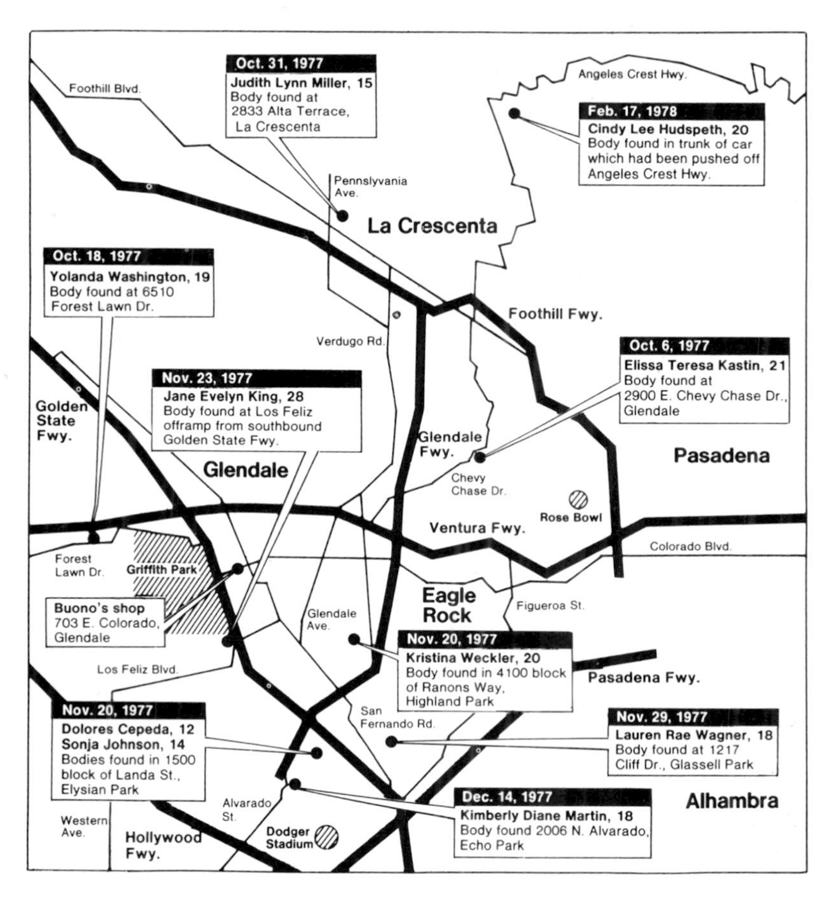

17. Map of where the victims' bodies were discovered. Courtesy of *Los Angeles Herald Examiner.*

18. Kenneth Bianchi appears to be deep in a hypnotic trance. Was it real or faked? Copyright, 1979, *Los Angeles Times*. Reprinted by permission.

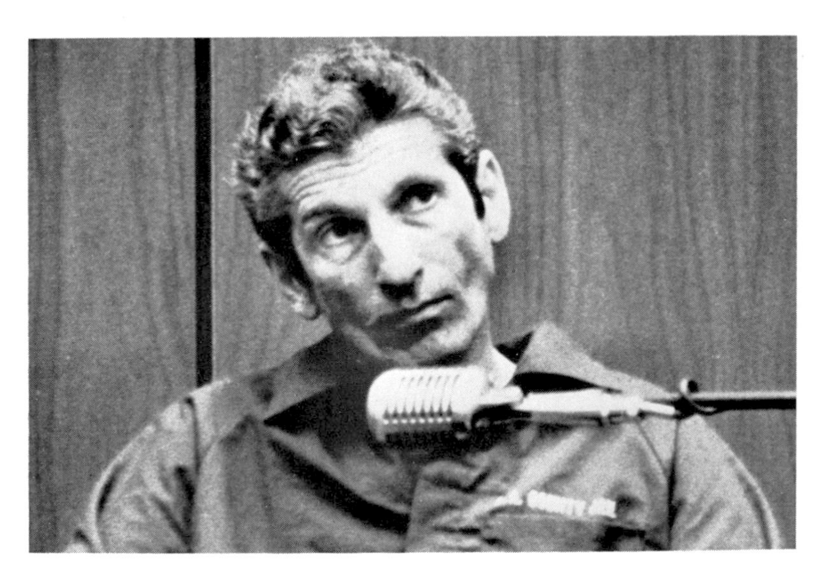

19. Angelo Buono speaks briefly to the court: "My moral and constitutional rights have been broken. I ain't taking any procedure in this trial. I stand mute." By permission of UPI/The Bettmann Archive.

bitterly to Buono and Bianchi: "I feel hate, absolute and complete, and I don't imagine forgiving them. Forgiveness is God's job."[16]

And then there are those in the families of the killers: Bianchi's mother who was driven from her house and home in Rochester, and forced to sell it at a deflated price to escape public scorn. Although she had no part in the killings, she had been cast by the press as the cause of Bianchi's deranged personality. Then there is young Sean Bianchi, who someday will have to face the embarrassment of his father's deeds.

PART III

RESOLVING MASS MURDER

CHAPTER 12

"WHAT TOOK YOU SO LONG?"

The operator received the frantic call at 4:13 in the morning of November 19, 1983 and put it through immediately to the Portland, Oregon police.

"My name's Galloway," cried the frightened voice of a teenage girl, "My father's shot me in the neck."[1]

Next followed the sounds of gunshots and then the crash of the phone onto the floor. The police response, although hastened, was not quick enough to find any life lingering in the bodies of 51-year-old Robert Galloway, his wife, two children, and his dog. Later that morning at Galloway's business, the J and J Remodeling Company, the police found the bodies of his two other children.

The crime scene left one disturbing question: Why? Why would a successful president of one of the ten largest home remodeling firms in the country suddenly go "berserk?" "He was a gentle man; he loved his children" remarked one of his relatives.[2] Why would such a man want to extinguish his entire family? Unfortunately, all the answers died with his suicide, leaving many perplexing questions unresolved. But one question was answered for certain: the killer was Galloway.

As in the Galloway slayings, the solution to a simultaneous mass murder is often no further than the crime scene itself. In some cases, the attack is so public that even the police are witnesses. When Charles Whitman opened fire from his perch high above the University of Texas campus, the police watched helplessly until a team of four officers finally made its way atop the tower to overtake Whitman. Similarly, the public slaughter in 1949 in which former World War II hero Howard Unruh began shooting at random on his street in Camden, New Jersey killing thirteen in as many minutes, left no doubt about what had happened or who had done it.

Even when the only witnesses to a massacre are all dead, there are glaring bits of evidence to indicate not only the enormity of the crime, but who was responsible for it. The police aren't always "blessed" by the suicide of the killer or by the killer remaining at the scene with smoking gun in hand, as James Ruppert did. Nevertheless, the many fingerprints, footprints, and other traces that surface in a bloodbath make it relatively easy to find the killer.

Throughout this book, we have emphasized the many distinctions between simultaneous and serial mass murder. The sharp contrast in characteristics of the killer, the setting, the situation, the motivation of the perpetrators as well as the public reaction is crucial to understanding the two types of mass murder. The most obvious distinction, however, is the difference in the relative difficulty in solving these two types of murder. Whereas simultaneous killings are solved with comparative ease and their perpetrators soon caught, serial murderers are far more elusive.

The serial killer, simply because he has murdered repeatedly without getting caught, must be considered a skillful practitioner. If he weren't, his murder spree would have been curtailed early on. Moreover, unless the serial murderer leaves unmistakable and unique signatures at the crime scenes—for example, specific marks on the victims or the same positioning of the bodies—the police may not recognize the homicides as the work of one person. Where a pattern does exist, it may be undetected because of the sheer volume of unsolved crimes under investigation, particularly in large cities. Even when the police are aware of the existence, though not the identity, of a serial murderer, the case may remain unsolved for a long period of time, if not permanently. Finally, those serial crimes that are solved are more often solved by luck than by thorough investigative techniques.

The case of David Berkowitz, "Son of Sam," illustrates that good fortune is sometimes necessary to identify patterns in serial killings and to solve the crimes. Before Berkowitz left a note confirming his identity as a serial killer, the New York police had been able to recognize the presence of a ".44 caliber killer" based on ballistics comparisons. Had Berkowitz changed weapons, not only might he never have been caught, but his killings might never have been linked and would have disappeared among the long list of unsolved homicides in New York City. One must wonder, therefore, just how many serial killers in large cities like New York have avoided detection by carefully varying their weapons—and perhaps, their entire *modus operandi.*

On the other hand, Berkowitz's unique proclivity for shooting couples sitting in cars might have eventually suggested the work of a single killer, even if he had switched guns. In addition, his bizarre behavior—shooting the dog of his neighbor Sam Carr, setting fire to the doorway of an apartment in his building, and sending threatening notes—was beginning to make him look suspicious to friends and neighbors. In most any urban environment with its diversity of residents, however, Berkowitz's strange actions would hardly have made him a prime suspect for mass murder. It took something as simple as a $35 parking ticket that he received at the time and place of his last shooting to lead the police to Berkowitz—the owner of the yellow Ford Galaxy bearing license plate number 561XLB. Only then, with hindsight, could Berkowitz's odd behavior in his apartment building be regarded as truly indicative of dangerousness.

In the late afternoon of August 10, 1977, police from several precincts moved in on 35 Pine Street in Yonkers, and waited for Berkowitz to appear. Hours later, he emerged from his building and walked toward his car. Police intercepted Berkowitz just as he was about to drive off, and pointed a gun at his head, ordering him to "freeze." Smiling and apparently unimpressed, Berkowitz responded "You've got me." He turned to Deputy Sheriff Craig Glassman, who ironically was also the neighbor he had tormented for months, and asked mockingly "What took you so long?"[3]

Even when unmistakable patterns emerge, that does not guarantee that the killer will be found quickly, if at all. In Columbus, Georgia, for example, it took no time to discern the consistent *modus operandi* of a rapist-killer known as the "Stocking Strangler," but it took six years after the murders stopped for a suspect to be indicted. From September 16, 1977 to April 20, 1978 seven victims were slain, and their similarities were overwhelming: all seven were women over 60 years old; all seven wore glasses; all were apparently widowed as their telephone listings suggested; all were found strangled with a stocking; and all but one lived within a one-mile radius and the other lived but two miles away. Yet when the stranglings stopped, the police were empty-handed despite an investigative task force and an all-out patrol effort. By the end of 1979, the manhunt was winding down and the case was beginning to look unsolvable, that is, until the May 1984 arrest of a suspect.

Most serial crimes do not have as uniform a pattern as the Columbus Stocking Strangler case. Yet, when police are faced with the possibility of a serial killer, however strong it is, their job takes on a greater sense of urgency: He might strike again at any time. Their job also tends to be more difficult because serial killers are the most successful at murder. Whereas most who commit homicide are identified fairly quickly, those who remain free to kill for the fourth, fifth, or sixth time—permitting the police to recognize a pattern—are obviously adroit at escaping apprehension. The usual law enforcement response in handling such difficult investigations is to form a task force.

The news that a task force has been established may temporarily give the plagued community a sense of security, but it is a false one, since these teams, as a rule, have never proven to be overly successful. In the Hillside Strangler case, for example, the task force was too large and decentralized. As we mentioned earlier, for example, information obtained from an interview with Kenneth Bianchi, following the murder of a call girl in his apartment complex, was never transmitted to those in charge.*

The Hillside Stranglings may never have been solved had Bianchi not ventured to kill on his own after his move to Bellingham, Washington. Indeed, his cousin, Angelo Buono, was more skillful at covering his tracks. When police searched his home for clues, nothing at all was found—he had cleaned it impeccably. By contrast, Bianchi, acting alone, was easy to catch because of the trail of clues he left surrounding the Bellingham murders. Until his arrest in Washington, however, the Los Angeles Task Force had been stumped for a year and had been labeled a total failure.

Shortly after the Hillside Task Force concluded its work in Los Angeles, another drama which would attract national attention began brewing in a different corner of the country. Over a span of two years, a number of black youths disappeared and were found dead in and around Atlanta, Georgia, leading to a similarly large-scaled manhunt.

The first of the twenty-eight Atlanta murders occurred in July 1979. The discovery of two bodies—Edward Smith, age 14, and Alfred Adams, 13—only 150 feet apart in a wooded lot led police to a theory that the boys were the victims of a dispute over drugs, an isolated incident.

By the fall of that year, the disappearance of two more black children (one in September and one in October) and the subse-

*Promising to assist police officials in managing the volume of information that surfaces in serial murder investigations, Information Access Systems, Inc., of Boulder, Colorado has developed information indexing and retrieval software that combines human judgement with automated decision-making. This computerized text management system is now being tested by the Green River Task Force in its continuing effort to solve the murders of dozens of women.

quent discovery of their corpses seemed more than coincidental, at least to their families. Mothers of the murdered children held a series of news conferences in which they insisted that the killings were related. However, according to Jeanne Blake who covered the killings for WAGA-TV in Atlanta, "the police weren't convinced until much later, until the bodies of seven or eight kids had been discovered." As a result, nearly a year of precious time passed before the Atlanta Task Force was established.

Chet Dettlinger, a former assistant to Atlanta's Chief of Police, charged that the investigation of the child murder spree was bungled by the police.[4] They failed to pursue leads, took the word of inexperienced police recruits, ignored the claims of alleged witnesses to the murders, and erroneously compiled their list of victims.

Dettlinger claimed that the police analysis of the geographic distribution of the crimes was one of the sloppiest aspects of the investigation. By focusing only on where the bodies were found, detectives overlooked an important pattern to the residences of the victims. The police map of the body sites suggested a "random" killer, but Dettlinger's own map of the addresses of the victims revealed a "path of murder." Twelve major streets were linked together to form a "misshapen boot," indicating that many of the victims may have known one another well.

Wayne B. Williams, a 23-year-old talent promoter and freelance photographer, was apprehended as a suspect in June 1981, after police on a stakeout had witnessed "someone" toss "something" off a bridge over the Chattahoochee River. At his trial for two of the murders, police argued that the "someone" was Williams, and the "something" was the body of 28-year-old Nathaniel Cater, the oldest of the missing persons.

Among the evidence against five-foot seven-inch Williams was the testimony of a 15-year-old black youth. The boy reported that in the summer of 1980 he was picked up by Williams and driven to a wooded area where he was fondled and asked to unzip his pants. When Williams stepped out of the car to get something from the trunk, the youth was able to flee. Also persuasive to the jury was testimony given by an FBI fiber specialist that hairs found underneath the shirt of one of the slain boys "could have originated from Wayne Williams," just as fibers from seventeen items in Williams's house and car matched fibers discovered on the bodies of twelve of the victims.

In February 1982, Williams was convicted of murdering two of the twenty-eight victims. Although no one was ever tried for the other twenty-six homicides, it is suspected that Williams is responsible for many of these too.

The Williams case, as with a number of serial murder investigations, leaves us with many "what ifs." What if the police had been quicker to mobilize a task force? What if the investigation had considered the geographic evidence in a broader context? Williams's capture may in fact have been hastened, perhaps even preventing several of the murders.

One of the most widespread manhunts was the one for the Boston Strangler by a task force headed by attorney John Bottomly.[5] Although the strangler was eventually found, there still remains some doubt as to whether Albert DeSalvo was in fact the strangler or simply a man who "took credit" for the strangler's deeds. With techniques as diverse as traditional forensics to untraditional psychics, the investigation was poorly focused. Indeed, the investigation should accurately be called more lucky than successful. The capture of Albert DeSalvo actually resulted from his arrest by the Cambridge Police for a breaking and entering and an assault, rather than for one of the stranglings.

The murders started with the strangling of older women in Boston, and expanded to younger women as well as surrounding communities. The murders also grew in brutality. The final victim, 19-year-old Mary Sullivan, was found propped up against her headboard, a broomstick protruding from her vagina, with her breasts exposed to a pool of semen that had dropped from her face and mouth where the killer had masturbated on her.

To assist the investigation, Bottomly established a Medical-Psychiatric Committee, which included a gynecologist, psychiatrists, clinical anthropologists, among others, to study all the evidence and to assemble a "psychiatric profile" of the strangler. One of the Committee members, psychiatrist Dr. James A. Brussel, had become renowned for his incredibly accurate profile of the "Mad Bomber" of New York. Brussel had been correct in predicting the description of the man who, for a period from 1940 to 1956, had plagued New York City with homemade bomb explosions and with letters to the newspapers after each incident. Dr. Brussel created a portrait of the bomber as a foreign-born, quiet, conservative, middle-aged man who lived alone. Brussel also hazarded to assert that the man, when found, would be dressed in a double-breasted suit buttoned all the way. Incredibly, when George Metesky was arrested for the bombings, he fit the profile precisely, down to the buttoned double-breasted suit!

The profiling of New York's Mad Bomber is a legendary accomplishment, which has never again been matched in its accuracy and precision. In the Boston Strangler case, at least, the profiling team was nowhere near as successful, and even sent the investigation onto the wrong track. The majority of the Medical-Psychiatric Committee (excluding Brussel) conjectured that there was more than one killer. The "old women," suggested the committee, were killed by a strangler whom they referred to as "Mr. S." On the other hand, "the girls" they believed were killed by at least one other person—quite possibly a homosexual—who may have known the young victims. In terms of character and history, the killer "Mr. S" was, according to the Committee's portrait, raised by a domineering, punishing, but at the same time, seductive mother. "Mr. S," unable to express his hostility toward her, instead displaced his expression of want and hatred against the "old women." The Strangler was described as a man who lived alone yet was still tormented by his confusion between hatred and sexual desire for his mother. Suffering from impotency rooted in his submissive childhood, he tried constantly to overcome his sexual inadequacy in sudden rages of passion and violence against his victims. The killer believed, speculated the Committee, that if only he could conquer his mother's domination over his life, he could live and love like a normal man.

When the Strangler was caught, he was but one man. Indeed, patterns may emerge that are very misleading. The ages of the women, which led the majority of the experts into believing there were two or more killers, just coincidentally fell into the two age groups. The Strangler picked out an address or an apartment to explore, and the age of the victims depended merely on whoever happened to be home at the time.

The Strangler, Albert DeSalvo, was actually known to the police for some time. Quite contrary to the psychological profile of the Strangler, Albert DeSalvo revered his mother, but hated his father for the brutal way he treated his mother. Far from a loner, he was married and had two young children. Also far from impotent, his wife Irmgard, whom Albert had met in Germany during World War II, described him as insatiable; he wanted her in the morning, during lunchtime, before dinner, after dinner, and later in the evening—five or six times a day. Since she was unwilling or unable to comply to such a demand, he called her frigid.

Albert expanded his lustful desires elsewhere. He had been known by the Cambridge police years earlier as "The Measuring Man." Long before the first strangling, DeSalvo would ring the doorbells of single women claiming to be from a modeling agency. After complimenting them on their beauty and figures, he suggested that they would be likely candidates for a modeling career. Flattered and intrigued, the women hardly minded when he produced a tape measure to record the key statistics. But they soon got the definite idea as his measuring of their legs, hips, and chests turned into fondling that he was nothing but a phony and a "sex maniac."

The police, however, considered him harmless. After his capture following an aborted burglary, The Measuring Man was arrested, convicted, and sentenced to two years for assault and battery against some of the women he measured as well as for attempted breaking and entering. He was paroled after eleven months in April 1962, just two months prior to the first strangling.

The thirteen stranglings tied to the Boston Strangler occurred between June 1962 and January 1964. Later in 1964, while Bottomly and his crew were hotly pursuing a variety of leads and a variety of suspects—none of whom was DeSalvo—Albert was arrested again.

On October 17, a 20-year-old newlywed was sleeping in her Cambridge apartment shortly after her husband's departure for work. She awoke to find a stranger dressed all in green coming toward her. Threatening to kill her, the man tied her to her bed, gagged her, and then raped her. But he didn't kill her. He just left after loosening her bonds. From the artist's sketch produced by the young woman's description of the intruder, a detective recognized a likeness to The Measuring Man, Albert DeSalvo.

DeSalvo's escalation from relatively harmless touching to sexual assault made him a good possibility for The Strangler. DeSalvo was never actually tried as the Strangler, however. Nor did he ever truly confess to the crime, except under hypnosis, which has encouraged many to ponder whether DeSalvo ever committed the stranglings or was just parroting what he possibly had heard from the real killer while in confinement. DeSalvo's incarceration for the rape, which eventually led to his arrest, was enough for the police. After several years of psychiatric observation at Bridgewater State Hospital, DeSalvo was transferred to the general population at Walpole State Prison, where threats against his life were carried out. His death in 1973 at the hands of fellow inmates, who detested his perverted crimes, left the Boston Strangler case permanently closed.

Not all profiling efforts are as wrong as the Medical-Psychiatric report in the Boston Strangler investigation. Regardless, psychological profiles tend to be so vague and general that they are basically useless in identifying a killer. John Godwin, author of *Murder USA*, concludes, "Nine out of ten of the profiles are . . .

vapid. They play at blindman's bluff, groping in all directions in the hope of touching a sleeve. Occasionally they do, but not firmly enough to seize it, for the behaviorists producing them must necessarily deal in generalities and types. But policemen can't arrest a type. They require hard data: names, faces, fingerprints, locations, times, dates. None of which the psychiatrists can offer."[6]

As with most things, however, the value and validity of a psychological profile depends mostly on the skills and experience of the profiler. Unlike a psychologist who might consult with police investigators on an occasional, ad hoc basis, a full-time team of FBI agents trained in behavioral sciences as well as law enforcement techniques prepares approximately three hundred criminal profiles each year. Because FBI profilers have extensive experience, they construct the most useful profiles. Unfortunately, this tool, no matter how expertly implemented, is inherently limited in its ability to help solve crimes.

The Behavioral Sciences Unit at the FBI Training Academy in Quantico, Virginia reviews crime scene photos, autopsy reports, and other evidence submitted to it by local police jurisdictions that request assistance in solving particularly sadistic and bizarre murders. From this information, the FBI team assembles a speculative profile of such things as the offender's sex, age, race, marital status, employment status, sexual maturity, and possible criminal record.

In addition to the Unit's unparalleled experience in the art of profiling, their interdisciplinary approach—including psychology, sociology, criminology, and political science—improves over more myopic psychological efforts. More important, notes Roger DePue, Chief of the Behavioral Sciences Department, "we draw on years of *investigative* experience with murderers, whereas most other psychologists have studied the killer from either an analytical or therapeutic perspective."[7] Interviews done by the FBI with known serial killers have emphasized questions related to their behavior at the scene of the crime, rather than their behavior in their family while growing up, to help interpret clues left in other unsolved cases.

Beyond the issue of accuracy, many expect too much from psychological profiles. The profile is intended as a tool to focus in on a range of suspects, rather than to point precisely to a particular suspect.

One FBI profile, for example, describes the likely killer in a sadistic murder of a 26-year-old Bronx woman as a white male in his late twenties or early thirties, who knew the victim and lived or worked nearby, was a high school dropout, lived by himself or with a single parent, and enjoyed pornography.[8] This profile, which proved to be quite accurate, describes, however, the usual characteristics of many sadistic killers as well as many people who do not kill.

The FBI's own recent evaluation of its profiling efforts, in our minds, underscores the limitations of this approach.[9] A survey of 192 users of these profiles indicated, first, that less than half the crimes for which the profiles had been solicited were eventually solved. Further, in only 17% of these 88 solved cases did the profile help directly to identify a suspect. While a "success" rate of 17% may appear low (and even lower if one includes the unsolved cases), the profiles are not expected, at least in most instances, to solve a case, but simply to provide an additional set of clues in cases found by local police to be unsolvable. Indeed, in over three-fourths of the solved cases, the profile did at least help focus the investigation. As Roy Hazelwood, one of the FBI profilers points out, "we're still in the stage where profiling is an art rather than a science."[10] It is doubtful, however, that this approach will ever prove to be anything but an art, or rather an educated guess.

The logic behind profiling is reasonable enough. If one accepts the premise that the killer acts out of some psychological need or defect, then patterns may emerge from the crimes which could reflect characteristics of the killer. The use of profiling—or, for that matter, any other strategy—requires that the police know that a crime has been committed. Unfortunately, they may not become aware of a murder or of a series of murders until it's too late.

Especially distressing are killers like Dean Corll of Houston, Texas who was responsible for the deaths of twenty-seven young boys from 1971 to 1973.[11] Such a murderer is not only unnerving in terms of the fiendish acts of sex and torture he committed, but more so by the fact that his crimes were completely unknown to the police.

On August 8, 1973 the police in Pasadena, a suburb of Houston, received a call from a young male reporting a shooting at 2020 Lamar Street. Upon their arrival at the address belonging to a dilapidated bungalow, the police found two teenaged boys and a teenaged girl, sitting on the stoop waiting for their arrival. One of the youths—Elmer Wayne Henley who had made the call to the police—was still holding the .22 caliber handgun that was used in the shooting. In the house, police discovered the dead, naked body of 33-year-old Dean Corll spread-eagled on the floor with several bullet wounds in his six-foot frame. The police also found as they searched the rooms, which smelled offensively of booze, dope, and acrylic paint, a scary array of apparatus for sex and torture, including a double-headed dildo a foot and a half long and a wooden "rack" cornered with handcuffs and ropes, just large enough for trussing a human being. But the discovery of Corll's body and his den of domination was just part of the grisly, sickening story to be unfolded in the next few days to the police.

The whole story actually began years earlier. Dean Corll, born on Christmas Eve 1939, was known around his Pasadena community as a quiet, reserved, and polite neighbor who seemed to enjoy the company of teenage boys, particularly that of David Brooks and Wayne Henley. Most, including Henley's mother, thought that Dean's preference for the kids was a bit odd; "He didn't act like a man his age" noted Mrs. Henley, yet no one really believed him to be dangerous.[12] In fact, most people considered him quite the opposite. Mrs. Henley remembered, "Dean treated Wayne like a son. And Wayne loved him like a father."

What Mrs. Henley and others didn't know about was the close sexual bond that had been developing between Corll and the young Brooks and Henley. Brooks was a very attractive youth who seemed almost mesmerized by Corll; and Henley, who was introduced to Corll by Brooks, found Corll to be the only one with whom he could really relate. They both came to love him and would do almost anything for him.

One of the things they would do was help him with his parties, wild parties with beer, drugs, music, and sometimes sex, to which Brooks and Henley would bring their friends and acquaintances. However, in 1971 these parties took a deadly turn. Boys, invited for drugs and booze, sometimes got more than they had expected. After drinking or snorting bags of toxic fumes until unconscious, Corll would tie them up, molest and sodomize them, and finally kill them and bury their bodies. And some of the time, Brooks and Henley would assist their friend in covering up the crimes, never telling on their beloved Dean.

But the parties ended on August 8, when Wayne made the mistake that so enraged Corll to turn against him. Wayne had brought a girl to Dean's house—15-year-old Rhonda Williams, who needed a place to stay for the night after running away. Wayne had promised Rhonda that his friend Dean would be happy to help her out; he was wrong—nearly dead wrong.

Dean blew up at the sight of the girl. "You weren't supposed to bring any girl," screamed Corll, "Goddamn you, you ruined everything."[13] But Corll calmed down, and Henley, Rhonda Williams, and another boy who had come along began sniffing bags of paint until they passed out.

When Henley awoke, he was tied up along with the other two teenagers, and Corll was threatening to kill them all. But Henley begged for his life, swearing to do anything for Dean. Dean decided to forgive his friend.

Dean ordered Henley to tear off Rhonda's clothes and to mount the girl, while he had fun with the other boy. But Henley saw his chance to free himself from his psychological bondage and grabbed a gun that was lying there, with which he slew his master.

Though the crime scene at 2020 Lamar Street was bizarre, Corll's shooting initially seemed routine for Houston, which in 1973 had been experiencing an average of one homicide per day. But that impression changed quickly as Henley led the police on a hunt that would uncover evidence suggesting years of torture and murder.

After his arrest, Henley directed the police to a boathouse a few miles south of Houston, where he claimed Corll had disposed of the bodies of the boys he had killed. The grisly task of digging for remains was given to trustees of the city jail, who had little choice in the matter.

The shed, numbered "Eleven" of the Southwest Boat Storage, had been rented to Corll for twenty dollars a month. It stood fifteen feet high and spanned thirty-four by twelve feet in area. Inside, the air was unbearably thick from the lack of ventilation and the heat of August in Houston. Shortly after breaking the surface of the ground inside the shed, the diggers found a layer of white substance, identified as lime, used to protect crops and plants from soil acidity. It was an ominous sign of what was to come: something—or someone—must be buried down there.

The excavation continued. Below the lime, the diggers came upon awful sights of skulls with bullet holes, trunks still bound in rope, as well as a variety of limbs and bones. The sights were no match, however, for the awful stench of fowl gases rising from the shallow graves. Digging deeper, the odor worsened as they reached bodies that had been there for longer and were more badly decomposed. And, of course, the hot and heavy summer air hardly helped matters. Each of the bodies had been wrapped in clear plastic sheets, making it somewhat possible for the police to distinguish one corpse from the other.

Body after body, the digging continued into the evening with the headlights of firetrucks providing the light for the nightmarish work of the diggers. Newspaper and television reporters gathered at the dig site, adding to the drama of each newly discovered victim; the count rose to eight by midnight when the work was called for the night.

The next day the digging crew found four before lunch and five after. They also found signs of some fiendish things that Corll had done to the young boys. One of the bodies, badly decomposed from the lime, lay beside a plastic bag in which his severed penis and testicles were preserved. Another boy's penis showed signs of having been bitten almost in half. Seventeen bodies in all were found at the boathouse. But that wasn't all. Two other sites around Houston added ten more bodies, making a total of twenty-seven.

The digging stopped at twenty-seven, a "record" at that time. There may have been more bodies in other places unknown to Henley and Brooks. Mary West, Dean Corll's mother, was not alone in her speculation: "I cannot help but wonder if the digging would have stopped if the record had not been broken."[14]

The most amazing part about the Corll–Henley–Brooks killings is that the police were completely ignorant of the murders in their own city. Although they had been receiving a variety of reports of missing teenaged boys, police passed them off as runaways, perhaps to California, though parents had insisted that their boys just weren't the type to take off without any notification.

Hardly a victory for the parents, they were proved right and the police wrong. But then what really could the police have done? Even ten years later, the horrible crimes of Dean Corll still take their toll; viewing a recent documentary recalling the event, a woman decided to inquire whether her missing child of ten years earlier was among the unidentified—he was.

The fact that this case was solved not by arduous investigative work on the part of the police, but rather by the confession of an accomplice, leaves some very unsettling questions. What if the fight between Corll and Henley had not occurred? How many more victims might there have been? Furthermore, because the case may never have come to the attention of the police, how many other killers are there like Dean Corll who prey on our children but ably cover their tracks?

The Corll case is not alone in showing the failure of police to investigate thoroughly missing persons reports or to see similarities in these reports. A very similar case occurring just a few years later further demonstrates how many of these crimes are "cracked" almost despite the efforts of police.

In 1978 the Chicago Police were lucky when they investigated John Gacy concerning the recent disappearance of Robert Piest, age 15.[15] Piest had asked his mother, who had come to pick him up after his part-time job at a pharmacy, to wait ten minutes in her car while he went to speak to a contractor. The contractor had expressed interest in hiring him for a summer job. Robert Piest never returned.

Robert Piest was not the type to run away. His mother knew that, and she was able to convince Lieutenant Joseph Kozenczak of it too. An immediate investigation of the contractor, John Wayne Gacy, uncovered his association with a number of boys who had been reported missing and a criminal record showing an incarceration in Iowa for a sodomy conviction. Next, a search of Gacy's home disclosed a wide range of implicating evidence: a pistol and a knife; a driver's license and a class ring belonging to missing boys, and even a receipt from the Nisson Pharmacy where Robert Piest worked. Further investigation continued to implicate Gacy. It culminated in the cold, horror-filled days in late 1978 when the police began digging up the floorboards of his house to discover the bodies of dozens of boys.

Had Gacy not continued his insatiable pursuit of muscular, pretty young boys for as long as three years, he may never have been caught. Certainly his gruesome activities were obscured in the thousands of missing persons reports that Chicago's large police department receives every year. Early on during Gacy's string of killings and burials, missing persons reports in Police

Areas Five and Six both cited Gacy as someone with whom them-issing boys were associated. However, the decentralized nature of the Chicago Police Department never permitted a link of these cases which would have highlighted Gacy as a common thread. Detection of this link might have prevented many deaths that did occur later.

Seeing a common element in several reports of missing or murdered persons in one large city is difficult enough. Seeing it across city or state lines magnifies the problem. Some killers are able to kill on the move so that they are already hundreds of miles away before police discover the crime. Henry Lee Lucas, for example, may have toured as many as thirty-six states during his decade of killing.

Some of these mobile serial killers will stay around one area for awhile and kill several victims; but when the police investigation gets too close, they move on to other places for a "fresh" start. By the time police investigators in Seattle, Washington were closing in on the man they called "Ted" who had killed as many as nine women in their state, Bundy had already moved on to Utah. After his arrest in Utah on a kidnapping charge, he was extradicted to Colorado to face a murder charge there. Months later he slipped out of his Colorado jail cell and fled successfully to Florida where he killed three more. On February 15, 1978, nearly a week following the murder of his final and youngest victim, 12-year-old Kimberly Leach, Bundy was stopped by the Pensacola Police—but only for driving in a suspicious manner. Although Bundy identified himself as "Kenneth Misner," police soon recognized him as a fugitive wanted by the FBI. Bundy's coast-to-coast spree lasting for four years ended for good when he was convicted and sentenced to death for his Florida murders.

Currently under development is a computerized information system designed precisely for the purpose of catching killers like Gacy, Lucas, and Bundy. Given the greater mobility of the modern-day killer, police investigators need to link up possible connections between murders and missing persons reports across town or across the country; these connections would ordinarily go unnoticed.

VICAP (*Vi*olent *C*riminal *A*pprehension *P*rogram) is described by its originator, Pierce Brooks, as "a centralized data information center and crime analysis system designed to collect, collate and analyze all aspects of the investigation of similar pattern multiple murders, on a nationwide basis, regardless of location or number of police agencies involved."[16] Once operational, it is planned that any police agency, having an unsolved murder involving mutilation or torture of victims or the disappearance of children, will submit to a central office at the FBI Academy a thorough description of the case, using a 27-page questionnaire that contains 285 pieces of information including suspect description, *modus operandi,* and types of evidence. VICAP will then alert the crime analyst to similar cases elsewhere.* The expectation, described by Robert O. Heck of the Justice Department who is partly responsible for its development, is that "VICAP will raise the probability that separate jurisdictions will recognize a serial killer, and the quicker this recognition, the greater the chance of interdiction."[18]

The VICAP concept originated from a multijurisdictional investigation of the disappearance and murder of children in Oakland County, Michigan in 1976 and 1977. During a fifteen-month period, four children—two boys aged 12 and 11, and two girls aged 10 and 12—were abducted from their neighborhoods in four different cities in the county and later found in ditches. Far from showing signs of bloody mutilation, each child was

*The value of the VICAP project is predicated in part on the presumption that serial killers roam the country, thereby not permitting similarities in their crimes to be detected. Recently, a Justice Department official stated in a televised interview: "For the most part, [the serial killer] goes from one place to another to do it."[17] The data, however, show that this is an exaggeration. Traveling serial killers like Bundy, Lucas, and Wilder are a minority to those like Williams, Gacy, Corll, Buono, and Berkowitz who "stay at home" and at their jobs, killing on a part-time basis.

found neatly groomed, even with a manicure and pedicure, well-fed, wearing freshly laundered clothes and with arms folded like a corpse in a mortuary. The boys had been sexually molested, which prompted police to speculate that the killer was a homosexual.

The ensuing investigation lasted two years and cost three million dollars. It has been called the most exhaustive investigation of its kind ever. The task force called in experts of all kinds—sociologists, forensic specialists, even a mortuary scientist and a psychic—in an all-out effort to find the killer. But after two years of investigation, involving thousands of tips and interviews, the effort was called off. Robert Robertson, an experienced investigator who coordinated the effort, admitted at the time "I don't feel we were ever near or close to solving the case or near to grabbing the person—or persons—responsible."[19]

Even though the Oakland County child killer was never caught, some don't view the investigation as a failure at all. According to Robert Heck, who had consulted on the case, it was an impeccable and thorough investigation demonstrating the advantages of multijurisdictional cooperation. It also indicates the limitations of any system, including VICAP, which attempts to routinize the investigation of serial murder.

Of course, computers will assist the police greatly in the future to recognize the work of a single killer, but even computer-aided investigations will have limits short of the human imagination. Computers can help only to the extent that the police encode the key items of data and to the extent that offenders really do exhibit patterns strong enough to detect. Moreover, the concept of "pattern similarity" is more complex than it may immediately appear.

No matter how voluminous the computer program supporting the data base of cases, it is doubtful that *precoded* checks of similarity will be a great benefit in discerning the unique features of each killer. While certain simple matches may be possible, such as offender hair color, etc., they will probably be of such broad characterizations that their usefulness will be limited. It is not inconceivable that a computer check of, for example, the circumstances of the disappearance of a child from a shopping mall could produce too many matches to be useful. On the other hand, the more specific circumstances of a case, for example, the particular manner in which a body is configured, might uniquely mark the work of one killer. Such specific information, however, might not fit into predesignated categories or codes.

In short, computer-assisted investigation may prove helpful, in some instances, by hastening the identification of a serial crime. In some cases, the killer might simply stop killing once he feels the police are "onto him." In other cases, a killer who feels that his apprehension is imminent may move on to other cities where he will continue to murder. Yet, if he maintains a pattern to his killing—which given the cleverness of some serial killers may be doubtful—VICAP will allow the investigation to move with him in a multijurisdictional effort to corner him.

At the same time, however, computers cannot actually catch criminals and, thus, must not be viewed as a panacea capable of stemming the tide of serial murder in this country. In the majority of cases, these killers are just too clever. If they are caught at all—before or after they stop killing—it is so often by luck.*

As we have seen, some investigations find the killer almost in spite of themselves because of chance or good fortune. Even a well-orchestrated and thorough manhunt is not guaranteed to succeed. As Robert Heck of the Justice Department points out, "It is most important to manage the process of investigation, including the tip file and other data. If the killer is not caught, then still you've done your best. But most serial killers are arrested by chance or happenstance."[20]

*VICAP will not assist the investigation of all cases of serial murder. A computer wasn't needed to find a similarity when several sets of bones were unearthed on Taylor Mountain twenty miles east of Seattle, or when seven elderly women, all with glasses, were murdered in Columbus, Georgia.

The hard truth is that serial killers, like Gacy, Corll, and Williams, are extremely skillful killers—"the cream of the crop." Unrestrained by either conscience or the law, they manage to slay dozens of human beings before their luck runs out, and they commit a fatal blunder. A few may even stop killing on their own accord and never become known to police.

But there may be many killers whose luck and expertise continue to protect them from apprehension. Some may be hiding in the anonymity of a large urban center where no one watches what they do or in the intimacy of a small town where they are beyond suspicion in the eyes of their neighbors. Others may travel across the country slaughtering scores of innocent victims, so cleverly altering their style and method of murder that the police do not even detect a pattern. Indeed, one can only speculate that many of the more than five thousand unsolved homicides in the nation each year are the work of a few very effective killers.

CHAPTER 13

THE BIG DEAL

Whoever says that crime doesn't pay hasn't heard about Clifford R. Olson—a 42-year-old construction worker in British Columbia, Canada, married and the father of an infant boy—who killed eleven times during a nine-month period.[1] From November 1980 to August 1981, the short and stocky Olson beat, strangled, or stabbed to death three boys and eight girls ranging in age from 9 to 18, all of whom were living in the Vancouver area. Some of the children were also sexually abused before they were killed.

As a child, Olson was a bully and a con artist. His teachers remember him as a promising young boxer who liked being at the center of attention. Instead, he grew up to be a part-time carpenter, and was convicted of some 94 offenses ranging from fraud to armed robbery. During the nine-month period when he was murdering children, Olson also managed to talk his way out of charges of sexual assault and rape.

Beginning on August 6, a surveillance team of Royal Canadian Mounties watched Olson's every move in the hope that he could somehow be linked to the unsolved murders. First, the surveillance team waited as Olson burglarized a house near Victoria. Then, they followed him to Vancouver Island, where he picked up a couple of young female hitchhikers. But fearing for the lives of the young women, the surveillance team quickly decided to stop Olson's rented van, rescue his passengers, and arrest him on a minor traffic charge. It was during the process of searching the van that the Mounties uncovered their first bit of incriminating evidence: an address book containing the name of one of the murder victims.

After spending six days in a local jail, Olson tried to consummate a deal with the prosecution. If he were to plead guilty to the murders, he would want to serve his time in a mental hospital rather than a prison, since in prison he'd be certain to be constantly threatened by fellow inmates for killing children. Despite their discussions, Olson was advised that the police could not determine where he was to serve his sentence, and the negotiations temporarily came to a halt.

Olson's next demand was more feasible, and more bizarre. He asked for $10,000 in exchange for each body to which he would direct the police. Suspicious that investigators might renege on their promise, he also demanded that $100,000 be deposited in a trust account from which $10,000 be paid to his family for every corpse he revealed.

Prosecutors were very much concerned that their bargain with Olson would set a dangerous legal precedent. Other criminals might even see this as a way to make murder pay. But they went along anyway, paying Olson's wife $90,000—based on a formula having a $40,000 base plus incentives for additional bodies and information. They feared that their circumstantial evidence was less then compelling enough to convict him of first-degree murder. In fact, they argued that he may well have been convicted of only a single second-degree murder charge and given a paltry ten-year prison sentence unless they made the deal with Olson. They also reasoned that the families of the missing youngsters deserved to know whether their children were dead or alive.

Meanwhile, some of the relatives of the murdered children didn't agree with the deal. They went so far as to demand a public inquiry into the handling of Olson's apprehension. They met together to discuss initiating a lawsuit against the government, based on the belief that the Mounties had botched the investigation.

Whatever the eventual outcome for families of the victims, Clifford Olson's own fate is settled: contrary to his wish to be hospitalized, he is serving his life sentence in Ontario's Kingston Penitentiary. Asked to reveal the whereabouts of the body of another missing child without being compensated, Olson snapped, "If I gave a shit about the parents, I wouldn't have killed the kid."[2] He is suspected of being responsible for as many as eight more murders.

The case of Clifford Olson represents an extreme and unusual version of plea bargaining.* In the more common example, a defendant agrees to plead guilty after negotiating with the prosecution for a reduced charge or a lighter sentence than he might have received had he pleaded innocent and gone to trial. Up to 90% of all felons plead guilty to a lesser charge or penalty as a result of a plea bargaining session. A defendant who kills might, for example, agree to plead guilty to second-degree murder or manslaughter rather than risk the more severe consequences of being convicted of first-degree murder in a jury trial. Or a defendant who commits several different murders may decide to plead guilty to one of them if all other charges are dropped. In this way, the prosecution is spared the time and expense of a lengthy trial, and the defendant obtains a lighter sentence and/or a better chance for early parole.

A variation on this theme is the case of 31-year-old Gerald Stano. From 1973 through 1980, he stabbed, strangled, beat, or shot to death at least twenty-seven and possibly as many as

*The idea that murderers might be compensated for their crimes is not something unique to Olson. Anticipating that David Berkowitz might profit from his celebrity status, the State of New York enacted the so-called "Son of Sam Law" prohibiting him from receiving any proceeds from the sale of his account of the crimes. His share of the royalties from Lawrence D. Klausner's *Son of Sam* was instead distributed among the families of his victims.

thirty-nine young women across central Florida because, as he put it, "I can't stand a bitchy chick."[3]

Stano's bargain with authorities gave him at least a temporary reprieve from death row. In exchange for confessions to three murders, Stano was sentenced to three consecutive life terms in three other cases. He may, however, still get the death penalty in any of the other twenty-one cases that have not yet gone to trial.

Serial murderers whose killing sprees cross state lines are rarely prosecuted by more than one state. The idea seems to be: Once you've captured a mass killer, make sure you keep him! In most cases, there would be nothing to gain in any practical sense by extraditing convicted mass murderers when they are waiting on death row or already serving a life sentence in another state.

After seven slayings in Washtenaw County, Michigan, John Norman Collins was found guilty of first-degree murder and sentenced to life imprisonment in the Southern Michigan State Prison at Jackson. But he was never tried for the brutal strangling-death of a pretty teenaged girl in California.

In 1970, the governor of California sought to extradite Collins, so that he could stand trial for the murder in Monterey County. California had a strong case against Collins. But after an exchange of messages between heads of state, Michigan Governor William Milliken vetoed the request on the grounds that Collins was already securely imprisoned. What more could be gained by his extradition to California? There is no statute of limitations covering murder. Should Collins ever be released in Michigan, he could have to face the indictment against him in California.

Even when all of the crimes of a serial killer are committed in the same jurisdiction, the killer is not necessarily charged or tried on all counts. Atlanta's Wayne Williams was a suspect in twenty-eight child slayings; but, for most of the deaths, the evidence against him was so weak that the prosecution went with its two strongest cases. Williams was then convicted on two counts of murder, sufficient to keep him locked up for life.

Opponents of plea bargaining point out that too many murderers and rapists "get off" by pleading guilty to a less serious charge. In contrast, proponents generally assert that the American system of justice would collapse if every case had to be tried. But neither opponents nor proponents generally appreciate the full extent to which plea bargaining influences the disposition of serious offenses. Few, on either side of the question, refer to Olson's use of plea bargaining to secure $90,000 for his wife and child; few cite the many cases of informants—killers themselves—who in exchange for information about their confederates in crime go scot-free or spend little time behind bars.

Successful prosecution of the Johnston brothers depended a good deal on gaining the cooperation of gang members and other criminals who were willing to "snitch." Bruce Mowday of Chester County's *Daily Local News* reported that "the heart of the prosecution's case . . . is made up of testimony from admitted murderers, burglars, and people who had committed various other crimes. . . . But for the Cambria County jury to believe the prosecution's theory of the killings and convict the Johnstons, it will have to credit the tale spun by the 'corrupt' prosecution witnesses."[4]

In return for his testimony, hitman Leslie Dale received ten to forty years. Informant Richard Donnell's deal was even better. Despite his admitted role in the 1970 beating and drowning of Jackie Baen, Donnell was permitted to plead to a charge of voluntary manslaughter with a sentence of one to three years concurrent with the term he was already serving for transportation of stolen goods. In effect, he would not spend even a day in prison for killing Baen.

Sometimes, a deal made to obtain testimony against a defendant can hurt the informant's credibility in the eyes of the jurors, if they suspect he is lying to gain some personal advantage. In the Johnstons' case, prosecutors made a deal with criminal Edward Otter: He would testify about his conversations with the Johnston brothers in which they alluded to their part in murdering members of their gang. In return, Otter would not be punished at all for fencing a million dollars' worth of stolen goods. Indeed, he would not even have to return any portion of the illegal money or pay taxes on it.

Defense attorneys for Norman and David Johnston attempted to attack Otter's credibility on the stand by getting him to admit under oath that he had been granted total immunity from prosecution—that Otter had absolutely nothing to lose and everything to gain by giving false testimony. But the jury would not be swayed from its belief in the guilt of the defendants, and the Johnston brothers were convicted anyway.

It is impossible to estimate how much lying does in fact occur in testimony given under immunity. Similarly, it is impossible to know how many innocent defendants have been convicted on the word of dishonest informants. Leslie Dale originally claimed to have been merely a passive onlooker—the driver of the car who, on July 17, 1977, sat in the front seat while Bruce Johnston shot Gary Crouch from the back seat of the car. Dale changed his testimony only after being caught in a lie—actually Dale was the one who shot Crouch from the back seat of the car, while Bruce Johnston sat in the front.

In a sense, it was the use of informants by the police that precipitated many of the murders carried out by the Johnston brothers. According to police, these killings took place to stop the informers from testifying before a federal grand jury investigating the Johnston's interstate burglary ring.

We are not necessarily arguing that investigators ought not solicit the testimony of informants. There is, however, a heavy obligation on the part of such investigators to see that their witnesses are protected from the defendants against whom they testify. Robin Miller might never have died, and Bruce Johnston Jr. might never have suffered serious injury, if the government had protected them from harm. Bruce Jr. probably should have been in the Witness Protection Program from the moment he was asked to inform. After all, he was pressured to give information which would surely have placed his life in danger. Yet he was allowed to walk the streets without surveillance days before he was scheduled to enter into the Federal Witness Protection Program, an easy prey for those who sought to stop his testimony.

Striking deals with accomplices to secure testimony against a defendant also raises ethical concerns about equal treatment under the law. That is, is it just to give a reduced sentence to a snitch and a harsher penalty to the person against whom he testifies? If a lighter sentence is awarded an accomplice for his willingness to testify against a defendant, then in certain cases it might be ethically proper to offer the defendant the same sentence in exchange for a guilty plea—assuming, of course, that both are equally culpable. For example, Hillside Strangler Angelo Buono was offered a life sentence with parole eligibility in exchange for a guilty plea—the same penalty as his cousin Kenneth Bianchi who testified against him; but Buono refused, and after a lengthy and expensive trial received the harsher sentence of life imprisonment without parole eligibility.

There are, on the other hand, situations in which equal treatment of informers and of defendants who plead guilty would not be feasible. Sometimes police claim it necessary to break a code of silence by awarding one partner in crime an absurdly light punishment or no punishment at all. Justifiable only as a last resort, this practice assures that at least some of the killers will be punished.

The resolution of the Zebra slayings, for instance, hinged largely on the eyewitness testimony of an informant—Anthony C. Harris who had recently been paroled from San Quentin. The 29-year-old convicted burglar and judo expert was the prosecution's key witness. Though an elementary school dropout, he was most able in educating the court about the six-month reign of terror in San Francisco.

Harris talked about the Death Angels' preaching of hatred for whites, described the slayings in detail, and identified the killers by name. Testifying under a grant of immunity from prosecution, he claimed to have first learned about the Death Angels from two of the defendants while they were all confined in San Quentin. Upon his release, Harris got a job at Black Self-Help, a moving company and front for the Death Angels cult, where he taught judo to teenaged members of the Fruit of Islam. He also alleged to have driven around with the defendants while they killed and maimed white "devils," but he never admitted his direct participation in any of the crimes.

Harris told the court about the night of October 20, 1973, the evening of the first Zebra killing. Richard and Quita Hague were taking a walk after dinner. They were holding hands as they strolled down Chestnut Street. Suddenly, two black men who had been waiting on each side of the sidewalk forced them at gunpoint into their waiting van. Thirty-year-old Richard Hague was hit repeatedly in the jaw with a lug wrench until he was unconscious. His face was then mutilated with a machete.

Twenty-eight-year-old Quita Hague's fate was even more horrible. First, she was made to watch as her abductors hacked away at her husband's face. Then, she was viciously dragged from the van by the roots of her hair and, while still begging for mercy, dropped to the ground where she was beheaded by the same machete that had just mutilated her husband.

Attorneys for the defense tried in vain to discredit Anthony Harris. They argued that Harris was insane and therefore unreliable; that he had perjured himself in order to hide the fact that he was really the Zebra slayer; and that he was after a $30,000 reward which the mayor of San Francisco had amassed from private donations and city funds for information leading to the arrest and conviction of the Zebra killers.

Actually, the reward had made a difference, but there was a lot more to it than $30,000. Harris was afraid, afraid that someone would recognize him as a suspect plastered across the front page of the local newspapers in a police artist's composite sketch. He also feared that he might be discovered in Mayor Alioto's massive springtime manhunt in which hundreds of black men throughout the city were being stopped and questioned. Later declared unconstitutional by a federal judge, the mayor's stop-and-frisk tactic blanketed San Francisco with both automobile and foot patrols—huge numbers of police officers who were instructed to stop anyone who vaguely resembled the newspaper sketches.

There were protest demonstrations around the city. The San Francisco Young Democrats were highly critical: Officers for Justice called the police actions "gestapo-like tactics." Pickets surrounded Mayor Alioto in front of city hall, blocked his way, and finally pounded and rocked his car. Demonstrators spat on him and hit him over the head with a picket sign.

Meanwhile, Anthony Harris had completely lost his nerve. He left Black Self-Help and called the San Francisco police. He was ready to cooperate, but only with a promise of immunity from the "top." Homicide inspectors Gus Coreris and John Fotinos were more than willing to comply. In the early morning hours, Mayor Alioto personally met with Harris to assure him that he would do "whatever the law permits to be done in such cases" and "see to it that [his] wife gets the reward."[5] Anthony Harris then talked, but never about himself.

Plea bargaining may in fact be a necessary element in the American system of criminal justice. But negotiations with brutal murderers in order to secure their testimony against other brutal murderers ought to be reserved as strictly a choice of last resort. Paying killers for information, risking the lives of criminals induced to turn informers, punishing accomplices unequally, and even letting some killers go free for the sake of information all raise difficult ethical and practical dilemmas. As a result, these practices should never be regarded as a substitute for thorough investigation and independent gathering of facts. The credibility of the entire criminal justice system would be jeopardized.

CHAPTER 14

SICK OR JUST SICKENING?

New York City's enigmatic mass murderer "Son of Sam" claimed he had been ordered to kill his six victims by demons who spoke to him through the voices of howling dogs. Two court-appointed psychiatrists agreed that David Berkowitz really believed his demon story and was legally insane. But an unconvinced court reached an opposite conclusion: It accepted Berkowitz's guilty plea to the charge of murder.

In February 1979, long after his 25-year-to-life prison sentence had been imposed, Berkowitz gathered together the press at Attica Prison and finally told the truth. He had indeed fabricated the tale about talking to dogs. His demon story was nothing more or less than a deliberately constructed fiction—an elaborate hoax designed and executed to place the blame for the killings outside of himself.

Psychiatrist David Abrahamsen had never been fooled. His testimony after holding lengthy interviews with the defendant had played a major role in the judges' decision that Berkowitz was sane and therefore mentally fit to stand trial for murder.[1] Abrahamsen had based his conclusion about Berkowitz on several important yet subtle factors. First, during their session together, Berkowitz failed to exhibit any of the confusion that so often accompanies insanity. Instead, he appeared to be "alert, perceptive, and highly intelligent." This only corroborated for Dr. Abrahamsen what he had already suspected: that it took "clear-headed cunning" for Berkowitz to have eluded for an entire year one of the most ambitious police manhunts in the history of crime.

Another clue as to Berkowitz's sanity came from constant relaying of stories about demons. Unlike most people who would prefer to forget their most frightening or threatening hallucinations, Berkowitz was all too eager to discuss them. Furthermore, he would protest vehemently whenever Dr. Abrahamsen attempted to change the subject. In some of their conversations, "Son of Sam" actually demanded to talk about nothing else but his demons and the dogs.

Berkowitz blamed his murderous behavior on the demons. At one point in his sessions with Abrahamsen, however, he admitted trying to slash to death a young woman who screamed so pitifully he was unable to kill her. This incident occurred on the day before Christmas, 1975, months before his first encounter with the demons which he claimed had ordered him to murder. In this assault, however, he was apparently on his own.

There were other important inconsistencies in Berkowitz's story. At first, he insisted that Sam was only a demon, not a human being. But when Abrahamsen confronted him with the existence of his neighbor Sam Carr, who had a dog, Berkowitz reluctantly changed his story, so that his neighbor became a part of it—Sam Carr was now the demon that spoke to him through barking dogs. "Sam" then existed in flesh and blood as well as fantasy.

Insanity cannot be turned on and off at will. Yet David Berkowitz's fellow workers at the post office saw nothing peculiar about him. Indeed, they described him as a boy scout type—courteous, reliable, and helpful. He was widely regarded as a person who "showed no disturbance," certainly not as a deranged lunatic who got messages from dogs.

Berkowitz claimed that he killed because the demons commanded him to do so. In at least one instance, however, he admitted completely ignoring their orders. During the first week of

August, he was "instructed" to travel to Southampton, Long Island, where he was to shoot a number of people on the beach. In the late afternoon, he drove to Asparagus Beach (actually in East Hampton) and waited there for two hours until nightfall. But Berkowitz's mission was aborted when it began to rain. Not wishing to get wet, he decided to leave. Apparently, then, Berkowitz could exercise at least some degree of control over his violent impulses.

Berkowitz was not the only one to see a personal benefit from faking insanity. Kenneth Bianchi, for months, had a number of psychiatrists fooled into believing that he had multiple personalities and therefore was not legally responsible for his crimes. As Prosecutor David McEachran indicated, if Bianchi could fool psychiatrists into believing he was insane, then he could just as easily convince them later that he was sane and earn his release. Like Berkowitz, Bianchi's ploy was unsuccessful, but it came close. Judge George remarked at Bianchi's sentencing, "Mr. Bianchi had faked memory loss; he had faked hypnosis; and he had faked multiple personalities. This action by Mr. Bianchi caused confusion and delay in the proceedings. In this, Mr. Bianchi was unwittingly aided and abetted by most of the psychiatrists who naively swallowed Mr. Bianchi's story hook, line, and sinker, almost confounding the criminal justice system."

Psychiatrists have traditionally been asked to give expert opinion in order to determine, among other things, whether a criminal defendant is capable of understanding the nature of the charges against him (his competence to stand trial) and whether he was legally sane at the time the crime was committed.

The insanity defense was developed in order to exclude from criminal responsibility those people who lack "blameworthiness"—the ability to choose between moral and immoral behavior.[2] Certain groups—for example, young children and idiots—are excused from legal responsibility because they are clearly incapable of understanding the nature and consequences of their behavior. But insanity is far more difficult to define and determine. Thus, for the purpose of guiding the decisions of judges, juries, and court-appointed psychiatrists, legislatures and courts have formulated certain tests to determine whether a particular defendant qualifies as insane and thereby falls beyond criminal responsibility or blame.

Twenty-one states continue to base their tests of insanity on the 1843 case of Daniel McNaughtan.* McNaughtan, a Scotsman, attempted to assassinate the British prime minister but mistakenly shot and killed the prime minister's secretary instead. By means of "expert medical testimony," McNaughtan's attorney argued that his client suffered from symptoms of paranoid schizophrenia; that he had believed for some time that members of the Tory party were following him everywhere and attempting to destroy him. The jury declared McNaughtan not guilty by reason of insanity. Since the public interpreted the verdict as overly lenient, the House of Lords met to draw up more restrictive guidelines for the use of the insanity defense. The so-called "McNaughtan test" grew out of these hearings: The defendant must be shown to be "labouring under such a defect of reason, from disease of the mind, as to not know the nature and quality of the act he was doing, or, if he did know it, that he did not know he was doing what was wrong."

Based on the McNaughtan test, some psychotic people could still be found legally sane. It is conceivable, for example, that a particular defendant might know that he is committing a criminal act and recognize that it is wrong, but not be able to stop himself. Thus, some states have adopted an "irresistible impulse" criterion to supplement the McNaughtan test. If a defendant is judged to be sane by the McNaughtan standard, his attorney may invoke

*Within legal circles, there has always been great controversy about the correct spelling of Daniel McNaughtan's name. At least twelve variations of the name have appeared. Until criminologist Richard Moran researched McNaughtan's signature for his 1981 book *Knowing Right from Wrong,* not a single legal scholar had spelled the name properly.

the irresistible impulse test to determine whether his client could have controlled his action even if he was aware it was wrong.

Psychiatrists have criticized the McNaughtan criteria for establishing legal insanity because they ignore the emotional aspects of mental illness and focus solely on whether the accused knows the nature of his act and knows right from wrong. Partially in response to this objection, the federal government and twenty-seven states now define legal insanity in terms of the broader criteria adopted by the American Law Institute (ALI) in 1962 as part of its Model Penal Code. This test states that a defendant is not criminally responsible if "as a result of mental disease or defect he lacks substantial capacity either to appreciate the criminality of his conduct or to conform his conduct to the requirement of the law."

A second section of the ALI test of insanity attempts to limit the definition of "mental disease or defect" by excluding "an abnormality manifested only by repeated criminal or otherwise antisocial conduct." But the vagueness inherent in the phrase "substantial capacity" is extremely problematic to both expert witnesses and jurors. For psychiatrists, the term "capacity" is a legal concept which may or may not be related to a psychiatric diagnosis of mental disorder. From the jury's viewpoint, the test gives no clue as to where it must draw the line between substantial and insubstantial lack of capacity. The test is therefore difficult to apply with consistency from one case to another.

If the question of a defendant's legal sanity is a complex one for psychiatrists, then it is an almost impossible one for lay jurors. Juries are frequently forced to decide, without any expertise in the matter, which of two conflicting psychiatric positions is correct. In what has been aptly termed "trial by label," opposing attorneys probe their respective expert witnesses for summary psychiatric labels with which to impress naive jurors.

The 1935 trial of 65-year-old, kindly looking Albert Fish, for example, contained extensive testimony regarding the mind of this perverse child-slayer. Fish's bizarre masochism took the form of devouring his own excrement, beating himself with a paddle spiked with nails, and inserting needles into his scrotum which he left there to rust. But he was on trial, not for his perversions, but for murder. Though suspected of six killings, Fish was tried for the grim murder of 12-year-old Grace Budd, whose body he had made into stew and eaten. Overwhelmed with persuasive evidence, on the one hand, that Fish was mentally deranged as well as compelling evidence, on the other, that he was sane and deliberate, the jury apparently went with its emotions and found him guilty. He was executed in 1936.

The insanity verdict—not guilty by reason of insanity (NGI)—is controversial in part because people assume it is so often used with success by cunning, streetwise criminals who would otherwise be imprisoned for life. Psychiatrists Pasewark and Seidenzahl conducted a study showing that college students incorrectly overestimated that 8150 or 37% of the 22,102 persons indicted for felonies in Wyoming had used the NGI plea and that 44% of these succeeded in being found not guilty because of insanity.[3] For the same 22,102 cases, Pasewark and Pantle asked state legislators in Wyoming for their estimates as to the use of NGI and its success rate. These legislators estimated that 20% of the accused entered a plea of NGI and that 40% of these resulted in a verdict of not guilty by reason of insanity.[4]

Apparently, many people—including college students and legislators—overestimate just how frequently the NGI plea is successfully applied. In Wyoming, for example, only 102 of the 22,102 defendants actually pleaded NGI and only one was found not guilty on that basis. Nationally, it is estimated that only 1% of all felony defendants plead NGI, of whom one in three is successful.

Our sample of forty-two mass killers yielded similar results, despite the fact that a large number of NGI verdicts might be expected in such a skewed group of offenders. Only nine of our defendants tried the NGI plea, of whom but four were successful. This is hardly the success rate claimed for NGI by those who fear that hordes of brutal murderers adjudicated not guilty by reason of insanity are being turned loose to prey on innocent citizens.

The insanity plea's low success rate may in part say more about the feelings of the citizenry, and thus of jurors, than about the defendants' state of mind. In the case of inexplicable or bizarre crimes, juries are often faced with a dilemma: they want, on the one hand, to place blame on the defendant who has clearly committed homicide, yet they want, on the other hand, to show compassion regarding his tortured mind. Since they can't both condemn and empathize, juries sometimes prefer to vent their outrage through a finding of guilty.

States' criminal procedures for applying the rules of the insanity plea are as varied and complex as the criteria for defining legal insanity. California employs a bifurcated process which sidesteps the jury's dilemma. The issue of guilt or innocence is decided in one phase of a jury trial, after which the question of sanity or insanity is explored in a completely separate phase of the trial. This permitted a jealous and enraged Edward Charles Allaway to be convicted of committing a mass murder and, at the same time, be adjudged insane.

Thirty-seven-year-old Edward Allaway came to work one day in July 1976 and shot nine co-workers. For a year Allaway had worked as a janitor in the library of California State University at Fullerton. Fellow workers and neighbors described him as "a typical nice guy." He was a clean-cut, good-looking campus custodian.

Apparently, Allaway's third wife, pretty 22-year-old Bonnie, a waitress at the nearby Hilton Inn, was less than satisfied with him. In fact, their arguments sometimes became so volatile that neighbors would call the police. Finally, Memorial Day weekend, 1976, Allaway packed his bags and moved out of their apartment. Despondent and jealous, he was now entirely alone.

The first indication that Allaway's separation was a continuing source of emotional turmoil for him came at work, where he was suddenly argumentative with the other members of his crew.

A week later, he walked into the local K-Mart and bought a .22 caliber semiautomatic rifle. Two days afterwards, he used it on nine co-workers whom he accused of "messing around with [his] wife."

Allaway's grim shooting spree took place in the basement and on the first floor of the campus library building. He had apparently selected those in the library whom he believed were responsible for his separation and had decided to leave unharmed those whom he considered innocent. With rifle in hand, he marched through the building from room to room and floor to floor looking for his victims. Within the space of a few minutes, seven persons had been killed and two others wounded.

Allaway was found guilty of six counts of first-degree murder, one count of second-degree murder, and two counts of assault with a deadly weapon. Indeed, there was no doubt in the jurors' minds that he had committed the shootings—particularly since he confessed and there were witnesses to the incident. In the subsequent sanity phase of the trial, however, the jury was not of one mind, splitting six to six on the question of Allaway's sanity or insanity. The hung jury necessitated another hearing before the judge, who declared him not guilty by reason of insanity, removed all criminal penalties for the crime, and ordered him sent to Atascadero State Hospital. Because of this disposition, should Allaway ever regain his sanity to the satisfaction of psychiatrists and the court, he would have to be freed.

At the heart of the public's distrust for the insanity plea is its perception that criminals like Allaway will "get off" on an insanity verdict and spend little time incarcerated. To the contrary, statistics actually reveal that offenders judged legally insane generally do not stay for shorter periods of time deprived of their freedom than if they had been found guilty. But the public tends to focus on the frightening exceptions—such as a man like Ed Kemper. Following his discharge from a mental institution to which he had been sent after murdering his grandparents, Kemper went on a murder spree lasting several months in which he killed eight women, including his mother, and had sex with their decapitated corpses. Similarly, the prosecution in the case against Kenneth Bianchi in Washington expressed concern over the implications of his attempted insanity plea. If Bianchi could fool psychiatrists into believing him to be a multiple personality and thus legally insane, then he could just as easily complete the con by later convincing the doctors that he had regained his sanity and thereby earn his release from custody.

Psychiatrist Seymour Halleck argues for the total elimination of the insanity defense, a defense currently recognized by all but two states.[5] By abolishing this plea, any defendant proven to have committed a criminal offense would be held accountable to society regardless of the state of his mental health. According to Halleck, no offender ought to be excused for his criminal behavior simply because he is judged to be mentally disturbed. Instead, all defendants—even if they are mentally ill—should be treated like mature members of our democratic society who bear a personal responsibility for their actions. Such a policy, Halleck believes, would ultimately help offenders by freeing mental health experts to treat rather than judge psychologically disturbed offenders. More important, this policy may have the more general effect of emphasizing an enlarged sense of responsibility for the behavior of all of us.

The problems invoked by the insanity plea may be addressed by modifying rather than abolishing it. In particular, eight states, beginning with Michigan in 1975, have adopted a "guilty but mentally ill" verdict to provide for those cases in which an offender, suffering from a psychiatric illness that influences his behavior or his perceptions of his behavior, shall still be held legally responsible for his actions. Under these statutes, the accused may still be found guilty, not guilty,or not guilty by reason of insanity; but he may also be found guilty but mentally ill. If the defendant is judged the latter, he is convicted of the crime as charged and then committed to the custody of the Department of Corrections where he receives further evaluation and treatment for his psychological condition.

The "guilty but mentally ill" verdict is in some ways not very much different from no insanity defense at all. According to Grant Morris of the University of San Diego School of Law, the guilty but mentally ill option may produce fewer NGI verdicts.[6] Jurors may see the "guilty but insane" alternative as a "compromise" which permits them to ignore evidence that a defendant is not criminally responsible, keep a dangerous offender locked away, but still assure that he is treated in a humane manner. In actuality, however, according to Morris, the psychiatric treatment provided under guilty but mentally ill is no different from that already available to all convicts. That is, any inmate needing psychiatric treatment can be transferred to a state hospital for the criminally insane until well enough to return to prison; a defendant adjudicated "guilty but mentally ill" is ordered directly to the hospital until well enough for transfer to prison.

There is, of course, another side to the story of the insanity defense, one that deserves equal emphasis. The NGI plea has been badly abused for purposes that have nothing to do with psychiatric diagnosis or humane treatment. Some criminologists assert that this verdict has been used to excuse rich and powerful defendants who might otherwise be convicted on the weight of the evidence. In one bizarre case, for example, a wealthy defendant was found NGI on the basis of expert testimony that he had a mental disorder "which had never been known, mentioned, or diagnosed."[7]

Criminologist Richard Moran argues, in addition, that beginning with the McNaughtan case itself, the insanity plea has been used to stigmatize political enemies. The label of insanity has the effect of discrediting the political cause of those who struggle against the status quo. Having been acquitted by reason of insanity, a political criminal can then be safely regarded as merely a lunatic whose views are hardly worth serious consideration. When Daniel McNaughtan was found NGI, he spent the rest of his life—twenty-one years—locked away in England's institutions for the insane. The validity of his grievances against the British government in power was totally ignored.

The insanity plea assumes an absolute: you are either insane or you are not. Given the requirements of tests of legal insanity, your act was either irrational and uncontrolled or planned and deliberate. There is usually no in-between because the conditions for sanity and insanity are regarded as mutually exclusive.

In reality, however, a defendant may be deliberate, cunning, vengeful, instrumental, and impulsive all at the same time. Jurors who must decide the sanity or insanity of the accused are, under such circumstances, left with an impossible task. In order to resolve the unresolvable, they may make decisions which seem inappropriate to those unfamiliar with the law.

Hamilton, Ohio's James Ruppert confessed to the simultaneous slaying of eleven members of his family. He admitted to psychiatrists having long been suspicious of his brother and mother. In his mind, they were out to sabotage his car as well as his career. The defense attempted to show grounds for Ruppert's innocence by reason of insanity. He had been unable to control the murderous response to his brother's mocking remark. Ruppert had gone berserk.

The prosecution found a more rational motive in Ruppert's sudden burst of anger: He had planned for some months to kill the members of his family. Broke and in debt, he was on the verge of getting kicked out of the house by his mother. If found innocent by reason of insanity, Ruppert would inherit all of their money—some $300,000.

Which side did the jury choose to believe? Ruppert was found guilty on two counts of aggravated murder; but he was also found not guilty by reason of insanity in the other nine deaths. Apparently, the jury believed that Ruppert was guilty when he shot his mother and brother (he did it for the money), but insane, and therefore innocent, when he then turned his guns on his sister-in-law, nieces, and nephews (he couldn't control himself).

Whether or not justifiable on logical grounds, the Ruppert decision has a consequence for the defendant not unlike that achieved by a verdict of guilty but mentally ill. James Ruppert would receive treatment at a psychiatric facility until such time that he was found to be sane. At that point, he would be imprisoned for the crime of murder.

As it happened, however, Ruppert wasn't hospitalized at all following the verdict. He was initially sent, as are all convicted felons in Ohio, to the Medical and Reception Center in Columbus for classification. Ruppert's psychiatric examination determined him to be sane, sane enough to go immediately to prison to serve his two consecutive life terms.

Few jurors want to treat insane people like criminals; and when a psychiatric disorder is obvious, clear-cut, and extreme enough, so is the verdict to be reached. Under such conditions, a jury typically agrees that a defendant lacks criminal intent or responsibility, hence he is legally insane. But the overwhelming majority of indicted felons including mass killers simply do not exhibit clear-cut signs of insanity, even when their offense appears to be disgusting and bizarre. It is easy under such circumstances to confuse what is sick with what is sickening; that is, to base a decision regarding the criminality of the accused on the repulsiveness of his act rather than on his mental state at the time he committed the offense. Attorney Gerard Sullivan refers to this misconception as the "he-killed-all-those-people-so-he-must-be-crazy" syndrome.

The problem with this argument is its circularity: Killing is crazy; therefore, anyone who kills must be crazy and ought to be found innocent by reason of insanity. By this faulty logic, no one who commits a heinous crime can be found guilty of murder.

Sullivan was the prosecuting attorney in the mass murder case of 23-year-old Ronald DeFeo, Jr., the Long Island man whose mass murder of his family in Amityville inspired the demon-ridden film, *The Amityville Horror.*[8] We do not know whether a supernatural horror ever existed there; we do know, however, that a brutal and tragic mass killing of six people did occur.

The prosecution in the case of Ronald DeFeo, Jr. called 57-year-old Dr. Harold Zolan, a forensic psychiatrist, to testify.[9] His distinction in the trial between psychosis and antisocial personality cut to the heart of the insanity defense.* Attorney Sullivan began by asking Dr. Zolan to define a psychosis:

> Dr. Zolan: A psychosis is a form of mental illness in which the patient has lost the capacity to deal with reality, to distinguish between reality and fantasy.
>
> Attorney Sullivan: Now, are there some forms of mental disorders, Doctor, which are not as grave or serious as a psychosis?
>
> Dr. Zolan: Yes.
>
> Attorney Sullivan: And is antisocial personality one of those?
>
> Dr. Zolan: Antisocial personality is a personality disorder, as opposed to a mental illness.
>
> Attorney Sullivan: What was your diagnosis of Ronald DeFeo, Jr.?
>
> Dr. Zolan: My diagnosis was that of an antisocial personality.
>
> Attorney Sullivan: What were its characteristics?
>
> Dr. Zolan: The antisocial personality runs a fairly wide gamut including people who appear different but actually basically are the same. And that gamut extends from a smooth persuasive con artist to the aggressive, destructive, rather obviously criminal activity that we are more apt to identify as an antisocial personality. The characteristics, the basic characteristics of all antisocial personalities are that they are people who have not been socialized into the society in which they live. They pretty much have a code of their own. They are people who are grossly selfish and callous, who are extremely egocentric, who have no capacity to experience or to feel guilt. They have a low frustration tolerance. They are easily aroused and at times often explosive. And

*The "antisocial personality" is synonymous with "sociopath" and "psychopath," the latter of which has been confused with psychosis.

> their main purpose in life is self-gratification generally regardless of the cost to others. I should add one other important thing, and that is that the antisocial personality fails to benefit from experience or punishment, and therefore is found to repeat antisocial acts despite the fact that they have been punished or warned or admonished. They probably constitute one of the largest groups of recidivists in our penal institutions.
>
> Attorney Sullivan: Now, Dr. Zolan, can you tell us how these or any of these characteristics of antisocial personality affect the ability or capacity of one to know and appreciate the wrongfulness of his conduct?
>
> Dr. Zolan: They do not affect it in any way at all.

We contend that characteristics of the antisocial or sociopathic personality can be attributed to a great many mass murderers, especially those who are serial killers. They are often evil but not crazy; they recognize the wrongfulness of their behavior but don't care. Serial killings generally involve sex and sadism; serial killers are having fun at the expense of their victims. For someone with a sociopathic personality, the act of murder is an end in itself. There is really nothing insane about the deed, except for the fact that the act itself is hideous and inhumane.

The public tends to confuse the behavior of the mass killer with the state of his mental health. In everyday conversation the term "crazy" is used loosely to refer to any extremely deviant act. In psychiatry, however, craziness or lunacy is part of the concept of psychosis—a form of mental illness in which an individual is out of touch with reality. In the legal notion, craziness or insanity refers to an individual's inability for psychological reasons to conform his behavior to the law. Therefore, the sociopath who commits a heinous and grotesque crime fits neither the psychiatric nor the legal standards of insanity: he knows he's doing something wrong, can stop himself from doing it, but simply chooses not to. Crazy minds and crazy acts do not always go hand in hand.

CHAPTER 15

PUNISHING THE MASS MURDERER

It was like a scene out of *Bonnie and Clyde.* In a stolen 1956 Packard, Charlie Starkweather and his girlfriend Caril Fugate sped westward on Highway 2 across Nebraska toward the Wyoming line, while baffled police hunted for them in southeast Nebraska and on toward Kansas City, Missouri.[1] But unlike 25-year-old Clyde Barrow and 23-year-old Bonnie Parker who made a career of bank robbery and murder, Charlie and Caril were just kids. He was a 19-year-old look-alike of James Dean in *Rebel Without a Cause* and she a ponytailed and spunky 14-year-old for whom their eight-day killing spree in 1958 was but a short-lived lark.

Charlie and Caril had been dating for some time when life grew more stressful. Charlie was kicked out of his house, never having really gotten along well with his father. And Caril's parents didn't like her seeing a boy who had dropped out of school in the ninth grade and was working as a garbage collector. The tension came to a head, however, when Charlie massacred her family.

The reasons for the family massacre are not exactly clear. Charlie later explained to the police that Caril's parents had threatened to inform on him concerning his murder of a gas station attendant two months earlier. Another story was that Caril's stepfather came at Charlie believing that he had gotten Caril pregnant. But for whatever the reason, if any reason at all, Charlie killed Caril's stepfather, mother, and half sister, while, according to Charlie, Caril watched.

Caril's stepfather, Marion Bartlett, was shot and stabbed to death, as was her mother, Velda Bartlett. Caril's half sister, 2½-year-old Betty Jean, was beaten around the head with the butt of a rifle, and when she wouldn't stop screaming, Charlie slashed her throat, finally killing the baby.

Charlie then wrapped up the bodies in sheets, blankets, and rugs and disposed of them on the Bartlett property. Marion Bartlett's body was in the chicken coop. Mrs. Bartlett was stuffed down the toilet hole of the outhouse, and Betty Jean was confined in a cardboard box which was placed near her mother's body.

Incredibly, rather than fleeing, Charlie and Caril remained in the house for six days, living as "man and wife": eating, making love, and watching television. Meanwhile, neighbors, relatives, and even the police came by the house suspiciously inquiring as to the whereabouts of the Bartlett family. Caril was, nonetheless, able to put them off—at least for almost a week—by telling them that they all had the flu. By the sixth day, Charlie and Caril decided they had better leave, because the charade couldn't be convincing for much longer.

They were right. Only hours after they departed in Charlie's beat-up Ford, driving south on Highway 77 and then east on a farm road toward the small town of Bennet, a relative discovered the bodies. The Lincoln Police were notified and issued the alert:

"Pick up for investigation, murder, Charles R. Starkweather. May live at 3024 N. Street, 19 years old. Also pick up Caril A. Fugate, 924 Belmont. Starkweather will be driving a 1949 Ford, black color, license 2-15628. This is a sedan, no grille, and is painted red where the grille was, and no hubcaps."[2]

Charlie and Caril headed toward the farm of 70-year-old August Meyer, whom Charlie had known for years. On the road up to Meyer's house, his car got stuck in snow, pushing his already frazzled patience to the limit.

Caril later told police "When we got stuck, when we were going out there and got stuck, and couldn't get it out, I think [Charlie] said he could kill him for it, and I said so could I."[3] And Charlie followed through too, shooting both Meyer and his dog.

The next day, still in the town of Bennet, Charlie and Caril killed again. This time their victims were a teenaged couple, very much different from themselves. Robert Jensen and Carol King, the perfect couple, were both good students and were active in the local church group. Bob was president of his junior class at Bennet High and a member of the football team, and Carol was a cheerleader. They were engaged.

Jensen and his girlfriend were out for a drive after dinner, when they stopped to assist two strangers walking along the road, who just happened to be Charlie and Caril. Once in the back, Starkweather pulled out a gun and ordered them out of the car and down into a storm cellar where they were executed.

Bob's body was found the next day at the bottom of the stairs of the cellar with six bullets in the side of his head. Carol's body lay on top of his, her coat pulled over her head and her jeans and panties encircling her ankles. She had obviously been sexually assaulted.

By the time the police found Starkweather's car still stuck in the mud and the three bodies slain in Bennet, Starkweather and Fugate were already back in Lincoln. They drove unnoticed in Robert Jensen's car past Caril's house which swarmed with police. Heading down to south Lincoln where the rich folk lived, they intruded upon the house of C. Lauer Ward, a wealthy lawyer and businessman. There they slew Mrs. Clara Ward and the maid Lillian Fencl. When Mr. Ward arrived home from a meeting with the governor, he too was killed. Charlie and Caril again fled Lincoln, only west this time and in Ward's luxury Packard.

Lincoln was panic-stricken. The news of nine dead in but two days was hardly ordinary in their peaceful community. Governor Victor Anderson, shaken not only by the suddenness of the murders but also by the fact that he was one of the last to see

Lauer Ward alive, called out the National Guard and announced a reward of $1000.

The police remained one step behind Starkweather. While southeast Nebraska residents fearfully remained in their homes, Starkweather and Fugate were in Wyoming, where radio bulletins of a stolen black 1956 Packard, license 2-17415 seemed strangely to fall on deaf ears. A short way past Douglas on Highway 87, Charlie pulled over to a Buick parked on the shoulder of the road. Charlie shot and killed the occupant, Merle Collison, a 37-year-old traveling shoe salesman, who had stopped for a nap.

Charlie started the Buick but couldn't seem to release the hand brake. A passing motorist, Joe Sprinkle, seeing both the Packard and the Buick at the sides of the road, thought there had been an accident and stopped to help. When Sprinkle spied Collison slumped over and Starkweather holding a rifle, he began wrestling heroically with Starkweather for the rifle. Deputy Sheriff William Romer, driving by on a routine tour, saw the two men fighting. Caril then ran over to the officer, shouting as though in need of help. Charlie seized the moment and sped off in the Packard back toward Douglas. Romer radioed ahead, and Starkweather was finally apprehended.

Wyoming had jurisdiction to hold the couple for the murder of Collison. Its governor, however, was willing to release them to their home state of Nebraska, since all but the last murder and the arrest had occurred there. Not knowing of the Wyoming governor's moral opposition to capital punishment, Charlie Starkweather signed the extradition waiver because he preferred Nebraska's electric chair to Wyoming's gas chamber.

From the point of their arrest, the Starkweather–Fugate case is one of sharp contrasts. Charlie played the role of a "cool dude" and a cool killer, almost daring to be given the chair, whereas Caril pleaded for sympathy and mercy.

Charlie's trial came first. He maintained a weak claim of self-defense, which hardly seemed reasonable given the number of victims and the fact that at least Jensen was shot from behind.

Charlie's attorneys put up an insanity defense against his wishes; after all, "Nobody remembers a crazy man," remarked Charlie.[4] The jury, nonetheless, was far from convinced of his insanity. They apparently found much more telling Charlie's sleeping—or feigned sleeping—during the reading in court of his earlier confession to the police. (This was a decade prior to the Miranda case which granted suspects the right to counsel during police interrogation.) The jury convicted Starkweather of first-degree murder and sentenced him to die in the electric chair.

Charlie's time spent on Nebraska's makeshift death row—the state really didn't have one—was brief by today's standards. There was no doubt as to his guilt, and little effort was mounted on his behalf to prevent his execution. In fact, his father, who throughout the trial had often been blamed for Charlie's antisocial character, wanted to sell his son's autograph and locks of his hair to the many souvenir hounds. The warden wisely prevented it. On July 25, 1959, Charlie Starkweather died from three charges of 2200 volts to his body.

Unlike Charlie's indifferent manner during his trial, Caril often cried during her prosecution. Her attorneys claimed that she had nothing to do with the actual murders. Further, they argued that she didn't know her parents had been killed and that Charlie had told her that they were still alive, threatening to kill them and her if she didn't go along with him. Her attorney said in court "Hers was really a story of a child in fear of her life for eight terrifying days, a child who believed that not only her own life was in danger but also the lives of her family. . . . She was a captive."[5]

Statements she made after her arrest, however, made her story implausible. For example, she had remarked to Deputy Sheriff Romer that she had witnessed all nine killings in Nebraska. How could she have remained with Charlie for the eight days to protect her parents when she had seen them die on the first day? The jury didn't believe her to be an unwilling participant, and convicted her. Mercifully or sympathetically on account of her youth, they spared her with a life sentence without parole eligibility.

As the day of Charlie's execution drew closer, Caril pleaded for Charlie to see her and to recant his testimony that had helped to convict her. She wanted him to admit that she was just along for the ride. But his position, allegedly, was that "if he fried in the electric chair, then Caril should be sitting on his lap."[6]

Charlie's imminent execution would end her hope for reprieve. In desperation, she telegraphed President Eisenhower[7]:

> I am now 15 years old. About a year and a half ago on a day when I was in public school, 19-year-old Starkweather who I had told several days before in front of my mother never to see me again went into my house and killed my 2-year-old baby sister, mother and step-father. Starkweather later confessed I had nothing to do with his murder which is true. Later he changed his story and said I helped him do his murder which is not true. He forced me to go with him when I got home from school against my will. Starkweather will be executed tomorrow. I have been denied by Governor Brooks a request to see him and see if he will tell the truth in front of a minister or someone else who would be fair before he is executed. I know of no one else to turn to because all of my family I was living with he killed. I know you are very busy but please help me in any way you can.

But the reply from the White House insisted that it was "a state matter." And her hope for a reprieve died with Starkweather in the electric chair.

As she grew into her thirties imprisoned at the Nebraska Center for Women at York, Caril became a different person. At fourteen, she had been the youngest woman ever to be tried for first-degree murder in this country; at thirty she was a model prisoner whose plight begged for pity.

By the 1970s, public sentiment began swinging her way, after a 1972 NBC-TV documentary, "Growing Up in Prison," reminded the American public about a young girl who had been banished to prison fourteen years earlier. NBC's report further inspired a 1974 biography entitled *Caril,* and a film dramatization of the case in *Badlands,* in which Martin Sheen and Sissy Spacek play characterizations of Starkweather and Fugate. Both the biography and the film portrayed Caril as a poor young girl victimized by her teenaged boyfriend as well as an unyielding criminal justice system.

Public sentiment was influenced and did have its effect. In 1973 the Nebraska Board of Pardons commuted her sentence from life to a term of 30 to 50 years, which would bring parole eligibility—but not until 1975. The Board of Pardons might have shortened the term even more, had their hearing not been attended by some vociferous opponents, including Robert Jensen, Jr.'s mother. She testified concerning Caril: "She was sentenced to serve all of her natural life in prison by a jury trial and a fine judge, now deceased, and I sincerely feel they meant for her sentence to be carried out and upheld by the courts."[8] Nevertheless, the groundswell of support on Caril's behalf far overshadowed the few who still carried torches for the victims. On June 20, 1976, Caril was released to start a new life, aspiring, as she put it, "to settle down, get married, have a couple of kids, dust the house, clean the toilet, be just an ordinary dumpy little housewife."[9]

While the nation cheered her release, the appeal of Mrs. Jensen is unsettling. Mass murder is unquestionably the most horrible of crimes, and the most severe of punishments is warranted. Further, although one may also feel for the plight of Caril Fugate, one must wonder what would have happened had not NBC documented her story. Should the fate of those serving life sentences so closely depend on volatile public mood? Would Caril Fugate have received the same form of compassion in a 1980s setting in which the public's tolerance for crime is much lower?

Caril Fugate is an exceptional case, not just in her age, but in her being released. Mass murderers, as a rule, do not get released. But then we must consider that few mass killers—convicted after 1970—have yet spent as much time in prison as Caril did. Will the criminal justice system similarly decide to release others involved in mass murder after they have served fifteen years? It may be doubtful, yet the public worries.

The public's sense of the fairness of the criminal justice system was dealt a severe blow by the publication of Vincent Bugliosi's *Helter Skelter.* The back cover reads: "Charles Milles Manson—eligible for parole 1978."* Readers were left to speculate whether Manson would be another Caril Fugate. If released, would he aspire for something more sinister than Caril's suburban dream? And if Charles Manson, perhaps America's most notorious mass killer, could get paroled, then isn't there any justice for the victims even in the case of mass murder?

The back cover of Bugliosi's book is most unfortunate, however. Manson's parole eligibility was a quirk of history. He was sentenced to death in 1971, but then in 1972 the California Supreme Court overturned its state's death penalty. This came just prior to the U.S. Supreme Court landmark decision in *Furman v. Georgia* that struck down the death penalty in America for its unequal and capricious application. The death sentences of all those on death row in California, and the rest of the country, were consequently reduced to the second most extreme punishment prescribed by law. Whereas in some states this meant life imprisonment without parole eligibility, in California there was only life with parole eligibility. Hence, Manson became eligible after seven years' incarceration, that is, in 1978.

The public often wrongly equates eligibility and release. Manson has been reviewed by the parole board each year since 1978, but he still remains behind bars. In his case, as would be the case of most any mass killer who has the opportunity for release, the public does not forget. It is the rare case in which they forgive. In Caril Fugate's case, her youth, gender, and secondary role in the crime accounted for the extraordinary public sentiment

*Since Manson was not released on parole in 1978, this phrase was removed from the revised edition of *Helter Skelter.*

on her behalf and thus for her special treatment by the correctional system.

As frightened citizens constantly point out, murderers get out on parole "all the time." Exaggeration notwithstanding, this claim applies, in truth, only to single-victim killers, whose release rarely attracts media attention unless they kill again. By contrast, mass killers are so notorious that their parole hearings are "media events," evoking widespread public outrage at the prospect of release. In Manson's 1982 hearing, for example, Sharon Tate's mother appeared with 19,000 signatures on a petition of protest; another citizens' group compiled a petition of 30,000 names. Manson still insists that he will get out someday; but nobody—not even Manson—can be so sure.

Public apprehension of the release of mass killers is based on cases prior to recent changes in the law. Richard Speck committed his offense in 1966, at a time when mass murder was such a rarity that the criminal justice system had not yet established special provisions for it. As with many single-victim murderers of that era, Speck was sentenced to die in the electric chair and waited for years on death row. When the U.S. Supreme Court abolished the death penalty in 1972, Speck's sentence was commuted to eight consecutive terms of 50 to 150 years. Under Illinois law, however, Speck became eligible for parole after ten years—in 1976, as though he had committed but one murder. Although eligible, he too has not been paroled.

A series of rulings by the U.S. Supreme Court in 1976 opened the way for states to enact new legislation for homicide and mass murder, in particular. Thirty-eight states have since restored the death penalty, building in stricter guidelines for its application to satisfy constitutional requirements. Illinois, for example, reinstituted a death penalty statute under which child-slayer John Wayne Gacy was scheduled to die.

Because of the tremendous growth of mass murder during the 1970s, the criminal justice system was compelled to recognize mass murder as a special type of homicide. California, which has had more than its share of mass killers, now employs a special provision for those who commit multiple murder. Specifically, whereas those convicted of first-degree murder are eligible for parole after seven years, a jury may add the special circumstance of multiple murder and then the only possible sentences are death or life imprisonment without parole eligibility. Sometimes, however, the "special circumstances" provision can be a potent bargaining position for the prosecutor. In the Hillside Strangler case, for example, Angelo Buono is not eligible for parole because of the finding of special circumstance. By constrast, his cousin, Kenneth Bianchi, pleaded guilty and received straight life with a seven-year parole eligibility, as part of his agreement to testify against Buono. But as Judge George said at sentencing: "I wish finally to place on the record my firm belief that neither Mr. Buono nor Mr. Bianchi should ever see the outside of prison walls once delivered there."*[10]

Many states have statutes that specifically prohibit the release of those convicted of mass murder. Even in the states with parole eligibility, mass killers are, nonetheless, unlikely candidates for release. Our survey of state laws governing the punishment of mass murderers reveals very wide diversity. On one extreme, Kansas has neither a death penalty nor a required life sentence; in Kansas a life sentence carries a fifteen-year parole eligibility, but this, of course, does not guarantee parole itself. On the other extreme, thirty-eight states have now restored the death penalty for murder since the moratorium on capital punishment following the 1972 Supreme Court decision.

According to the 1976 Supreme Court ruling, these new statutes must specify particular categories of murder where the death sentence can be applied as well as mitigating circumstances—

*Kenneth Bianchi failed, however, to fulfill the conditions of his plea bargain by wavering on his testimony against Angelo Buono. As a result, he was transferred to Washington to serve a life sentence there, for which he will not be eligible for parole for twenty-six years, eight months.

such as insanity—where the death penalty is inappropriate. Many states have designated multiple murder as one of the aggravating categories for the death penalty. Virginia, for example, delineates "the willful, deliberate and premeditated killing of more than one person as part of the same act or transaction"[11] as one of seven conditions making murder a capital offense. Since, on the face of it, this and similar multiple murder statutes cover only simultaneous killings, serial murder must be covered by the special classes of "homicide-rape" or "heinous murder." Some other states, including California, define multiple murder more broadly to include killings on separate occasions to encompass both simultaneous and serial mass murder.

Overall, our survey indicates that most states employ in the case of mass murder either the death sentence, life imprisonment without parole, or both. Those states that permit parole to murderers would, however, still be unlikely to award it to mass killers.

Public support for the execution of mass killers is now overwhelming. Gallup polls indicate that two of every three Americans now approve of the death penalty for murder.[12] Furthermore, we found in a survey of almost four hundred Bostonians even stronger support for the death penalty in the case of mass murder than in the case of other forms of murder.[13] For example, as many as 85% of these respondents—including a number who initially claimed to be "totally" against the death penalty—endorsed executions for the serial murder of children.

It cannot be denied, therefore, that the death penalty has considerable public support in this country, particularly for certain mass murderers. Because this support is so grounded in emotion, perhaps no degree of reasoning, debate, and research will alter it. A 1981 survey conducted by ABC News and the *Washington Post* indicated that revenge was the most often stated reason for supporting the death penalty: 42% of its proponents cited this as the basis for their view.[14]

The thirst for revenge is keenest in the case of mass murder, however, especially when it includes elements of sadism and brutality against innocent victims. Prosecutor Stephen Kay commented about Lawrence Bittaker and Roy Norris, who tortured and killed five teenaged girls in Southern California: "I don't want to call them animals; I like animals, and I don't want to degrade animals."[15] Kay, who was quite familiar with the inhumanity of mass murder, having served on the prosecution team in the Manson trial, apologized to Bittaker's jury that the maximum penalty was "only" the death penalty.

Professor Walter Berns in his provocative book *For Capital Punishment* initiates his argument for "the morality of capital punishment" based on revenge by making examples of the most notorious mass killers[16]:

> The real issue is whether justice permits or even requires the death penalty. I am aware that it is a terrible punishment, but then there are terrible crimes and terrible criminals: Richard Speck, killer of eight Chicago nursing students; Charles Manson and his 'family,' killers of actress Sharon Tate and others; and Elmer Wayne Henley and the man for whom he 'worked' (and whom he eventually murdered), Dean Allen Corll, the leader of the Houston, Texas, homosexual torture ring, killers of some twenty-seven young men. Henley was sentenced to 594 years in prison, but it is questionable whether even that sentence is appropriate repayment for what he did.

For people like Walter Berns, who view revenge as a primary objective of punishment, capital punishment makes sense: the most extreme crime deserves the most extreme sanction.* From our point of view, however, punishment must serve a utilitarian rather than an emotional purpose. In the case of mass murder,

*It's easy to mistake the root of the word "capital" in capital punishment. Rather than an adjective describing the extremity of the penalty, it is derived from "decapitation" or "punishment of the head," a method of execution used for centuries in many parts of the world.

protection of society is the primary objective, and "getting even" is secondary. This end is well-served by life imprisonment without parole.

The overburdened taxpayer may view the prospect of incarcerating a mass murderer for life as an enormous and unnecessary expense. He may ask why we should spend all that money to house and feed a "worthless" killer, when he could be executed instead. The figures typically thrown out to establish these costs and to fortify the argument—usually in the neighborhood of $20,000 per year—are severely distorted.

In 1979, nearly $3.5 billion was spent directly in this country on state corrections (that is, excluding local jails that house pretrial defendants and misdemeanants, as well as federal institutions that incarcerate violators of federal laws). These state institutions had a combined population for that year of 281,233, which translates to an expenditure of $12,368 per prisoner per year.

There is also wide variation in the extent to which the states support corrections. A recent survey by George and Camille Camp of the Criminal Justice Institute reports that per capita operating costs—excluding construction costs and capital outlay—range from as low as $5121 to as high as $22,748.[17] The angry taxpayer can calculate that over the life expectancy of a mass murderer sentenced to life, as much as a million dollars might go to housing him, and that ignores effects of future inflation!

The logic is flawed, however. By executing one mass killer, or in any way emptying a cell, the saving is far short of this range. A large portion of the per prisoner cost consists of salaries of correctional personnel, including central administration, as well as utilities, which are unaffected by minor changes in prison population.

On the opposite side of the ledger, the small annual savings in actual cost realized by executing a mass murderer—with the unlikely assumption that his space would remain vacant—are surpassed many times over by the increased costs to the state of prosecuting a capital case, particularly post-trial. In its 1976 decision, the U.S. Supreme Court endorsed the use of a two-stage process, separating the determination of guilt from sentencing, and suggested the necessity for state supreme court review of death penalty cases. The direct cost of prosecution and court-appointed defense through these required steps can easily surpass the expenses for imprisonment.

There are those extremists who recommend speedy executions without a lengthy appeals process; they half-seriously suggest, "Take them in the back and shoot them." The Supreme Court and most of us realize the need for careful judicial review in order to prevent irrevocable miscarriages of justice. And all of this costs considerably. Death penalty cases run in the millions. The New York State Defender's Association estimated that on the average in capital cases each trial costs $1.5 million, which then could even be doubled before the appeals process is concluded.[18] Of course, noncapital trials are expensive, but the appeals to higher courts are not as drawn out.

In the murder trial of Angelo Buono, the jury opted for life imprisonment over death in the penalty portion of the trial. The trial cost over $2 million before any appeals were even filed. Buono's accomplice and cousin, Kenneth Bianchi, plea bargained for life imprisonment with parole eligibility. Who really got the bargain in the Bianchi deal? Assuming he never gets paroled—and this is a pretty fair assumption—the taxpayers benefited by his guilty plea in exchange for the lesser punishment.

Whether the sentence be life imprisonment or death, a mass killer will never again roam the streets. In either case, the main goal of protecting society is achieved. A more controversial question, nonetheless, is which is more effective in deterring others from committing similar offenses.

We believe that most mass murderers cannot be deterred simply by making the penalty more severe. The weight of scientific evidence suggests that it is the certainty or probability of punishment—not its harshness—that deters. In other words, a penalty will not stop someone from killing if he does not think he will get caught. And as we have noted, a number of serial killers would not have been apprehended had it not been for their bad luck.

Some criminals, in fact, have committed mass murder in order to avoid getting caught for other offenses, even though they risked a greater penalty as a consequence. For example, the possibility of capital punishment didn't stop three youths in Seattle's Chinatown from slaying thirteen witnesses to their armed robbery; life sentences for murder didn't prevent the Johnston Brothers from killing their accomplices in grand larceny whom they believed would inform on their lesser crimes to a grand jury.

Men who slay their families out of revenge or despondency find the need to murder more compelling than its legal consequences. For those who commit murder-suicide, the concept of state punishment is irrelevant. For those who live to be tried for their crime, juries typically view them more as victims of their own impulses than as cold, calculating killers, and thus choose imprisonment over death. Therefore, the notion of the death penalty as a deterrent is largely irrelevant in family murder.

Finally, the serial killer, motivated by sex and sadism, is hardly deterrable. His sociopathic disposition favors immediate gratification, regardless of consequences. In the extreme case, he doesn't consider the risk of punishment or simply doesn't care. As Douglas Clark reacted when condemned to death for the sadistic murders of six young women, "It doesn't bother me in the least. . . . There are a hell of a lot worse things that can happen than to die in the gas chamber."[19]

PART IV

CONCLUSION

CHAPTER 16

LIVING WITH MASS MURDER

Our primary purpose in this book was to examine the validity of a number of popular beliefs concerning the mass killer and his crime that pervade both psychiatric journals as well as popular books and movies. Psychiatric case studies and best-selling biographies describe the vicious acts and troubled childhoods of a very biased selection of mass killers—only those mass killers who are so bizarre in their behavior that psychiatric experts are consulted regarding their sanity. Reinforcing this distorted picture, the popular media fictionalize the mass murderer as a glassy-eyed, crazed lunatic who kills out of an irresistible hunger for human destruction and sadism.

In truth, this view bears only some resemblance to one type of mass murderer, the serial killer. This individual travels around, sometimes from state to state, searching for victims whom he can rape and sodomize, torture and dismember, stab and strangle. Even these truly sadistic killers are, however, more evil than crazy. Few of them can be said to be driven by delusions or hallucinations; almost none of them talks to demons or hears strange voices in empty rooms. Though their crimes may be sickening, they are not sick in either a medical or a legal sense. Instead, the serial killer is typically a sociopathic personality who lacks internal control—guilt or conscience—to guide his own behavior, but has an excessive need to control and dominate others. He definitely knows right from wrong, definitely realizes he has committed a sinful act, but simply doesn't care about his human prey. The sociopath has never internalized a moral code that prohibits murder. Having fun is all that counts.

Not all sociopaths kill. For most, external controls—especially family and community pressures—hold in check the aggressive impulses which would otherwise go uninhibited due to their lack of conscience. However, when a sociopath is freed from these external controls through, for example, divorce or relocation, he may try to outmaneuver the law to get exactly what he wants.

Serial murderers make front-page headlines nationally because of the macabre nature and extended drama of their crimes. Despite their newsworthiness, however, these killers constitute a minority of mass murderers. More commonly, mass killings occur all at once in a single massacre as a means to a specific end.

Many mass slaughters are executed for profit or expediency. Murder is committed for the sake of a rational goal—to get rid of the eyewitnesses to a crime, or to eliminate "snitches." Though immoral, mass murder is seen as an effective way of achieving this objective. The killer may neither wish to kill nor enjoy it. But the end justifies the means: mass murder is perceived to be necessary for survival.

The annihilation of an entire family by one of its members is the most frequent form of mass murder. In the typical scenario, a husband/father executes his wife and children after being threatened with marital separation or losing his job. These events which precipitate murder are "final straws" in lives long overburdened with frustration and failure. External controls are weakened by the sudden change of life, and anger temporarily overrides their inner sense of morality. For family killers whose conscience is ordinarily strong, suicide may be the only way to handle the aftermath of murder.

Despite the extreme nature of his crime, the mass killer appears to be extraordinarily ordinary. He is indistinguishable from everyone else. Indeed, he may be the neighbor next door, a co-worker at the next desk, or a member of the family. Because of his ordinary role in the community, those who know him best are astonished when they learn of his murderous behavior.

No one can predict who will turn out to be a mass killer. Beyond personality and background, there are significant elements in a setting—the availability of weapons, obedience to authority, membership in a group whose theme is murder—that encourage "normal" people to kill.

Like murder generally, few mass murderers prey on total strangers. The extent to which the victims of mass murder are specifically chosen by the killer or are simply unfortunate to be "in the wrong place at the wrong time" depends on the type and motivation of the crime. Simultaneous slaughters rarely involve total strangers. Those that do—such as public snipings in which dozens of passersby are shot down—are particularly fearsome; they happen as suddenly as the explosion of a bomb.

The serial killer typically picks on innocent strangers who may possess a certain physical feature or may just be accessible. Nearly without exception, serial killers select the vulnerable—prostitutes who willingly enter cars of strangers and subject themselves to submissive roles, hitchhikers who similarly place themselves within the domain controlled by the killer, old women who live alone and are defenseless, and children whose trusting nature or lack of strength make them easy marks.

The obvious advice is to be careful: whenever possible, to avoid situations in which you are at the mercy of strangers. We must also recognize, at the same time, that some risk is unavoidable. Can we truly expect a stranded motorist to refuse the assistance of a kind-looking man who stops to give aid or a ride? Can we expect a young child to ignore a man with a police badge when he says that a parent is ill? Could we expect an adult not to do the same? The answer is obvious—No! Advising people to take reasonable caution is one thing; but teaching people to consider everyone they encounter as a potential killer victimizes our entire society. It breeds a general sense of cynicism and distrust which ultimately affects all of our human relationships.

When serial killers were on the loose in cities like New York, Los Angeles, and Atlanta, local residents wisely modified their daily activities to take greater precautions against being the next victim. But citizens everywhere experience another kind of fear associated with mass murder: Many believe that the criminal justice system is soft and that the most dangerous killers, if caught, will eventually get released on parole, or worse, be acquitted.

Do mass killers really get away with murder? This depends on the type of killing. Simultaneous massacres usually leave behind a houseful of evidence leading a trail to the perpetrator. And sometimes, the killer himself is left behind at the scene when the police arrive. Family killings, in particular, are usually committed for a purpose, to eradicate a situation that has been a source of continuing torment. To the family slayer, the likelihood of capture and punishment is often secondary to his purpose.

The police have far more difficulty with serial killers. In the first place, some time may pass before law enforcement investigators realize that a series of seemingly unrelated homicides is actually the work of a single individual—by that time, he may be long gone. The Justice Department is taking initiatives to try to stem the tide of serial murders in the United States. Both psychological profiling of the unknown killer from clues at the scene of the crime and computerized linking of crimes in separate jurisdictions hold some promise. Besides their intrinsic limitations, however, these methods must challenge the cunning and skill of the most successful of all killers. As we have seen, when a serial murderer is caught, it is often more a result of luck or the cooperation of snitches than of the matching skill of the investigators.

When mass killers are caught and prosecuted, they rarely get treated with leniency. Very few benefit from the insanity plea—if in fact such is a benefit—and most get extremely severe penalties: either death or life imprisonment. Under recent laws, many states employ sentences for mass killers that explicitly prohibit their release on parole. Because of the notoriety associated with their crimes, even mass killers of years past who remain in prison with parole eligibility will most likely never be released. These men perhaps realize what the public misunderstands: their fate has been guaranteed by the enormity of the acts which they committed.

ENDNOTES

Chapter 1

[1]Much of the information about the case of Edward Gein came from Judge Robert H. Gollmar, *Edward Gein: America's Most Bizarre Murderer* (Delavan, Wisconsin: Chas. Hallberg and Company, 1981).
[2]" . . . Mrs. Worden had . . ." *ibid.*, p. 32.
[3]"What did Gein . . ." George Arndt, M.D., "Gein humor," *ibid.*, Appendix A.

Chapter 2

[1]Information on the case of Ted Bundy was drawn primarily from three books: Ann Rule, *The Stranger Beside Me* (New York: W. W. Norton and Company, 1980); Richard W. Larsen, *Bundy: The Deliberate Stranger* (Englewood Cliffs, New Jersey: Prentice-Hall, 1980); and Stephen G. Michaud and Hugh Aynesworth, *The Only Living Witness* (New York: Linden Press, 1983).
[2]"I have never . . ." Michaud and Aynesworth, p. 95.
[3]"They are all . . ." *The New York Times*, July 15, 1966.
[4]"oozing with hostility" *Newsweek*, August 15, 1966.
[5]"going up on . . ." *ibid.*
[6]"He was always . . ." *ibid.*
[7]Information concerning the 1898 copycat murders was obtained from Albert I. Borowitz, "Packaged Death: Forerunners of the Tylenol Poisonings," *American Bar Association Journal* 69 (1983), pp. 282–286.
[8]David P. Phillips, "The Impact of Mass Media Violence on U.S. Homicides," *American Sociological Review* 48 (1983), pp. 560–568.

[9]Donnerstein's study was cited in Walter Sullivan, "Violent Pornography Elevates Aggression, Researchers Say," *The New York Times*, September 30, 1980.

[10]Murray A. Straus and Larry Baron, "Sexual Stratification, Pornography, and Rape," Family Research Laboratory, University of New Hampshire, Durham, 1983.

Chapter 3

[1]John M. Macdonald, "The Threat to Kill," *American Journal of Psychiatry* 120 (1963), pp. 125–130.

[2]Daniel S. Hellman and Nathan Blackman, "Enuresis, Firesetting, and Cruelty to Animals," *American Journal of Psychiatry* 122 (1966), pp. 1431–1435.

[3]Alan R. Felthous, "Childhood Cruelty to Cats, Dogs and Other Animals," *Bulletin of the American Academy of Psychiatry and the Law* 9, (1981), pp. 48–53.

[4]Description and analysis of the Graham case were drawn from James A. V. Galvin and John M. Macdonald, "Psychiatric Study of a Mass Murderer," *American Journal of Psychiatry* 115 (1959), pp. 1057–1061.

[5]G. S. Evseeff and E. M. Wisniewski, "A Psychiatric Study of a Violent Mass Murderer," *Journal of Forensic Science* 17 (1972), pp. 371–376.

[6]A comprehensive discussion of the XYY debate can be found in Saleem A. Shah, "The 47, XYY Chromsomal Abnormality: A Critical Appraisal with Respect to Antisocial and Violent Behavior," in W. Lynn Smith and Arthur Kling, eds., *Issues in Brain/Behavior Control* (New York: Spectrum Publications, 1976), pp. 49–67.

[7]"There is a . . ." in "The Mind of a Murderer," *Medical World News*, November 23, 1973, p. 42.

[8]Marvin Ziporyn was cited in *ibid.*, p. 43.

[9]Elliot S. Valenstein, "Brain Stimulation and the Origin of Violent Behavior," in Smith and Kling, eds., pp. 43–48.

[10]"I have just . . ." *Time*, August 12, 1966.

[11]Carlton Fredericks, *Psycho-Nutrition* (New York: Grosset and Dunlap, 1976).

[12]Donald T. Lunde, *Murder and Madness* (San Francisco: San Francisco Book Company, 1976).

[13]" . . . if I killed . . ." *ibid.*, p. 55.

[14]"It is the . . ." Hellman and Blackman, p. 1434.

Chapter 4

[1]In addition to newspaper accounts, information concerning "Son of Sam" was extracted from two books about the case: Lawrence D. Klausner, *Son of Sam* (New York: McGraw–Hill, 1981); and Charles Willeford, *Off the Wall* (Montclair, New Jersey: Pegasus Rex Press, 1980).
[2]Berkowitz's famous "Son of Sam" note to the police has been reprinted in many places, including Klausner, pp. 141–143.

Chapter 5

[1]Information on the Cowan case was obtained from issues of *The Reporter Dispatch*, White Plains, New York, and from Jay Robert Nash, *Murder, America: Homicide in the United States from the Revolution to the Present* (New York: Simon and Schuster, 1980), pp. 303–309.
[2]"Nothing is Lower . . ." *ibid.*, p. 304.
[3]"causing the city . . ." *The New York Times*, February 15, 1977.
[4]"I will give . . ." *The Reporter Dispatch*, February 20, 1977.
[5]Marvin E. Wolfgang and Franco Ferracuti, *The Subculture of Violence: Towards an Integrated Theory in Criminology* (London: Tavistock, 1967).
[6]"a ladies' man . . ." *The New York Times*, May 5, 1977.
[7]L. Berkowitz and A. LePage, "Weapons as Aggression-Eliciting Stimuli," *Journal of Personality and Social Psychology* 7 (1967), pp. 202–207.
[8]In addition to newspaper reports, information on the case of Harry De La Roche, Jr. was extracted from Roberta Roesche with Harry De La Roche, Jr., *Anyone's Son* (Kansas City, Kansas: Andrews and McMeel, 1979).
[9]"You're the stupidest . . ." *ibid.*, p. 64.
[10]"As I considered . . ." *ibid.*, p. 53.
[11]"No matter how . . ." *ibid.*, p. 85.
[12]"sexual elements are . . ." David Abrahamsen, *The Murdering Mind* (New York: Harper and Row, 1973), p. 11.

Chapter 6

[1]Information on the Bittaker–Norris case was obtained from the transcript of Bittaker's trial and from an interview with Prosecutor Stephen Kay.

[2]"If you are . . ." *State of California v. Lawrence Bittaker.*

[3]Paul Cameron's study was reported in *The Times-Picayune,* New Orleans, October 1, 1976.

[4]"the rape wasn't . . ." *State of California v. Lawrence Bittaker.*

[5]Erich Fromm, *The Anatomy of Human Destructiveness* (New York: Holt, Rinehart and Winston, 1973).

[6]Stuart Palmer, *The Psychology of Murder* (New York: Thomas Y. Crowell Company, 1960).

[7]"It's a tragedy . . ." Larsen, p. 278.

[8]In addition to newspaper reports, information about the case of Calvin Jackson was drawn from Nash, pp. 300–303.

[9]"We're going to . . ." Marshall Kilduff and Ron Javers, *The Suicide Cult* (New York: Bantam Books, 1978).

[10]"I'd rather bring . . ." *The Boston Globe,* April 26, 1981.

Chapter 7

[1]Stanley Milgram, "Behavioral Study of Obedience," *Journal of Abnormal and Social Psychology* 67 (1963), pp. 371–378.

[2]Henry V. Dicks, *Licensed Mass Murder: A Socio-Psychological Study of Some S. S. Killers* (New York: Basic Books, 1972).

[3]"one 'only' drove . . ." *ibid.,* p. 262.

[4]In addition to newspaper accounts, information concerning the Zebra killings was taken from Clark Howard, *Zebra* (New York: Berkley Books, 1979).

[5]In addition to newspaper reports, information concerning the Manson family was drawn from two books: Vincent Bugliosi with Curt Gentry, *Helter Skelter* (New York: W. W. Norton and Company, 1974); and Clara Livsey, *The Manson Women: A 'Family' Portrait* (New York: Richard Marek Publishers, 1980).

[6]Information concerning the Hennessey murder was obtained from Richard Gambino, *Vendetta* (Garden City, New York: Doubleday and Company, 1977).

[7]"follow and see . . ." *ibid.,* p. 79.

Chapter 8

[1]Shervert H. Frazier, "Violence and Social Impact" in Joseph C. Schoolar and Charles M. Gaitz, eds., *Research and the Psychiatric Patient* (New York: Brunner/Mazel, Inc., 1975).

[2]"makes me happy . . ." *The Boston Globe,* October 27, 1982.
[3]"I maintained all . . ." *The Boston Sunday Globe,* February 28, 1982.

Chapter 9

[1]Information in this chapter was taken from various reports in the *Journal-News,* Hamilton, Ohio, written by Nancy Baker, Joe Cella, Jim Newton, and Ken Bunting; in the *Cincinnati Enquirer* written by John R. Clark; and in the *Cincinnati Post* written by Dick Perry; and from personal interviews with attorney John F. Holcomb, attorney Hugh D. Holbrock, Police Chief George McNally, Judge Fred B. Cramer, reporter Dick Perry, and Lucille Tabler.
[2]"He's one of . . ." personal interview with attorney Hugh Holbrock.
[3]"There's been a . . ." *Citizen-Journal,* Columbus, Ohio, March 31, 1975.
[4]"It was a . . ." personal interview with Dick Perry.
[5]"Babies asleep in . . ." *Journal-News,* April 24, 1976.
[6]"Jimmie and his . . ." *ibid.,* April 1, 1975.
[7]"I just don't . . ." *ibid.*
[8]"Why was the . . ." personal interview with Lucille Tabler.
[9]"Everybody wanted to . . ." *ibid.*
[10]"At work they . . ." personal interview with Donald Ruppert.
[11]Testimony of Drs. Howard Sokolov, Philip Meehanick, and Lester Grinspoon was taken from Ruppert's trial in 1975.
[12]"to enter a . . ." *State of Ohio v. James Ruppert.*
[13]"pretty much of . . ." *Cincinnati Enquirer,* April 1, 1975.
[14]"if he could . . ." *Journal-News,* June 25, 1975.

Chapter 10

[1]Information in this chapter was obtained from various articles in the *Daily Local News* most of which were written by Bruce Mowday and in *The Johnstown Tribune-Democrat* by Sandra K. Reabuck, and from personal interviews with attorneys Dolores Troiani, William H. Lamb, Anthony List, Sheri Desaretz, Detective Charles Zagorskie, and reporters Bruce Mowday and Allen Davis.
[2]"like a zombie . . ." *Daily Local News,* February 22, 1980.
[3]"Bruce shined the . . ." *ibid.,* March 7, 1979.
[4]"one of the . . ." *ibid.,* August 30, 1978.
[5]"Robin's been shot . . ." Julia Cass, "The Gang That Caught the Johnston Gang," *Today* (Magazine of the *Philadelphia Inquirer*), February 22, 1981, p. 13.

[6]"If it weren't . . ." *The Johnstown Tribune-Democrat,* November 24, 1980.
[7]"either life in . . ." personal interview with attorney Dolores Troiani.
[8]"They always said . . ." personal interview with Allen Davis.
[9]"Junior and Jimmy . . ." personal interview with attorney William H. Lamb.
[10]"If you didn't . . ." personal interview with Dolores Troiani.
[11]Testimony from *Commonwealth of Pennsylvania v. David and Norman Johnston* and *Commonwealth of Pennsylvania v. Bruce Johnston.*

Chapter 11

[1]Information in this chapter was drawn mainly from various reports in the *Lost Angeles Herald Examiner,* many of which were written by Frank Candida; from issues of the *Los Angeles Times,* particularly a November 15, 1983 feature by Bella Stumbo; from Public Broadcasting Service's *Frontline,* #206, "The Mind of a Murderer", March, 1984; from Ted Schwarz, *The Hillside Strangler: A Murderer's Mind* (Garden City, New York: Doubleday, 1981); and from personal interviews with Judge Ronald M. George, attorneys Roger Boren, Michael Nash, Alan Simons, author Neville Frankel, reporter Frank Candida, and an anonymous court-watcher. Finally, some of the courtroom events described were observed by the authors.
[2]"I came hoping . . ." PBS, *Frontline.*
[3]"When you expand . . ." *Daily News,* Los Angeles, November 15, 1983.
[4]"The Ken I . . ." PBS, *Frontline.*
[5]"Are you Ken?" and ensuing conversation between Bianchi and Dr. John Watkins, *ibid.*
[6]"I fuckin' killed . . ." and ensuing conversation between Bianchi and Dr. Ralph Allison, PBS, *Frontline* and Ted Schwarz, pp. 170–175.
[7]Conversation between Bianchi and Dr. Martin Orne, PBS, *Frontline.*
[8]"Bianchi was almost . . ." *Time,* January 14, 1980.
[9]"I can't find . . ." *State of Washington v. Kenneth A. Bianchi.* See also PBS, *Frontline.*
[10]"I see more . . ." personal interview with Judge Ronald M. George.
[11]"My moral and . . ." *State of California v. Angelo Buono, Jr.*
[12]Statements of witnesses, *ibid.*
[13]"Death is too . . ." *Los Angeles Herald Examiner,* January 10, 1984.
[14]"I'm sure, Mr. Buono . . ." *State of California V. Angelo Buono, Jr.* and *State of California v. Kenneth A. Bianchi.* See also PBS, *Frontline.*

[15]"The Lord spoke . . ." *Los Angles Times,* November 1, 1983.
[16]"I feel hate . . ." *ibid.*

Chapter 12

[1]"My name's Galloway . . ." *The Oregonian,* November 20, 1983.
[2]"He was a . . ." *ibid.*
[3]Statements during the capture of "Son of Sam" were extracted from Klausner, pp. 350–351 and Willeford, p. 228.
[4]Chet Dettlinger with Jeff Prugh, *The List* (Atlanta: Philmay Enterprises, Inc., 1983) excerpted in the *Chicago Sun-Times,* February 26, 1984, pp. 48–50.
[5]Information on the case of the Boston Strangler was taken from Gerold Frank, *The Boston Strangler* (New York: The New American Library, 1966); and Eustace Chesser, *Strange Loves: The Human Aspects of Sexual Deviation* (New York: William Morrow and Company, 1971), pp. 92–96.
[6]"Nine out of . . ." John Godwin, *Murder USA: The Ways We Kill Each Other* (New York: Ballantine Books, 1978), p. 276.
[7]"We draw on . . ." personal interview with Roger DePue.
[8]This illustrative profile is taken from Bruce Porter, "Mind Hunters," *Psychology Today* 17 (April 1983), pp. 10–11.
[9]The success rates for the FBI profiling team were taken from Institutional Research and Development Unit, "Evaluation of the Psychological Profiling Program," FBI Academy, Quantico, Virginia, 1981.
[10]"we're still in . . ." Porter, p. 52.
[11]Information concerning the Corll case is drawn primarily from Jack Olsen, *The Man with the Candy: The Story of the Houston Mass Murders* (New York: Simon and Schuster, 1974).
[12]"He didn't act . . ." *ibid.*, p. 226.
[13]"You weren't supposed . . ." *ibid.*, p. 119.
[14]"I cannot help . . ." *ibid.*, p. 195.
[15]Information concerning the Gacy case was taken from Clifford L. Linedecker, *The Man Who Killed Boys* (New York: St. Martin's Press, 1980).
[16]"a centralized data . . ." Pierce Brooks, "The Violent Criminal Apprehension Program," Vida, Oregon.
[17]"For the most . . ." ABC-TV, *20/20,* July 5, 1984.
[18]"VICAP will raise . . ." personal interview with Robert O. Heck.
[19]"I don't feel . . ." *Chicago Tribune,* April 3, 1979.
[20]"It is most . . ." personal interview with Robert O. Heck.

Chapter 13

[1]Information about the case of Clifford Olson was taken from a number of reports in *Maclean's* including a feature story dated January 25, 1982.
[2]"If I gave . . ." *ibid.*, p. 20.
[3]"I can't stand . . ." *Chicago Tribune*, October 21, 1982.
[4]"the heart of . . ." *Daily Local News*, February 25, 1980.
[5]"whatever the law . . ." Howard, p. 354.

Chapter 14

[1]The analysis of David Berkowitz's state of mind was taken from David Abrahamsen, "Unmasking 'Son of Sam's' Demons," *The New York Times Magazine*, July 1, 1979, pp. 20–22.
[2]Discussion of the insanity plea benefited from Edward Dolnick, "The Psychiatrist's Role in the Courtroom is on Trial," *The Boston Globe*, May 28, 1984, pp. 45, 48; and two books: John Monahan and Henry J. Steadman, eds., *Mentally Disordered Offenders: Perspectives from Law and Social Science* (New York: Plenum Press, 1983), and Richard Moran, *Knowing Right from Wrong: The Insanity Defense of Daniel McNaughtan* (New York: The Free Press, 1981).
[3]R. A. Pasewark and D. Seidenzahl, "Opinions Concerning the Insanity Plea and Criminality Among Mental Patients," *Bulletin of the American Academy of Psychiatry and Law* 8 (1980), pp. 199–202, cited by Grant Morris, "Aquittal by Reason of Insanity: Developments in the Law," in Monahan and Steadman, eds., pp. 65–108.
[4]R. A. Pasewark and M. L. Pantle, "Insanity Plea: Legislator's View," (1979), pp. 222–223, cited in Grant Morris, *ibid.*
[5]Seymour L. Halleck, *Psychiatry and the Dilemmas of Crime: A Study of Causes, Punishment and Treatment* (Berkeley, California: University of California Press, 1971).
[6]Grant Morris, in Monahan and Steadman, eds., pp. 65–108.
[7]"which had never . . ." Harry E. Allen, Paul C. Friday, Julian B. Roebuck, and Edward Sagarin, *Crime and Punishment* (New York: The Free Press, 1981), p. 336.
[8]Information concerning Robert DeFeo and testimony from his trial were taken from Gerard Sullivan and Harvey Aronson, *High Hopes: The Amityville Murders* (New York: Coward, McCann and Geoghegan, 1981).
[9]Dr. Zolan's testimony was given in *State of New York v. Ronald DeFeo.*

Chapter 15

[1]The main source of information on the Starkweather–Fugate case was William Allen, *Starkweather: The Story of a Mass Murderer* (Boston: Houghton Mifflin Company, 1976), supplemented with Marilyn Coffey, "Badlands Revisited," *The Atlantic* 234 (December 1974), pp. 70–81.

[2]"Pick up for . . ." Allen, p. 71.

[3]"When we got . . ." *ibid.*, p. 77.

[4]"Nobody remembers a . . ." *ibid.*, p. 140.

[5]"Hers was really . . ." *ibid*, p. 53.

[6]"if he fried . . ." *ibid*, p. 162.

[7]"I am now . . ." *ibid.*, p. 173.

[8]"She was sentenced . . ." *ibid.*, pp. 182–183.

[9]"to settle down . . ." *Time*, June 21, 1976, p. 22.

[10]"I wish finally . . ." *State of California v. Angelo Buono, Jr.* and *State of California v. Kenneth A. Bianchi.* See also PBS, *Frontline.*

[11]"the willful, diliberate . . ." Code of Virginia, para. 18.2–31(g).

[12]George H. Gallup, *The Gallup Report,* No. 187 (Princeton, New Jersey: The Gallup Poll, April 1981), pp. 18, 19 reprinted in Bureau of Justice Statistics, United States Department of Justice, *Sourcebook of Criminal Justice Statistics—1982* (Washington, D.C.: United States Government Printing Office, 1983), p. 264.

[13]The survey of Bostonians was conducted at the College of Criminal Justice, Northeastern University.

[14]Jeffrey D. Alderman, Linda A. Cranney, and Peter Begans, *ABC News–Washington Post Poll,* Survey No. 0034 (New York: ABC News, June 8, 1981) reprinted and adapted in Bureau of Justice Statistics, *ibid.*, p. 265.

[15]"I don't want . . ." personal interview with Stephen Kay.

[16]"The real issue . . ." Walter Berns, *For Capital Punishment: Crime and the Morality of the Death Penalty* (New York: Basic Books, 1979), pp. 8–9.

[17]George Camp and Camille Camp, *The Correctional Yearbook: Instant Answers to Key Questions in Corrections* (Pound Ridge, New York: Criminal Justice Institute, 1982) cited by Bureau of Justice Statistics, United States Department of Justice, *Report to the Nation on Crime and Justice: The Data* (Washington, D.C.: United States Government Printing Office, 1983), p. 93.

[18]New York State Defenders Association study cited in *Time,* January 24, 1983, p. 39.

[19]"It doesn't bother . . ." *Los Angeles Herald Examiner,* February 16, 1983.

[18]New York State Defenders Association study cited in *Time,* January 24, 1983, p. 39.

[19]"It doesn't bother . . ." *Los Angeles Herald Examiner,* February 16, 1983.

SELECTED BIBLIOGRAPHY

Abrahamsen, David, *The Murdering Mind.* New York: Harper and Row, 1973.

Abrahamsen, David, *The Psychology of Crime.* New York: Columbia University Press, 1960.

Allen, William, *Starkweather: The Story of a Mass Murderer.* Boston: Houghton Mifflin Company, 1976.

Berns, Walter, *For Capital Punishment: Crime and the Morality of the Death Penalty.* New York: Basic Books, 1979.

Brussel, James A., *Casebook of a Crime Psychiatrist.* New York: Bernard Geis Associates, 1968.

Bugliosi, Vincent with Gentry, Curt, *Helter Skelter.* New York: W. W. Norton and Company, 1974.

Bureau of Justice Statistics, United States Department of Justice, *Report to the Nation on Crime and Justice: The Data.* Washington, D.C.: United States Government Printing Office, 1983.

Chesser, Eustace, *Strange Loves: The Human Aspects of Sexual Deviation.* New York: William Morrow and Company, 1971.

Dettlinger, Chet with Prugh, Jeff, *The List.* Atlanta: Philmay Enterprises, Inc., 1983.

Dicks, Henry V., *Licensed Mass Murder; A Socio-Psychological Study of Some S. S. Killers.* New York: Basic Books, 1972.

Dickson, Grierson, *Murder by Numbers.* London: Robert Hale Limited, 1958.

Frank, Gerold, *The Boston Strangler.* New York: The New American Library, 1966.

Gambino, Richard, *Vendetta.* Garden City, New York: Doubleday and Company, 1977.

Godwin, John, *Murder USA: The Ways We Kill Each Other.* New York: Ballantine Books, 1978.

Gollmar, Judge Robert H., *Edward Gein: America's Most Bizzarre Murderer.* Delavan, Wisconsin: Chas. Hallberg and Company, 1981.

Harrington, Alan, *Psychopaths.* New York: Simon and Schuster, 1972.

Howard, Clark, *Zebra.* New York: Berkley Books, 1979.

Keyes, Edward, *The Michigan Murders.* New York: Thomas Y. Crowell, 1976.

Keylin, Arleen and DeMirjian, Arto, Jr., *Crime: As Reported by the New York Times.* New York: Arno Press, 1976.

Kilduff, Marshall and Javers, Ron, *The Suicide Cult.* New York: Bantam Books, 1978.

Klausner, Lawrence D., *Son of Sam,* New York: McGraw Hill, 1981.

Lane, Mark, *The Strongest Poison.* New York: Hawthorn Books, 1980.

Larsen, Richard W., *Bundy: The Deliberate Stranger.* Englewood Cliffs, New Jersey: Prentice–Hall, 1980.

Linedecker, Clifford L., *The Man Who Killed Boys.* New York: St. Martin's Press, 1980.

Lunde, Donald T., *Murder and Madness.* San Francisco: San Francisco Book Company, 1976.

Lundsgaarde, Henry P., *Murder in Space City: A Cultural Analysis of Houston Homicide Patterns.* New York: Oxford University Press, 1977.

Macdonald, John M., *Homicidal Threats.* Springfield, Illionis: Charles C. Thomas, 1968.

Macdonald, John M., *Psychiatry and the Criminal.* Springfield, Illinois: Charles C. Thomas, 1976.

Michaud, Stephen G. and Aynesworth, Hugh, *The Only Living Witness.* New York: Linden Press, 1983.

Monahan, John and Steadman, Henry J., eds., *Mentally Disordered Offenders: Perspectives from Law and Social Science.* New York: Plenum Press, 1983.

Moran, Richard, *Knowing Right from Wrong: The Insanity Defense of Daniel McNaughtan.* New York: The Free Press, 1981.

Nash, Jay Robert, *Murder, America: Homicide in the United States from the Revolution to the Present.* New York: Simon and Schuster, 1980.

Olsen, Jack, *The Man with the Candy: The Story of the Houston Mass Murders.* New York: Simon and Schuster, 1974.

Palmer, Stuart, *The Psychology of Murder.* New York: Thomas Y. Crowell Company, 1960.

Roesche, Roberta with De La Roche, Harry, Jr., *Anyone's Son.* Kansas City, Kansas: Andrews and McMeel, 1979.

Rule, Ann, *The Stranger Beside Me*. New York: W. W. Norton and Company, 1980.

Schwarz, Ted, *The Hillside Strangler: A Murderer's Mind.* Garden City, New York: Doubleday, 1981.

Sifakis, Carl, *The Encyclopedia of American Crime.* New York: Facts on File, Inc., 1982.

Smith, W. Lynn and Kling, Arthur, eds., *Issues in Brain/Behavior Control.* New York: Spectrum Publications, 1976.

Stoller, Robert J., *Perversion: The Erotic Form of Hatred.* New York: Pantheon Books, 1975.

Sullivan, Gerard and Aronson, Harvey, *High Hopes: The Amityville Murders.* New York: Coward, McCann and Geoghegan, 1981.

Sullivan, Terry with Maiken, Peter T., *Killer Clown.* New York: Grosset and Dunlap, 1983.

Van den Haag, Ernest and Conrad, John P., *The Death Penalty: A Debate.* New York: Plenum Press, 1983.

Willeford, Charles, *Off the Wall.* Montclair, New Jersey: The Pegasus Rex Press, 1980.

Winn, Stephen and Merrill, David, *Ted Bundy: The Killer Next Door.* New York: Bantam Books, 1980.

Wolfgang, Marvin E. and Ferracuti, Franco, *The Subculture of Violence: Towards an Integrated Theory in Criminology.* London: Tavistock, 1967.

INDEX